D1648626

A MOMMY, A DADDY, TWO SISTERS, AND A JIMMY: AUTISM AND THE DIFFERENCE IT MAKES

By Richard D. Bucher, Ph. D.

Contributing Editor
Patricia L. Bucher

Title by Suzy Bucher (Painter), age 4

When I was little, people would ask me about my family and whether I had any brothers or sisters. I would answer, 'I have a mommy, a daddy, a sister, and a Jimmy.' He's not your everyday brother who picks on you and puts gum in your hair. He buys me presents and gives me hugs and kisses, and when I was little, he sang to me.[1]
    --a sister (Suzy)

Cover illustration by Katie Bucher (Hessen), age 9

https://ajimmy.com/
https://www.facebook.com/RichardDBucherPh.D/

Dedication

To my wife and children, our Linwood family, and Jimmy's best friend, Tai Mitchell.

Foreword

When I began working as a young intern at Linwood 42 years ago, autism was a concept that very few people understood or had even heard of. In fact, if you were not a parent, a caregiver or a researcher, it was not likely that autism was on your radar. It was not long after I began working at Linwood that Jimmy's parents brought him in for a visit to be evaluated for admission. Was he a good fit for Linwood? Was Linwood a good fit for him? Jimmy sat in a room with Linwood's founder, Jeanne Simons, who was the director of the program. When I say "sat," I use that term loosely. I was in the room with them. Jimmy was not going to sit for anyone when he entered the room. If memory serves me, after about 20 minutes of shrieking and flying around the room, he finally sat with Miss Simons and engaged in a few brief moments of "work." Linwood was one of only a few programs at that time that provided educational and residential services for children living with autism. The Buchers had exhausted all other options. As it turned out, Jimmy was a great fit.

Jimmy and I grew up together at Linwood. Education goes both ways. As a young man just entering the world of special education, I probably learned more from Jimmy and his family than they ever learned from me. After all, they lived with Jimmy for 11 years before we ever met. Reflecting on the world as it was then, autism was an irregularity – a variance from the norm. It was a childhood disorder that the medical world was just getting attuned to. Educators were simply baffled.

I am blessed to have witnessed the growth of the Bucher family. I remember Katie as a little girl.

And I remember when Suzy was born. I also remember a family in crisis. The Buchers had always exuded high energy. Jimmy's impact on the family seemed to have magnified that energy making it all the more difficult for each of them to settle into their respective lives. This was a highly educated family that prided themselves on their accomplishments. They were never ashamed of or disappointed with Jimmy. Their unconditional love for him was ever present. Affecting them more than anything else was that they did not have all the answers. "Why does he behave the way he does?" "Why am I unable to calm his overwhelming anxiety?" "What am I doing or not doing that is causing him to be different?" But that was then. The family always loved and accepted Jimmy just the way he was. That was never an issue. Today, that unconditional love and acceptance has led the family to a peace that they perhaps could not envision when Jimmy was a child; family vacations, holidays, Christmas cards, weddings, the birth of grandchildren. Jimmy is part of it all. And, as any adult does, Jimmy and his sisters say goodbye at the end of the day and retire to their respective homes with their respective families and friends (Jimmy's family being his Linwood family).

Although autism is not completely understood today, it is no longer regarded by reasonable people as a childhood disorder. It is a fact that individuals living with autism have a different way of perceiving and navigating the world in which they live. Regardless of the causes or explanations that are offered, we, as reasonable people, no longer judge these individuals.

Jimmy and his family were present and accounted for, as was I, when the autism community became front and center in our world. Jimmy ultimately, and very gradually grew into a fine young man – a contributing member of the community in which he lives, works and plays. I too have grown up, along with Jimmy, and with Linwood. Jimmy still receives support from Linwood; I imagine he always will.

--Bill Moss, Executive Director of Linwood Center

TABLE OF CONTENTS

Before We Begin

Before I moved ahead with this labor of love, I told my wife, my two daughters, and my son Jimmy what I had in mind. With their blessing and a deep sense of responsibility, I started writing.

I don't see this story being told elsewhere. Spanning more than forty years, it's the kind of informative and brutally honest account I wish I could've read years ago. It will resonate with those who want or need to know more about autism or "autisms"[2] for whatever reason.

A Mommy, A Daddy, Two Sisters, and A Jimmy: Autism and the Difference it Makes follows a family who knows from trial and error there are no easy answers; no magic pill if you will. Like many other families, we continue to be transformed by experiences that are exhausting, awe-inspiring, gut-wrenching and challenging, consuming, funny, sad, and uplifting. We share our vulnerabilities and concerns as well as what makes our lives special and full of surprises. Each of us opens up about how we struggle within ourselves, with each other, and with the outside world. But in spite of or perhaps because of these struggles, we find ourselves coming together and growing more appreciative of the journey over time.

Of course, Jimmy's voice is included. As a child, right before bedtime, we asked him about his day and then recorded exactly what he said. Some of these journal entries appear in the book. Once I got his permission to write this book, Pat and I spent lots of time discussing memories with Jimmy. When we did, he would repeatedly ask if "this" was going in the book. Usually, my answer was, "Maybe." After asking him if that was okay, he would say, "Sure!"

When you raise someone with autism, it's not just a family thing. Consequently, many other voices and experiences are included, such as those of caregivers, health professionals, pastors, educators, coaches, and others who remain a big part of Jimmy's life and ours.

My hope is that this book will nudge us toward a world in which we value and respect what makes each of us unique and special, regardless of who we are, what we look like, or how our brains work. To do this requires us to change ourselves and reach out to others, regardless of where we fall on the spectrum of autism or for that matter, the spectrum of humanity.

I welcome any and all feedback. You may email me at **rdbucher@aol.com**, or access my website at **https://ajimmy.com**, which includes a link to my blog. If you want to read or watch videos containing information about up-to-date research and stories about autism, you may access this book's Facebook page at

https://www.facebook.com/RichardDBucherPh.D/ .

1   As Long as It's Healthy

Prenatal education classes attempt to make pregnancy and childbirth less overwhelming by building confidence and providing information. One mother (Tessa) recalls one class in particular. "Our instructor briefly talked to us about 'expectations' and what could happen if our baby wasn't quite what we expected." The instructor "mentioned birth marks and minor abnormalities. She even equated her daughter being a redhead as being one of these expectations." Like most, Tessa assumed her baby would be "healthy and normal in the medical sense of the word." But reality set in when her child was born. Within days, Tessa found out her child was blind and deaf.[3]

The birth of a child with a disability may be seen as the loss of a "perfect" baby. It catches parents off-guard and leaves them with far more questions than answers Mothers may blame themselves, especially if they suspect heredity had something to do with it. One study estimates that mothers may take as long as a year to fully process their infant's disability.[4]

If she learns her toddler has a disability like autism, a mother might think, "This is not my child that I expected and planned for. This is not the child I waited for through all those months of pregnancy and all those hours of labor. This is not the child I made all those plans to share all those experiences with."[5]

In October of 1976, my wife Pat was feeling significant contractions, and unlike previous false alarms, she sensed that this time it was for real. I hopped, and my wife plopped into our car and drove to Sinai Hospital in Baltimore. As I drove to the hospital, trying to dodge the bumps in the road, I felt tense but ready. For the last few months, we had taken Lamaze natural childbirth classes, practicing breathing exercises, asking questions, talking with other couples, and preparing for an uneventful, safe labor and childbirth. We read, we prayed, and we knew the basics of Lamaze inside out.

Pat had a 24-hour long, difficult labor. It was nothing like the joy-of childbirth we had visualized during our Lamaze class. In the back of our minds, we were planning on a natural childbirth, but it wasn't meant to be. Anesthesia was ordered. While a C-section was discussed at one point, Jimmy had a high forceps delivery only after hours and hours of Pat's intense labor and pushing; as well as coaching by yours truly. Unfortunately, the anesthesia never took. He was a big baby with a birth weight of eight pounds, fourteen ounces. It seemed as if his head was nearly as big as the rest of his body.

Stupidly, a few hours later, I drove home. I was exhausted and had no business driving. I chowed down some breakfast, got my fix of caffeine, and headed to Baltimore City Community College. As a professor of sociology, I decided to bag my lesson plans for the day and talk about my amazing wife, my son Jimmy, and the unbelievable experience of watching Pat give birth.

For two days, we experienced all of the highs of new parenthood; but then we began to sense something was wrong. In dribs and drabs, we were alerted to the possibility that Jimmy might have some pretty severe medical issues. When the nurses brought Jimmy to Pat, they never left the room. Doctors informed us that our son had been twitching, which might be seizure activity. Jimmy was moved to the Newborn Intensive Care Unit at Sinai. I remember many more questions than answers. I was focused almost entirely on getting through each day and being there for my wife and my child. On the other hand, Pat was much more attuned to Jimmy's future from the very beginning.

Pat's recovery took a while. After five days, she was sent home without him. A few days later, doctors felt all was well and were ready to send Jimmy home. When we arrived at the hospital with his best outfit in hand and his brand-new car seat already to go, we were told Jimmy had developed severe grand mal seizures. He was being transferred to Johns Hopkins Pediatric Intensive Care Unit, where he spent the next three weeks of his life, as did Pat. She lived in a reclining chair, pushed up next to Jimmy's hospital crib.

To this day, I can remember helplessly observing my little baby boy as I watched him repeatedly jerk for what seemed like an eternity. We didn't really know too much at that time. But being at Pat's side through the entire labor and recovery was critically important in terms of preparing me for what was to come. I didn't have to imagine all that she and Jimmy went through; I was there.

We soon learned there was a chance Jimmy suffered brain damage during delivery. Before long, we began to wonder whether Pat's twenty-four-hour labor had anything to do with these seizures. After a very long month of experimenting with the right meds and doses, doctors sent Jimmy home. Even though he was now more stable, Pat had to monitor Jimmy's seizures the entire day, each and every day. While I was at work, Jimmy was never more than six inches apart from her, even during naptime. We moved his crib into our bedroom, right up against Pat's side of the bed. Since baby monitors were not available at this time, Pat slept with her hand resting on Jimmy's chest for the next two years.

*Figure 1 BABY JIMMY BACK HOME
UNDER OUR WATCHFUL EYE.*

On Jimmy's first birthday, we were sent to what was then called the Kennedy Institute in Baltimore. After talking with a number of doctors and reviewing Jimmy's development up to that point, we were informed that Jimmy was mentally retarded and uneducable. Formal evaluations showed that Jimmy's communication and fine motor skills were extremely delayed. (Only later did we learn that he had mild cerebral palsy as well as autism.) Once we listened to the so-called experts and analyzed their test results, we decided we weren't about to lower our expectations; it was far too early, and the evidence was way too flimsy.

We found ourselves second-guessing the complete faith and trust we placed in Pat's doctor. The next day, another OB-GYN said, "If I'd been there, I would have never let you go through all that. I would have given you a C-section." Over time, Pat knew she would heal. But what about Jimmy?

A few years after Jimmy's birth and his subsequent developmental delays, Pat and I considered a possible lawsuit against the doctor who delivered Jimmy. We wondered why he didn't do a C-section on my wife. Once we consulted with an attorney, we discovered that proving medical malpractice would be extremely difficult. A strong argument could be made that the doctor's choices did not constitute malpractice, only "mediocre medicine." Besides, there were any number of variables that might explain Jimmy's condition. We were told a routine medical malpractice case typically takes between four and five hundred hours of preparation, and much of that time would involve us. The attorney made it clear that the odds were stacked against us, so we didn't pursue it.

By three years of age, Jimmy's seizures were gone. By the time he was six, he knew how to read, type, and do math. Jimmy spent several hours each day screaming, hand-flapping, and spinning in panic attacks, which the professionals liked to call tantrums. He was a tremendous danger to himself; he destroyed furniture and anything else in his path. But when he was calm, he was a sweet, adorable, giggling, and smiling child. Doctors were at a loss; they had no diagnosis and the only help they could provide was sympathy.

Prior to Jimmy's birth, we were constantly asked the same question, "What do you want, a girl or a boy?" And without thought or hesitation, we simply responded, "It really doesn't matter, as long as it's healthy." The sex of our child didn't matter, as long as we had a healthy child. We didn't give that canned, socially-conditioned response a second thought. Now we do.

When I hear that response, it goes right to my gut. It makes me feel totally excluded. What if your child is not healthy? Then what?
--the mommy

2   A Perfect Storm

Parents of children with autism find themselves in a "perfect storm" of stress, according to Dr. Susan Parish, Professor of Disability Policy at Brandeis University. Overnight, they have to become experts on a wide range of complex matters, including early intervention, insurance laws, educational policy, and the ins and outs of the health-care system. To make matters worse, our social system fails to adequately support these families who are desperate for knowledge and assistance. Parish says, "We expect families to care for their kids, but we don't provide them adequate support to do so."[6]

Navigating through "the system" is a big stressor. Using military terminology, fathers in one study talked about "fighting for everything," and battling a system in which there was no "route map" or "welcome pack." Finding sources of support was a logistical nightmare for these fathers. Robert, a father, describes the toll it takes, "…I regard myself as quite articulate and …able to look after myself, but you wonder just how other people survive this sort of minefield, and that's what worries me because some people just can't cope with it…"[7]

One couple who found themselves in this perfect storm regrets not reaching out for help early on. "We didn't know whom to tell. We just hunkered down and saw our marriage get worse." According to Dorothea Iannuzzi, a clinical social worker who works with families impacted by autism, turning to friends, grandparents, and others for help can make a difference. "You need to pull in as many supports as you have," she says. Find time to breathe and relax a bit, "even if it's just one hour a week."[8]

For Pat and me, the perfect storm described by Parish was compounded by my wife's feelings of guilt, doctors who couldn't provide us with answers to our questions, and a son who seemed to defy everyone's attempt at a diagnosis or treatment.

My wife had a normal, healthy pregnancy. Pat did everything the doctor told her to do. If her doctor told her to eat three slices of wheat bread a day, she ate three slices of wheat bread a day. She was going to have the perfect Lamaze baby, and smile during delivery. "Well," as she says, "it didn't work out that way."

For months after Jimmy's birth, Pat's personality was basically wiped out. She had always been so bubbly and enthusiastic. Pat recollects, "I just couldn't smile. I felt on the verge of tears all the time." Her questions had no answers. "Why me? Why am I being punished? What did I do to deserve this?" Feelings of guilt were ever-present, and each day, "I found myself thinking of all the bad things about me and promised to change" so that this nightmare would stop, for Jimmy's sake and my family.

A movie came out in the 60s called "Stop the World: I Want to Get Off." I remember thinking that very thing.
        --the mommy

At one point, when he was a three-month-old infant, Jimmy stopped breathing in Pat's arms. After several attempts to revive him with CPR, Jimmy started to breathe again. Pat rushed him to the emergency room, and medical staff whisked him away. After rushing to the hospital to join my wife, we both waited anxiously, not sure if Jimmy would make it. Later, when the doctor brought him out to us, he had no muscle tone, his body was limp, and his eyes focused on nothing. The doctor asked, "Is this how he is normally?" In response, my wife simply said, "No." Then, the doctor warned us, "Prepare yourself for the fact that this may be all he ever is." During this 4-day hospitalization, Pat hit "rock bottom." She recalls, "Going into a room, crying my soul out, and asking God to make me go crazy because I couldn't take it anymore." In order to sleep by Jimmy's side in the Pediatric ICU, Pat found a large unused crib and pushed it up against his smaller crib. Her prayers were answered when he awoke on the third day and gave Pat a huge smile as he lifted his head. Jimmy was back.

As he grew, help was hard to come by. Pat looked everywhere for information that might provide insight into raising a child with symptoms like Jimmy. She finally found a book by Dr. Benjamin Spock, an American pediatrician whose advice on child care influenced generations of parents. The last chapter, which was very short, was devoted to parents of "handicapped children." Dr. Spock warned these parents to make sure their children didn't feel that they were a disappointment. This resonated with my wife, who said she never wanted Jimmy to feel he was a disappointment in any way, shape, or form.

In addition, Pat found comfort and strength in an autobiography titled *Joni*. Joni Eareckson Tada, a world-wide advocate for the disabled, is very open about her struggles to understand her paralysis as a result of a diving accident in her youth. Much of her writing deals with her journey in coming to accept God's design in her life. Joni shared her image of God as a loving father, and that a loving father does not just make you happy all of the time. Rather, a loving father does things that hurt; and even though you may not understand, it's for your own good. Pat could accept that.

It would have been easy to point our finger at each other and play the blame game. For some reason, we didn't. Rather, we dealt with stress and uncertainty in our own ways. Pat is future-oriented; she's always looking ahead, sometimes months and years down the road. On the other hand, I am very much locked into the present. I tend to focus on getting through today and maybe tomorrow and the weeks ahead. For the longest time, thinking about the future was a luxury I felt I couldn't afford. Rather, I was all about meeting the challenges of the here and now, and somehow getting through another day.

Jimmy would not be diagnosed with autism until age 11. Not knowing what we were up against made finding emotional, educational, psychological, and medical support that much more difficult. As we looked to each other and our faith for help and guidance, we began to think that maybe God had given us more than we could handle. In the midst of this perfect storm, we redoubled our efforts and thoroughly committed ourselves to do everything we could to try to help Jimmy.

3 More Guilt and Blame

In 1971, a new "rock star" in the field of autism and medicine appeared on Dick Cavett's late-night talk show. *The New Republic* referred to Professor Bettelheim as a "Hero of Our Time." Popular media and the medical establishment praised and touted his ideas. When Cavett, a TV personality whose show was seen by hundreds of thousands of viewers, asked his guest to describe autism, Bettelheim referred to autism as the most "severe psychotic disturbance of childhood known to man," a condition so severe that "there was a wish that it would be much better if the child wouldn't live."

Bettelheim's best-selling book, *The Empty Fortress*, popularized the "refrigerator mother" theory of autism. As he saw it, mothers never really wanted their autistic children. They were more concerned with their own lives than they were with providing their children with the physical and emotional support they needed. Bettelheim found these mothers to be depressed, stressed out, overwhelmed and unavailable. Furthermore, he reasoned they were in need of intense psychological treatment, which could very well necessitate removing the child from the mother's care for long periods of time.[9]

Dr. Ruth Sullivan, a mother of a child who was diagnosed with autism in 1960, remembers the damage done by Bettelheim. She says, "Everything you read, and there wasn't much, but everything you read said mothers caused autism; poor mothers that hated their children. They were cold, refrigerator mothers."[10] Blame-the-parent theories have since been totally discredited, but unfortunately there are still people, including some medical professionals, who cling to the idea that the causes of autism can be connected to the choices parents make in raising their children.

Once Jimmy was born, it wasn't long before my wife was being grilled by one health care professional after another. She was repeatedly asked, "During pregnancy, did you smoke?" "Did you drink any alcoholic beverages?" "Did you take prescriptions, any illegal drugs?" Thankfully, for her sake and mine, her answer to each of these questions was an unequivocal "No!" She was exacting when it came to following doctors' orders. As Pat was struggling with guilt, constant questioning from professionals reinforced the idea that *she* must have done something wrong. I think back to this time in our lives and remember seeing mothers who abused their bodies in some fashion and yet had babies who did not appear to have serious medical issues. Seemingly, there were no answers to questions like "Why Jimmy?" and "Why us?"

Fortunately, I was able to avoid this guilt trip. In part, this was due to my gender. As a father, I was not the one being grilled by doctors. Furthermore, I had to go back to my job as a professor and there, I managed to get away from it all for a good part of each work day.

As a social scientist, I learned to be critical. I knew that theories were just that, theories. And I needed to save whatever energy I had so I could focus entirely on my wife and my son. While Pat and I felt physically and emotionally overwhelmed at times, we wanted a child more than anything. When Jimmy was born, even with all of his health issues, we felt extremely blessed. Our prayers had been answered.

However, guilt lingered for Pat. We thought and talked for hours about each of our family histories, hoping to discover some rational, genetic link to explain Jimmy's condition. We examined our own quirks and personalities, looking for answers. Looking back, my wife did regret trying to be so stoic throughout childbirth. She wondered whether things might have turned out differently if the doctor knew just how much pain she was experiencing during her long labor.

It's worth noting that Jeanne Simons, one of the pioneers in this field, was motivated in part by the guilt that was unfairly and mistakenly placed on parents of children with autism. "Her empathy for parents of autistic children was profound and almost unique at that time."[11] In 1955, she established the Linwood Center for Disturbed Children, a school and residential facility for children with autism. Simons emphasized on more than one occasion that in addition to serving as an environment in which children with autism can grow and reach their potential, Linwood provided much-needed relief and support for parents who are made to feel guilty. Years later, the Linwood Center would dramatically impact our family's life.

4 The China Doll and the Fishbowl

It's not at all unusual for parents with autistic children to experience social isolation and outright rejection. Interviews with more than 500 parents revealed that almost two out of three autistic children "were sometimes or often avoided or left out of activities by other kids." The vast majority of parents said their children found it difficult to make friends. These children were often viewed as "weird" or "odd;" and roughly 13% were physically bullied. One mother, whose son was bullied in school, shared how he was called names and teased, often because of his passion for superheroes and other things about which he cared deeply. She said, "He was hurt badly by this."[12]

When he was a young boy, our natural inclination was to walk in front of Jimmy, protecting him from the "big, bad world." We knew what was out there; the inevitable hurt, isolation, and intolerance he would encounter outside of our inner social circle. There was a good chance that people would misinterpret or misunderstand his behaviors, such as hand-flapping, screaming, or invading someone's personal space.

For his safety, we had to almost always be by his side. Jimmy had a knack for putting himself in danger. He would reach for hot stoves and sharp knives. My wife remembers having to stop Jimmy from trying to touch cars as they drove by. We avoided railings on the upper floors of hotels and shopping malls since Jimmy seemed to have no fear of heights. He was drawn to high places and had to be restrained so he wouldn't jump. For some reason, these behaviors are no longer an issue.

Whenever possible, we advocated for Jimmy so we could loosen our hold on him. We educated neighbors, community groups, members of our church, and teachers and aides in Jimmy's school. My wife created a summer camp for children like Jimmy because no such camp existed nearby. She took time out of her busy schedule to speak to Maryland lawmakers in order to press for laws and funding for children with disabilities.

When Jimmy was little, we received considerable advice from professionals, some good but much of it forgettable. One of the most valuable things we were told came from our pediatric neurologist, Dr. Kenton Holden of Johns Hopkins University Hospital in Baltimore, MD. He warned us, "Don't treat Jimmy as if he was a China doll." Dr. Holden understood why we might want to protect Jimmy, but he encouraged us to push Jimmy to try new things and enter new, unfamiliar worlds. Let him be himself as much as possible and learn from the bumps and bruises he will encounter along the way. Also, Dr. Holden used the analogy of a fishbowl. As he put it, "Don't keep Jimmy at a distance, as if he were in a fishbowl." In other words, love him, hold him, and hug him.

Due to Jimmy's disability, he didn't want to be touched, much less hugged. As an infant, he was more content lying on the floor than in our arms. We could have left him on the floor all day long and he would have been just fine. But as parents, we refused to let Jimmy keep us at arm's length; even if that meant putting up with his screaming and fussing when we tried to embrace him. We both needed to hold him, and we figured out ways to do it. We held him as we danced, sang, swung on our outdoor swing set, and rocked back and forth in our rocking chair. Over time, Jimmy learned to put up with our non-stop, loving displays of affection. In a way, I firmly believe our persistence in fighting through his standoffishness helped us connect with our son, and Jimmy with us.

Holding Jimmy for longer periods of time was only possible if he was dancing in the arms of my wife or me. Consequently, Pat spent hours each day dancing with Jimmy, with Barry Manilow and Motown tunes in the background. She would wrap her arms around Jimmy, squeeze him, and sing from time to time as they moved and spun around to the music. He loved it! Not only would this help Jimmy stop crying, it also seemed to soothe him. Pat felt an intense need to hold him, and dancing gave her the opportunity to do this for lengthy periods of time. Unfortunately, when he reached age seven, this daily routine had to stop because he became too big and heavy to carry in her arms.

For the longest time, Jimmy wanted to experience the larger world, however difficult that might be. He wasn't content to sit in a corner of a room, hum, thump on the floor, and talk to himself all day, although that was a favorite activity. Even though we were tempted to overprotect him, we followed Dr. Holden's advice. We pushed Jimmy out of his comfort zone and let him venture outside his inner circle as much as possible, protecting him the best we could. Yes, some people would be unkind and mean to Jimmy, but that didn't stop us. We knew we had to keep on pushing, expanding his boundaries and changing his day-to-day routines.

Don't you hide that boy in your house. You take him out wherever you're going.
        --a grandfather (Lloyd Lawrence)

5   The "Bucher Method"

38,000 families use a total of 381 different treatments. On the average, a family uses five treatments at a cost of $500.00 a month. One family uses 56 treatments at the same time. This data comes from the National Database for Autism Research (NDAR), the largest electronic filing cabinet on autism in the world.[13] Many parents are extremely vulnerable when their child is diagnosed with autism; therefore, rash decisions and emotion may replace rationality. Out of desperation and hope, parents may decide to do whatever it takes to lessen the symptoms of autism or maybe even find a cure. This might mean discovering a miraculous book, using a hyped concoction of drugs, or trying some radical parenting technique. In his book, *Far from the Tree*, Andrew Solomon talks about the "literature of miracles" which motivates parents to try every imaginable treatment, even if it costs gobs of money and has no scientific basis.[14]

According to experts, mainstream medicine has had an extremely difficult time nailing down what causes autism and identifying effective treatments. Dr. Paul Law, Director of IAN and the father of a young adult with autism, says, "When there are no good treatments for a disorder…there's a proliferation of treatments." Liane Carter, a mother of a son diagnosed with ASD, warns, "There's a sense of desperation, that for every treatment out there that you consider and don't do, what if that was the one thing that would make a difference? There's a lot of guilt, a feeling there's something you haven't tried."[15]

I t's one thing to hear a single person express concerns about a product or rave about a treatment. It's quite another when numerous scientists collect data and report findings. While scholarly research indicates that certain treatments show promise, others are at best a waste of time and money. At worst, they can cause serious health problems and even death. An absurd number have not been proven scientifically. These treatments include dietary and nutritional supplements, certain "revolutionary" teaching techniques, hyperbaric oxygen chambers, and physical manipulation. As an example, something called the Miracle Mineral Solution (MMS) has been marketed online as a cure for autism, even though the Food and Drug Administration (FDA) has warned people of its potentially life-threatening side effects.

Parents are extremely vulnerable when their children are diagnosed with ASD. Often, they look far and wide for anything they think might help. In today's world, they're confronted with a plethora of so-called new "breakthroughs" that claim to produce unheard-of results. Without the benefit of hard, scientific evidence, people have to depend on their own intuition, empathy, resources, and gut feelings to determine the impact of a particular treatment.

One danger is that people, in an effort to find a treatment that works, convince themselves that a treatment works. This is known as the self-fulfilling prophecy. Another danger is that a child with autism might seem to show positive signs in response to a treatment, but the changes might have absolutely nothing to do with the treatment itself. For instance, children tend to respond favorably to positive interaction and positive attention. How can we be sure that any observed changes are due to the treatment in question rather than the fact that families and caregivers are suddenly giving more time and attention to their autistic child?

The ongoing litany of so-called cures or breakthroughs for autism brings back a conversation my wife and I had with our neurologist. When Jimmy was in kindergarten, our neurologist said, "Some of these kids will get 'better' if you wave a wand over their head." In other words, a child might start developing certain abilities regardless of any program or treatment. Progress might simply reflect growth and maturation. Likewise, he added with a hint of sarcasm, "You could identify what you're doing with Jimmy that's helping him and call it the 'Bucher Method.'"

In the mid-1970s, autism was almost hidden from the public eye. At this time, there was no diagnosis termed the "autism *spectrum disorder.*" It was not until the early 1980s when Jimmy was six that our neurologist, who was affiliated with Johns Hopkins, suspected Jimmy might be autistic. He referred us to Dr. Whitehouse, Head of the Kennedy Krieger Institute in Baltimore, Maryland. After a battery of tests, Dr. Whitehouse suspected autism, but was hesitant to make this diagnosis since he felt Jimmy was "too emotionally connected" to people. He told us that our son was the most hyperactive, "functional" child he ever met. Amidst all of this, Jimmy was developing a charming personality and at times, could be very sweet and anxious to please.

Today, hardly a week passes when there doesn't seem to be a new study, finding, or theory on autism. A plethora of books, journal articles, blogs, videos, and other social media now focus on the possible causes, cures, and implications of autism. Parents are told there is no cure for ASD, yet they hold out hope that their child is different. Many sources of information prescribe simple answers to complex problems that seem to defy solutions.

As we look back, how do we make sense of Jimmy's development and progress? It would be easy to identify something we did or didn't do in raising Jimmy. We might want to focus on some behavioral routine, a diet, a physical therapy regimen, our decision to administer or withhold a drug or vaccine, or some educational television show that Jimmy watched religiously. But isolating on one of these variables does not do justice to his story and uniqueness. Nor does it take into account the collective impact of Jimmy's immediate and extended family, friends, therapists, teachers, and others too numerous to mention.

As with any individual, Jimmy's development represents the complex interaction between nature and nurture. Assessing Jimmy and trying to partial out biological, social, and psychological variables was something we tried to do early on. Was it a particularly difficult labor? Could the answer be found in our genetic backgrounds? What about my wife's pregnancy? Was the doctor negligent in not doing a C-section? As we grappled with questions such as these, we realized the futility of this kind of assessment. But coming to this realization took time.

As parents, we came to the realization that it made much more sense for us to *stop* over-analyzing Jimmy and ourselves. We decided not to revisit our genetic family trees any more, and to cease second-guessing the circumstances under which he was born. Whatever we did from now on, we would continue to do it with love and with faith in God, Jimmy, and ourselves.

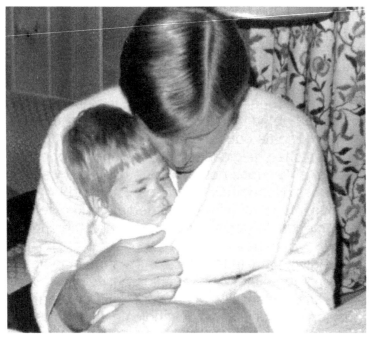

Figure 2

Jimmy is wonderful, whatever he turns out to be.
*   --the mommy*

6   Falling Through the Cracks

1 in 68 school-age children in the U.S. has autism as reported by the CDC (Centers for Disease Control and Prevention).[16] However, the CDC acknowledges that this estimate might miss a significant number of children on the spectrum. A more recent government survey of parents shows that a 1 in 45 estimate might be more accurate.[17] Regardless of the data, we know that we need better methods of recognizing autism and estimating its prevalence. Indeed, when Jimmy was finally diagnosed in 1987, autism was much less common; at least that's what we were led to believe.

According to the CDC, autism diagnoses vary greatly from community to community. In some areas, children may be falling through the cracks because they do not have adequate educational, economic, and medical resources to evaluate and diagnose them, especially at an early age. As they grow into adolescence, many children with autism are not getting the services and support they desperately need. Dr. Shapira of the CDC says, "The most powerful tool we have right now to make a difference in the lives of children with ASD is early identification."[18]

I distinctly remember Jimmy's first day of Early Intervention Kindergarten. The driver of the special ed bus opened the door and greeted him with a big, warm smile. Jimmy didn't hesitate; he got on and took his seat as the Oak Ridge Boys' country hit, "Elvira," blared from the bus's speakers. When the bus pulled away, I was overcome with emotion and tears welled up in my eyes.

"I go to my first day of school. I go on the school bus number 202. I see my teacher Ms. Weyrauch. Ms. Weyrauch's children came to my school too."

"I go to school. Tonight, Mommy promised me see "Real People" – some of it. I do reading games with Ms. Weyrauch. I play Frisbee. John threw the Frisbee and the leaves start to fall."

"I go to school. BJ and Robert built a big tower. Ms. Weyrauch said, 'That's enough things in the high corners.' Ms. Weyrauch said to Robert, 'Not make a big mess. This is a clean place.'"
  --Jimmy (from his journal)

Taking the bus soon became part of Jimmy's routine. One morning, Pat and Jimmy walked down our driveway hand-in-hand, just like always. Only this time, Jimmy started screaming "NO! NO! NO!" as he got closer to the bus. Fortunately, I was home and could see Jimmy getting hysterical, flapping his hands and spinning. Since Pat wasn't strong enough to control him, she called for my help.

I sprinted down our driveway, and firmly but lovingly wrapped my arms around Jimmy as we boarded the bus. Having never seen this behavior before, we assumed he just didn't want to go to school that day. As I managed to buckle him into his seat, Pat noticed that the bus looked the same but the number was different. Once we said our "goodbyes" and "love you's," we got off. As it pulled away, Pat was distraught. "What have we done to make him act this way? We've been working so hard to give him everything he needs – have we turned him into a spoiled brat? What difference does it make if the school bus is a different number?"

At the school where he attended kindergarten, a mainstream elementary school, my wife and I were invited to attend a meeting with his teacher as well as other professionals who worked with Jimmy. We were informed that Jimmy was unable to use the bathroom and clean himself independently. To say that we were taken aback is putting it mildly since Jimmy managed just fine at home. There was talk about the appropriateness of his school placement, and whether he would need to be transferred from a regular school to a self-contained school for severe and profoundly retarded students.

As the meeting wore on, one of the staff members raised a question that gave us pause, "What kind of toilet paper dispensers is Jimmy using at the school? Were they the resistant-type dispensers?" To save money, this type of dispenser made about 6 inches of toilet paper available with each tug of the roll.   An earlier diagnosis revealed that Jimmy had mild cerebral palsy (CP), affecting his speech and his hands. Perhaps his CP was making it difficult for him to get enough toilet paper. Once the staff confirmed that this was indeed the case, they simply installed resistance-free toilet paper dispensers. Problem solved. If it wasn't for the staff member's ability to think outside of the box, Jimmy would have been forced to transfer to a school which clearly didn't meet his needs.

In elementary school, Jimmy was constantly falling through the cracks of the public-school system. At age 10, he was placed in what was called a "transitional class," designed for special children who were capable of a greater degree of mainstreaming. But staff was still unable to control his behaviors. He was in perpetual motion in the classroom. Unable to stay in his seat, he was constantly touching everyone and everything in his reach. Frustration on his part gave way to lengthy bouts of screaming.

One of his mainstream classes was social studies. As part of the curriculum, Jimmy and his classmates spent three weeks preparing for a field trip to the National Museum of Natural History in Washington, D.C. Jimmy was given numerous homework assignments on the upcoming trip. Two days before the trip, Pat was informed that Jimmy would not be allowed to go. Because of his so-called uncontrollable behaviors, she was told it wouldn't be safe for him or his classmates. In spite of Pat's offer to chaperone and take full responsibility for Jimmy, his teachers refused to budge. This decision by his teachers was all the more difficult to understand since they had seen Pat keep Jimmy under control whenever she visited the classroom. Pat spent the next day trying to allay the fears of teachers and administrators, but it was no use. So, she did what any good mother might do. While I stayed home with Katie for the day, Pat drove Jimmy to Washington, D.C. on the day of the trip. They joined Jimmy's class at the Museum, walked with them during the tour, and then left when his class boarded the bus. All in all, the two of them had a great time.

Months later, Jimmy was spending most of his time at school in his very own room (a small, unused closet) and his own aide. Only on rare occasions did he interact with other students and teachers. We knew full well that this was *not* appropriate and could *not* continue. Clearly, the public-school system in our county was not capable of meeting Jimmy's needs. They knew it, and so did we.

After carefully looking over the remaining options for the new school year, the closest we came, which was not close at all, was a class for emotionally disturbed children. However, because of this placement, a school psychologist by the name of Pete Zerheusen evaluated Jimmy and suggested that he might have autism. At that time, we knew very little about this disability. We knew it was serious and thought people with autism didn't talk. But Jimmy talked non-stop.

When Jimmy was diagnosed with autism at eleven years of age, we had no blueprint to follow. In the 1980s, relatively little information about autism was available. We went to libraries, expanded and diversified our social network, and picked the brains of special educators, doctors, and parents. We read everything we could get our hands on. There was no Internet at that time, so it was a challenge to find any information, much less relevant and reliable information.

Dr. Holden, our neurologist, told us that the odds of having a child with autism were 10,000 to 1. As I tried to process these odds, my immediate reaction was part disbelief and part numbness. But I also felt a sense of relief. Finally, we had a diagnosis that explained a great deal; behaviors that used to defy explanation became easier to understand. Now, at least we had a better idea of what we were dealing with and how we might plan to help our son moving forward. We were ready to get to work.

7 Juggling Work and Family

Today, it's not unusual to hear someone ask a mom how she balances work and family. Rarely do I ever hear this same question asked of a father. Nevertheless, we know that fathers today are concerned about work demands that require too much time away from their families. In a culture that still tells them to put work first, men struggle with priorities. A recent Pew Research Center report finds half of full-time working fathers say they spend "too little time with their children."[19] Balancing work and family life is a challenge, with close to one-third saying they "always feel rushed." Further, only 39% of working dads say they are doing a "very good job" raising their children.

Bronnie Ware, an Australian nurse, spent years in palliative care, caring for and developing relationships with people who were close to dying and knew they were dying. During this time, she listened and kept a blog, recording the most common regrets voiced by her patients. In her book, The Top Five Regrets of the Dying, she mentions something she heard from every male patient in her care; namely, "I wish I hadn't worked so hard." These men deeply regretted missing their children's youth and the companionship of their partner. To a man, they regretted the lack of balance between work and their lives outside of work. What's more, they wished they had made different choices on a daily basis to maintain that balance. [20]

On my drive into work, I used to pass a billboard on the side of the road which spoke to dads. Its message was simple and straightforward; "Set aside time to be a father each and every day." While I understand its value, it is difficult for me to wrap my mind around this idea. To me, it makes being a father sound like something you put on your list of things to do each day. I really, really enjoy spending time with my children and grandchildren. It feels natural to me, it's fun, and I learn so much. Being a father defines me. It is who I am, rather than something I make sure I do on a daily basis.

Recently, I read an article that provided pointers for balancing work and family life. I had to laugh. Thinking back to those early days of raising Jimmy, it seems like I spent my life literally running and never stopped. When I left work, I ran to the parking lot and headed home. I remember going on errands, running from the car to the store; and then running from aisle to aisle within the store. When I was done shopping, I ran back to the car and then drove straight home.

Time was extremely precious; almost too precious. Years after Jimmy was born, my wife and I finally found a babysitter we felt we could trust with Jimmy. When we went out, our time together was something to cherish. However, our exhaustion from our daily routine made it difficult for us to unwind and focus on each other. Sometimes, even staying awake on a date was a challenge. Leaving Jimmy with a sitter was not easy for the two of us, but it was something we had to do once in a while. Pat and I learned we could not afford to ignore our relationship; rather, we absolutely needed to make time for ourselves.

Playing golf or basketball with the guys or taking part in some other time-consuming recreational activity on weekends was not even a consideration. That's why I ran for exercise. In less than one hour, I could get a good workout by simply running around our neighborhood. I could fit this into our family's schedule, and I soon discovered I needed this time to unwind, space out, and at times reflect. When I needed to "get away from it all," I ran.

Increasingly, it's no longer news to hear about a father who changes jobs or cuts back on his responsibilities at work to spend more time with his family. When it comes to making time for your children, results from a recent study point to the importance of quality versus quantity.[21] In other words, what we do with our children, such as eating meals together, and spending time reading, talking and playing together, is more important than simply putting in the time and sharing space. In our family, quality time was critically important, but so too was the *quantity of quality time*.

When I spent time with Jimmy, vegging out in front of the TV for extended periods of time wasn't an option. Furthermore, both of us needed more than just a few minutes of quality time each day. I can appreciate how my job as a college professor, social class, the support of my wife, and my personal priorities made it possible for *me* to integrate quality and quantity. As a working father, no one ever thought to ask me how I was able to juggle professional and family responsibilities. I just did it.

Paul Raeburn, author of *Do Fathers Matter? What Science Is Telling Us about the Parent We've Overlooked*, observes, "If you asked a psychologist in the 1970s what fathers do for their kids, especially young kids, the answer would have been, 'Not much.'" He adds, "The most important thing people thought fathers did was earn money and keep their kids out of poverty – which is a good thing – but that was the beginning and the end of it."[22]

I've never questioned my importance to my family's well-being. As a father, my emotional, psychological, and physiological connections with each of my children began before birth and continued through childhood, adolescence, and now adulthood. These connections didn't just evolve naturally; rather they're an outgrowth of my relationship with each of my children. Our family's economic stability was a team effort. My income, along with money from my wife's piano lessons, food from her garden, and our family's ability to live within our means, allowed me to work one job and made it possible for Pat to stay home and take care of Jimmy.

Family took priority; taking care of Jimmy and meeting his needs and those of my other children was number one. Family concerns and responsibilities spilled over into work and everything else for that matter. As an example, in the morning I was there, helping my children get ready for school. Fortunately, as a professor, I had a considerable amount of flexibility in my schedule. That flexibility allowed me to leave home as late as possible and return home shortly after my last class or the occasional afternoon meeting at school.

I vividly remember days when I felt like I had already put in a full day by the time I arrived at work around 7:30 a.m. And unlike my wife, I could then escape from the daily grind at home. When I began work on my Ph.D. at Howard University shortly after Jimmy was born, I would get up around 4 a.m., hoping to get at least some quiet study time before Jimmy awoke. Unfortunately, his sleeping patterns were anything but regular.

From age 3 to 6, Jimmy spent mornings in a public-school program for children with special needs. When he got home, a typical day for Jimmy was divided into three parts: education, physical therapy, and social/emotional growth. After he had lunch and listened to his favorite tapes for a short period of time, Pat focused on his education. While there was no set routine, language, spelling, letters, numbers, colors, math, and reading somehow all came together during this time. I taught a schedule that usually allowed me to be home by 3 p.m. When I arrived, I was "on." For the next three hours, it was time for me, Jimmy, and later his sisters to play outside if possible, to reinforce the physical therapy he was receiving each week.

Figure 3 OUR TIME TOGETHER GOT EVERYBODY MOVING.

From 6 to 6:30 p.m., meal time was an opportunity for the entire family to eat together and try to talk about our day amidst semi-controlled chaos. Playing around, reading books, and just having fun took us to bedtime at 8 p.m.

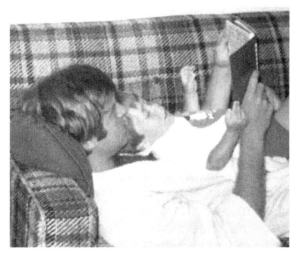

Figure 4 READING A FAVORITE BOOK SETTLED JIMMY

By design, my colleagues at Baltimore City Community College (BCCC) knew very little about my family life. My inner circle at work knew that my son had serious developmental issues, but rarely did I go into detail. For some reason, my guard was up when I went to work. Perhaps I didn't want anyone questioning my commitment to work, nor what I did on my own time.

When Jimmy was young, I remember a meeting I had with the sociologists in my department. Stan, who was leading the meeting, began discussing our activities and accomplishments as a department. He then proceeded to list the many accomplishments of each of my colleagues that semester, all the while going on and on about how productive they were. When he got to me, all he could say was "Bucher, what have you been up to?" I suddenly felt overcome with emotion, disrespected and misunderstood. After all, Stan was one person who knew full well that I had a young son with autism. Didn't he know that each and every day I was doing everything in my power to be a good father, a good husband, *and* a good teacher? Didn't he have the ability to put himself in my shoes? At that moment, words would not come to me. I fought back my tears, got up and left the room. Stan and I never spoke about that moment again.

A few years later, my nine-year old daughter, Katie, nominated me for *The Carroll County Sun* "Father of the Year Award." Out of all the awards for which I have been nominated, this was the most special. In an essay, Katie described what made her dad special. To my surprise, I won the award. However, as much as that award meant to me, I didn't include it on my resume or on my annual BCCC evaluation, even though my commitment to be a good father made me a much better teacher. In retrospect, I wish I had.

In her essay, Katie wrote, "He's the best because he thinks it's more important to stay home than to work all the time on his job. Daddy doesn't let my mom do all the work. My brother is autistic. Dad plays with him or takes him somewhere all the time. He takes my brother to basketball courts, shopping malls, and playgrounds. I couldn't do all that." Finally, Katie mentioned her "special time" when she doesn't share her dad with her brother or younger sister, Suzy. Weekdays, Katie and her dad ate breakfast together before he took her to the bus stop.

8   Run and Jump

Sometimes, fathers are referred to as the peripheral or invisible parent. Perhaps that explains why they are largely absent in the research on parenting children with autism. Fortunately, some recent studies in the U.S. and abroad buck this trend and conclude that dads are increasingly hands-on in the care, play, and the education of their autistic children. For example, one small-scale study examines seven fathers and their sons with autism. In-depth interviews reveal men who connect with their sons in a variety of ways, including "shared activities" and "developmental sensitivity." Often, father and son's "shared activities" took the form of physical activity, such as playing at the playground, swimming, and wrestling indoors. These fathers were tuned into how their sons learned, as well as their achievements, however small. One father mentioned his son jumping off the ground as a major breakthrough given his development up to that point.[23]

In a recent study done in the United Kingdom, more than 300 fathers (biological, adoptive, foster, or step-fathers) described their involvement in their autistic children's lives. Almost every day, dads played with their children, including "rough and tumble play, looking at books, computing, and going for walks." Dads were also highly engaged in their child's education, often helping out with homework and attending meetings at school. Given that employment posed the greatest obstacle to spending more time with their children, nearly half of these dads opted for part–time or shift work or became self-employed.[24]

When I got home from work each day, I'd play with Jimmy for hours. Our world was our yard and a nearby school playground. We would play "run and jump," a variation of tag. He'd chase me around our yard, giggling and smiling as he ran as fast as possible. When he eventually caught me, I'd either throw him high in the air or spin him around with his feet off the ground. In addition to developing Jimmy's gross motor skills, this type of exercise made him less agitated and built up his stamina. And he absolutely loved chasing and catching me. Jimmy never seemed to tire of "run and jump," and as long as he was happy, I was happy. We'd then play soccer, one on one in our front yard. Fortunately, we had a pretty big front yard. Next, I'd typically push Jimmy on our swing set, or go back and forth with him on the swing's glider as we talked and sang songs.

When his sister Katie was old enough to join us, we created some pretty amazing obstacle courses in the backyard. Then it was time for me to pull the two of them in a wagon that I had built entirely from lumber, wheels, and metal that I had found in a nearby trash heap. Typically, our destination was a nearby school playground within walking distance of our home. We repeated this routine almost every day of the week.

Figure 5 KATIE AND JIMMY ON THEIR WAY

Besides being lots of fun, this time became "our time." We were on our own, while my wife was inside teaching piano lessons, paying bills, making dinner, or simply catching her breath. Without mobile technology to distract us; my children and I were completely engaged in whatever we were doing at the moment.

I sometimes wonder how my relationship with my children would have been different if my wife and I hadn't become, out of necessity, Jimmy's peer group. My time with Jimmy was one more reminder of our outsider status in our own community. Jimmy was largely invisible to our neighbors. While he was not picked on, at least in my presence, he was never included in games, birthday parties, or any other activities in our neighborhood. It was our reality, and we adapted to it as best as we could.

9 Misdiagnoses

In *Nobody Nowhere: The Remarkable Autobiography of an Autistic Girl*, Donna Williams provides a first-person account of the world of autism. Williams, born in 1963 in Melbourne, Australia, was variously labeled as retarded, disturbed, insane, and psychotic early in her life. It wasn't until she became a young adult that she would be diagnosed as autistic. Williams' intelligence, insight, sense of humor, and creativity defied commonly held assumptions about autism, so much so that some questioned whether she was "faking" autism. After all, autism was assumed to be so debilitating that someone like Williams could not write like she did. Interestingly, the same doubts were aired about Temple Grandin. People are now much more aware of the wide range of capabilities along the spectrum. Smukler writes, "Today, Williams' and Grandins' 'credentials' are rarely challenged. Rather than being doubted, they are more likely to be commended for offering us an 'inside out' view of autism."[25]

Dr. Lawrence Bartak, a highly respected teacher and educational psychologist, provided Williams with her diagnosis of autism, even though she was sociable. Dr. Bartak, whose work revolves around professionals who provide services to individuals with autism, wrote the "Introduction" to *Nobody Nowhere*. He cautions against putting professionals on a pedestal, "Professionals are not superhuman, and are just as prone to making incorrect, if not downright silly interpretations of what they observe as anybody else. Many of the things we notice in people with autism remain puzzling, even after some 40 to 50 years of research in this field."[26]

Why do some professionals feel the need to take our dreams away from us?
*   --the mommy*

At three months, Jimmy had a massive seizure. He lost all muscle tone and visual contact. Our doctor said we needed to prepare ourselves for the fact that this was all he might ever be. Just three days later, he was once again rolling over and smiling back at us. Soon thereafter, we saw Dr. Holden, his neurologist, and asked, "Will Jimmy be able to talk? Will he be able to walk?" He simply responded, "We won't know until Jimmy talks or walks."

Early on, some prognoses were on target, but most were not. For instance, one doctor diagnosed him as having a "weak side," probably due to brain injury which caused cerebral palsy (CP). Shortly thereafter, his first physical therapist noticed that Jimmy showed a tendency to drag his leg, and then informed us, "He will never walk normally." Years later, Jimmy became the first athlete to run two miles in the Maryland State Special Olympics.

During those early years, Jimmy's diagnoses were "all over the place." Pat and I tried to be objective and positive at the same time, critically evaluating each one. At age one, Jimmy was given his first round of developmental tests. A well-known child development specialist at what is now the Kennedy Krieger Institute was very straightforward and definitive in his explanation of Jimmy's capabilities. "In a race where everybody else is going 100, Jimmy will go 50 at best." When we think back to this doctor and his assessment of Jimmy, we distinctly remember one of our dialogues with him:

Doctor: "If you asked him (Jimmy) to get

something for you, would he get it and bring it back?"

*Pat: "*I don't think so."

*Doctor: "*Well even a dog could do that!"

This doctor's people skills were not his strong suit to say the least. But that didn't matter; we could not and would not accept that diagnosis or many others that followed. Even in the face of highly respected professionals who told us we were being unrealistic, we persisted, kept our focus and clung to our dreams.

Everybody was ripping away our dreams. It's the parent's job to be unrealistic. Parents' unrealistic goals for their children often result in miraculous things.

--the mommy

The testing continued. Right after our visit to Kennedy-Krieger, a home school professional began to visit Jimmy on a weekly basis. She advised us that it was too early to conclude anything about Jimmy's potential.

In the early twentieth century, one of the world's foremost surgeons said, "A smart mother often makes a better diagnosis than a poor doctor." I would add that there are times when a smart and engaged mother, or father, can make a diagnosis that is just as good if not better than that made by a *good* doctor.

My wife is one smart lady. In many ways, she had a better handle on Jimmy's development than anyone else. And yet, her veracity was often questioned by doctors and other professionals.

Never in my life have I felt that my honesty was being

questioned as much as when I spoke to professionals, including doctors, as the mother of a child with disabilities. I clearly remember two early evaluations – one said repeatedly stated "mother claims" while the other used the words "mother reports."

--the mommy

Pat's experiences aren't unique. For instance, other mothers of children on the autism spectrum talk about feeling invisible. "I was still very hurt and upset because no one was listening to me, you know the doctors, nurses, psychologists, the specialist just did not listen to me (Maria). In this same study, Anne expresses her disillusionment with health care professionals, "You just think they don't believe you, and you think, they think you're just making a fuss."[27]

By age three, Dr. Holden determined that Jimmy wasn't talking or using his hands normally due to his mild cerebral palsy. Three years later (1982), he diagnosed Jimmy as having ADD, Attention Deficit Disorder, adding that ADD was a new term we'd be hearing a lot about.

Other than mild CP, we knew the other diagnoses were at best educated guesses. At age ten, Jimmy received a diagnosis of Pervasive Developmental Disorder (PDD). The PDD diagnosis was an ambiguous, catch-all term that didn't tell us very much. So, we proceeded to ask questions and educate ourselves to the best of our abilities. What do we do, what are his needs, and how can we help? A subsequent written evaluation from a doctor at Johns Hopkins stated that "one of Jimmy's biggest problems was an overzealous mother."

After spending eleven years looking for a diagnosis that fit our son, we took him to Linwood. Unknown to us, we discovered that this program for children with autism was less than an hour's drive from us. Upon entering a large old stone mansion, we were greeted by a staff member who took Jimmy while we met with Linwood's director as well as key educational and residential personnel. We weren't interested in "selling" Jimmy. We wanted this facility to know everything about our son and our family. When it came time to describe his challenging behaviors, we wouldn't hold back.

Figure 6 FOUNDER JEANNE SIMONS PAINTED THE HISTORIC LINWOOD HOME

After introducing ourselves, the discussion turned toward Jimmy. We were ready for the typical questions we'd been asked by staff at other institutions. For instance, does he try to set fires? Does he try to hurt his sisters? What violent tendencies does he have? Instead, we were asked questions we had never heard before. When he was a baby, did he arch his back when we tried to hold him? Did he whisper before he talked? Did he tiptoe on grass, sand, or other surfaces? (He still does.) We responded, "Yes," "Yes," and "Yes."

In a matter of six hours, Linwood nailed the diagnosis. Jimmy had autism. At the end of the meeting, the head of this facility said "Yes, we want him, and we can help him." Pat began to cry tears of joy as I tried to process what they were saying. Before we left, one of the senior staff members told us, "Don't ever forget he's still your son." There was no chance of that. We were going to be highly involved every step of the way, just as we had been up to that point in Jimmy's life.

The diagnosis of autism was far from tragic. For us, it was a relief.
--the mommy

The Linwood staff did not go on and on about how Jimmy would be a constant source of stress and ruin our lives if we didn't get help. They didn't talk about Jimmy as if he had some dreaded disease. Rather, one staff member by the name of Bill Moss offered insight into Jimmy's future. "Don't be surprised if Jimmy grows up to be a relatively mellow and delightful adult." Nobody had ever said this was even a possibility.

Soon, Jimmy would start taking the bus to Linwood. The bus would pick him up Monday morning and bring him back Friday afternoon. Sending him off to Linwood wasn't easy by any means. In a way, it was as if we were sending our eleven-year-old son off to college. Yes, we did our homework on Linwood, but we still had reservations and it was difficult to entrust our "little boy" to someone else. Suzy was an infant, but 7-year-old Katie vividly remembers how it felt to "lose" her brother. Pat did her best to explain to Katie that our family and Jimmy's teachers couldn't give him everything he needed. She tried hard to comfort Katie, offering to set up "regular visits" with Ms. Nunnelly, her wonderful school guidance counselor. Talking with Ms. Nunnelly seemed to help, but Katie still struggled. Like us, she was trying to process all that was going on, and she wasn't sure this was in Jimmy's best interests. Pat remembers shedding quite a few tears throughout this transition, which as she said probably didn't help matters. She couldn't put Katie's fears to rest and soothe her like she wanted to, but that didn't stop my wife from trying.

Recently, Katie confided in me that Jimmy going off to Linwood affected her deeply. "They took my brother away," she said. Clearly, this was a hellish adjustment for her, especially since it wasn't long before Pat went back to work and Suzy went to day-care. What boggles my mind is that as her daddy, I wasn't more tuned into what she was thinking and feeling when Jimmy first left home. Yes, this was a big life change for Jimmy, but it was also a big life change for Katie. And in the midst of doing what we determined was in Jimmy's best interest, I lost sight of Katie and all the support she needed throughout this process.

Early in their lives, our daughters endured and internalized a lot of emotional pain. They knew we were stretched beyond our limits with Jimmy, and I suspect there were times they kept things to themselves because they didn't want to add to all of the emotional strain in our family. Thinking back to that time is still difficult for us.

We were so grateful for Linwood, but that doesn't hide the fact putting Jimmy's care in somebody else's hands was extremely painful.
--the daddy

10 Tumtime

Many on the spectrum find it difficult to gauge and track time. This can make it difficult for them to process and understand abstract concepts like three weeks from now, yesterday, and 20 years ago; or the idea that time only moves forward, not backward. Estimating how long it will take to complete a task can also be a challenge. It's one thing to be told something will take about an hour, it's quite another for one's brain to understand and gauge the length of time in an hour. Developing a sense of time is a very important skill that makes it possible to do many things, including planning one's daily schedule and transitioning from one activity to another.

How can we help autistic children improve their understanding of the passing of time? In a study by faculty at Eindhoven University of Technology in The Netherlands, researchers examined this question. Using a timer designed for this study, music was used to help autistic children anticipate the end of time spans. The timer, which displayed a row of red lights growing shorter with the passage of time (visual feedback), combined with familiar and favorite songs played in a particular sequence, (auditory feedback) allowed children on the spectrum to measure time. Moreover, researchers found that this intervention reduced the anxiety and repetitive behaviors of these children, allowing the children to focus more on what they were doing rather than the timer itself. The timer helped in a variety of situations, including waiting for dinner, gauging time for a specific activity, having a shower, or monitoring how long until a family member comes home.[28]

When he was a child, Pat and I talked with his neurologist about Jimmy's inability to interpret the passage of time. According to Dr. Holden, it was possible that Jimmy's brain made it difficult for him to understand the concept of time. Dr. Holden believed that Jimmy was so obsessed with time because he had no sense of time.

As a preschooler, Jimmy was incapable of waiting for anything. One of his first words was "when?" At first, we would try to explain – after lunch, after naptime, or after Daddy gets home. But he would just persist and persist with his "when?" Pat's first strategy was to teach him to use the word "sometime." For some reason, that would satisfy him for a while. Once he learned to say "tumtime" – his best approximation of sometime, things got better. We could turn the question around to him and say, "when Jimmy?" and he would answer "tumtime." But even that didn't last for long.

As soon as we discovered that Jimmy could identify numbers around age 4, Pat taught him how to read a digital clock. What a blessing that was! Once he outgrew naps, she could put him in his room for "tape" time. Pat would set out a few cassette tapes full of his favorites that she recorded off the TV, and tell him that tape time was over at say, 2:30. He would know to play his tapes until the digital clock said 2:30. This routine, combining auditory and visual cues, seemed to provide him with the structure he needed, and he picked up on this VERY quickly. Now, when Jimmy asked "when," Pat could give him a time. However, her timing better be impeccable or there was hell to pay.

Locking in on a particular time proved to be a double-edged sword. Jimmy would do most anything to make sure he was able to watch a certain TV show, whether it be his favorite game show, anything having to do with the Muppets, or more recently, *Its Academic*. My wife remembers not making any appointments that might interfere with reruns of *The Muppet Show*, Channel 8, at 3:30 p.m., Monday through Friday. If Jimmy and Pat happened to be out, he would grow extremely anxious if it got past 3:00 and they weren't yet home. He'd start flapping and squealing, asking over and over again, "What time is it now?"

Jimmy would sometimes ask neighborhood children to "play" although he really had no idea how to "play" or even relate to other children. One time, three little boys were walking by our house and Jimmy asked them to play. Their first response was "sure – later." Of course, Jimmy replied with "when?" When pressed, the boys finally told him "4 o'clock." Sure enough at 4:00, Jimmy was standing at the end of our driveway, waiting for his "friends" to come play. Little did they know Jimmy could tell time. The boys never came.

Early in Jimmy's life, it seemed like hardly a day went by when we weren't visiting a doctor or a health care professional. These visits were for everyday health concerns, or at times, we were trying to gain further insight into the nature of Jimmy's disability. Since I was working a full-time job, my wife would take Jimmy to see various doctors, especially for routine procedures and care. Although she would volunteer to remain with Jimmy while the doctor attended to him, Pat was often told that her assistance wasn't necessary and to have a seat in the waiting room. Typically, Jimmy's constant movement and extreme agitation would make it virtually impossible for a nurse or doctor to look into his ear, put a needle in his arm, stitch up a wound, or perform any kind of medical procedure. Invariably, someone would eventually come out to take Pat up on her offer to help.

One visit stands out in Pat's mind. She took Jimmy for outpatient surgery at a nearby hospital when he was eight years of age. When medical staff came out to get Jimmy for the procedure, Pat told them, "I think you're gonna need me." They assured my wife that Jimmy would be fine and took him back to the examining room. Some five minutes later, the call went out for Pat. The nurse said they were having problems getting an IV into Jimmy. When she went back to help, she could see the doctor and his staff were frazzled after trying in vain to settle Jimmy down. Jimmy was sobbing.

Nothing seemed to work. Hugging did not soothe Jimmy. Promises of treats if he sat still or saying something like "it will be over soon" were totally worthless. Enlisting the help of several adults to hold him down only made his agitation worse. Pat felt she had to come up with something in her "bag of tricks." What if Dr. Holden was right? If Jimmy had no sense of time, perhaps this was making him more anxious because he had no idea how long something would last.

In Jimmy's case, the magic was counting. Before any procedure, she would inquire about the length of time Jimmy would have to stay still. If the nurse told her twenty seconds, she would say to Jimmy, "I am going to count to twenty slowly; and if you sit quietly, it will be over by then." Next, Pat proceeded to rest gently on top of Jimmy and in a very, very calm and loving manner, she slowly counted to twenty. Then the nurse could administer an IV quite easily or do whatever had to be done.

As a middle-aged adult, Jimmy's concept of time continues to make it difficult for him to make sense of the world. For instance, after a twenty-year hiatus, we recently returned to the church he attended as a young child. We had already told him that Ms. Straub, his favorite Sunday school teacher, died a while back. Death is a concept Jimmy now understands as well as any of us. On our way to visit his old classroom after the service, he saw a painting on the wall honoring his teacher. However, he had no sense that things had changed since he was last there. Once he saw the painting, his first question dealt with the whereabouts of Ms. Straub. "Where is she?" Jimmy asked, as he continued to look for his dear old friend.

11 Colorful Communication

Donna Williams, an author, singer-songwriter, and screenwriter, knew a thing or two about autism and communication. In her autobiography, she distinguishes between her world and "the world." As someone whose autistic diagnosis was confirmed at age twenty, she gained newfound understanding through her communication with others with disabilities. "I have been with the mentally ill, the backward, and the physically disabled. I have also had the pleasure of being with others labeled 'autistic.' This was the only group who spoke my own language so well that I realized that much of what I thought of as my personality was in fact my individual expression of many of the misunderstood and confusing symptoms of autism."[29]

While she was promoting her book, *Nobody Nowhere: The Extraordinary Autobiography of an Autistic*, Donna Williams met Jim Sinclair, another autistic adult. Like Williams, Sinclair speaks and writes about autism and communication. In his well-known essay, "Don't Mourn for Us," Sinclair emphasizes that autism is not some "impenetrable wall." Rather, people with autism have the potential to communicate; they just might use different sounds, body language, and symbols to express themselves. If parents or caregivers think they cannot communicate with their autistic children, Sinclair advises them to work harder, move into "unfamiliar territory," be more creative, and question their own assumptions. Talking and communication are *not* the same. Just as children are expected to learn from their parents, parents must also let their children teach them about their language and world.[30]

The word autism is derived from the Greek word, "autos," meaning self. Individuals with autism tend to be stereotyped as self-absorbed, socially disengaged, and cooped up in their own private world. The inability to reach out to others and communicate effectively is described in the literature as a defining feature and core deficit of autism. For our son Jimmy, communication is not easy, but when people show interest and make an effort to really listen to him, he can be very social, engaged, and even charming.

Jimmy enjoys stepping outside of his world and interacting with others on his terms. Asking appropriate questions in the eyes of society, beginning and maintaining conversations, adjusting to different topics of discussion, and reading body language can make daily social interaction overwhelming. Nevertheless, he is highly adept at discerning who's really tuned into him and who's not.

At age two, Jimmy started speech therapy. It wasn't until two years later that he started to say a few words clearly enough to understand. Up until about four years of age, Jimmy was essentially non-verbal. He talked so fast and dropped so many sounds he was unintelligible. When he wanted anything, he would scream. Jimmy would go from smile to scream in less than a second and often we had no idea why. By age five, he was speaking in phrases, many of them memorized. A year later, he learned to type. Due to his cerebral palsy, Jimmy could not write longhand. But typing enhanced his ability to communicate and opened up all kinds of worlds to him.

Like many children with autism, Jimmy used words in unusual ways. For example, he repeated certain phrases he heard elsewhere. As a child, he made a habit of waking up, saying, "Good morning morning," because this is something he heard on Garfield television specials. Or during the course of talking to himself, which he did on a regular basis, he would utter a long, drawn out and high pitched "Sheeeesh." Jimmy was simply repeating what Kermit used to say on *The Muppet Show*. "You guessed it buster," from *Garfield* and "No way José," from *Alf* were two other phrases that frequently found their way into Jimmy's speech. When he was ten, we heard from one of Jimmy's teachers who reprimanded him for laughing at another child who was acting up. When she said, "Jimmy that is NOT funny," Jimmy replied," I disagree." This was a phrase he heard repeatedly watching *Hollywood Squares* on television.

Keeping context in mind and shifting perspectives allows us to communicate with Jimmy. Often, episodes from *The Muppet Show*, game shows, and *Sesame Street* serve as reference points. For instance, Jimmy will begin talking about Dr. Marty to a stranger or a casual acquaintance. Who is Dr. Marty? He was a contestant on *Name That Tune* many, many years ago. Another time, Jimmy went to see the show *Pirates of Penzance* at a local dinner theater. Afterwards, we asked him about the show. "How was the music?" His response, "'Hail, Hail, The Gang's All Here,' Ms. Shirley Wooten." (Wooten, a contestant on *Name That Tune*, guessed the name of this song). Jimmy continued, "Gilda Radner (guest star on *The Muppets*) sang 'Modern Major General' with the Talking Carrot" (both of these songs are from *Pirates of Penzance*). It took me a while, but I finally began to make sense of these connections once I asked Jimmy, and then my wife, to explain them to me.

Jimmy's language can be very colorful, funny,

and difficult to understand. When I visit Jimmy on weekends, I often check his appearance as well as the cleanliness of his room. Usually, he asks me to take note of his personal hygiene, but in a roundabout, obtuse way.

Jimmy: "Two of my thumbs are no good. You know what's wrong with my toes? Toes too long, way long!"
Translation: Can you check my toenails and fingernails, and if they're too long, can you cut them?

Jimmy: "I need an h.c."
Translation: (short for head check) Do I need a haircut?

Then, in the middle of our discussion about his hygiene, Jimmy may change the focus of his questions.

Jimmy: "There are too many wires coming out of my TV."
Translation: My television isn't working.

While Jimmy and I were shopping one Saturday over the summer, he started having some "fun" with me:

Jimmy: "Look!" pointing to the front of his tee shirt which read Deep Creek Lake. Then he extends his hand to me and says "Shake." When I start to shake his hand, he pulls back and says, "Not handshake, milkshake." Jimmy repeats this sequence a few times until I catch on.
Translation: In a few weeks, Jimmy will be visiting us. At that time, his friends at Linwood will be going to Deep Creek Lake for a few days. Jimmy wants a milkshake when he comes home to visit us. I might add a chocolate milkshake.

Over the years, Pat has taught Jimmy some useful phrases that allow him to communicate with us. When he started talking, phrases such as "All done" and "Momma down please" enabled Jimmy to tell us what he was feeling. As an example, he gradually learned to say "all done" when he got frustrated and could not hold it together anymore. If he was working with his occupational therapist, saying "all done" was certainly more socially appropriate than screaming or throwing stuff on the floor. "Momma down please" let us know when he had finished eating and was tired of sitting in his booster chair. Gradually, he learned to use these phrases in public to make his needs known. At age six, on a roller-coaster ride at a local amusement park, he spent the entire time politely saying, "Momma down please, momma down please."

Doctors called Jimmy's outbursts tantrums. I hated that. To me, this was his way of telling us, "I'm dying inside, and I need to stop."
    --the mommy

Jimmy has taught us a number of creative phrases as well, some of which have become part of our everyday vocabulary. Last year, my daughter Suzy got a birthday present from her coworkers with a note that read, "Happy Birthday Eve Eve, only 367 days till your next birthday." Who came up with the idea of wishing someone "Happy Birthday Eve" the day before one's birthday, or "Merry Christmas Eve Eve" two days before Christmas? Jimmy, of course.
    The concept, neurodiversity, asserts that Jimmy, like every other individual on the autism spectrum, has his own distinctive set of communication skills. Simply describing Jimmy's ability to communicate as a core deficit ignores his

strengths in this area. To illustrate, Jimmy possesses an uncanny ability to remember information for a long period of time. That skill allows him to communicate with family and friends on their birthdays by sending cards that convey his heartfelt thoughts. Our family doctor, who recently got a birthday card from Jimmy, shared with us that Jimmy was the only person who remembered his birthday.

One day, Jimmy came to our house for a swimming party. It didn't take long until he got bored with the pool, so he came inside and watched TV. While inside, he saw my calendar with all of our family members' birthdays on it. Before I knew it, we were all getting birthday cards from Jimmy every year. Now, twenty years later, he never forgets my birthday and I cherish the birthday cards he sends me. He's amazing!
--a friend (Lynn Clarke)

In a world full of superfluous language and people who say one thing but mean another, Jimmy is totally honest. In spite of his lack of formal education, his narrow interests allow him to develop expertise in specific areas. As an example, he knows store hours and aisle numbers of the grocery stores we typically shop. He knows the capitol of each state in the U.S. But his wisdom goes much deeper. Jimmy understands the importance of sharing, gratitude, and kindness. More importantly, he consistently models these human traits. His manners are excellent. When Jimmy speaks, he makes liberal use of "Please," "Thank you very much," "Excuse me," "Yes sir" and "No sir," and "May I ask a question?" Jimmy never just says no. He *always* says, "No thank you."

When I ask my wife to describe Jimmy's communication style, the first words out of her mouth are persistent and circuitous. Circuitous persistence allows him to keep "going at it" until someone understands him. As someone who needs structure and consistency, he's smart enough to keep asking questions until he gets the information he needs.

For the longest time, Jimmy has understood more than people give him credit for. Communication, like empathy, is a two-way street. Too often, Jimmy finds communication difficult because people do not make the effort and show the requisite patience. Our focus is on respecting and understanding Jimmy's colorful speech, not extinguishing it. There are times when Jimmy saves his questions for us because he knows we will listen intently and empathetically. It must be terribly frustrating for him that many people don't care enough and don't put forth the effort to converse with him to find out what's on his mind. His speech is not meaningless by any stretch of the imagination.

Having raised Jimmy, I am confident I can understand anybody.
--the mommy

12 Underwear is Underwear

Dr. Darold Treffert, one of the world's foremost experts on savant syndrome and a consultant for the movie *Rain Man*, takes pride in the fact that this award-winning film introduced so many people throughout the world to autism. He stresses that *Rain Man* is entertainment, *not* a documentary. Nevertheless, the movie received critical acclaim for its authenticity in addition to its respectful and dignified portrayal of people with disabilities.[31]

Professor Ginny Russell studies autism, ADHD, and dyslexia at the University of Exeter (UK). In the University's *Screen Talks* blog, Dr. Russell discusses the movie *Rain Man* and its impact on our understanding of autism. She writes, the movie had "two important consequences." First, it inadvertently promoted a stereotype that all people with autism have savant or extraordinary abilities, when in fact, such savant skills rarely occur in individuals with autism. Second, *Rain Man* raised the public's awareness of autism. This movie's "high profile media coverage led to far greater recognition and application of the diagnostic label."[32]

Nearly three decades after the movie *Rain Man*, a team of researchers from Scotland found that portrayals of autism on screen may still reinforce stereotypes. Developmental psychologist Dr. Fletcher-Watson elaborates, "To deepen public understanding of autism spectrum disorders, we need more autistic characters on our screens. These characters should reflect the diversity we see in real life, rather than being artificially built from a textbook diagnosis of somebody with autism."[33]

I vividly remember watching the movie *Rain Man* soon after it came out in 1988; one year after Jimmy received a diagnosis of autism and began attending Linwood. It was a cathartic and eye-opening experience for my wife and me. Just prior to seeing the movie, we were a bit apprehensive, nervous, and guarded. Anytime anyone tries to tell "your story," there is a tendency to feel very vulnerable, especially when that story is deeply personal. In the back of our minds, we knew *Rain Man* could hurt us deeply if it took shortcuts and misrepresented people like Jimmy and people in his life. *Rain Man* dealt with a part of our lives that was extremely painful at times, and we were still not much past the "survival stage" in terms of dealing with Jimmy's autism.

Before going, I read reviews of the movie and they were generally excellent. The star of the movie, Dustin Hoffman, had evidently done his homework to prepare for playing the lead role of Raymond Babbitt, a man with savant syndrome. In addition to watching tapes and movies of many savants with autism, Hoffman studied scientific research and read journals, talked with professionals, visited a number of institutions that care for savants, and interacted with savants and their families. Even though Hoffman studied a number of savants and got to know them up close and personal, he did not try to imitate them. Rather, he learned what it might be like to have autism, and fashioned his own character based on that understanding.

Walking into the theatre, we felt as if we were as qualified as anyone to critique this movie, given our personal experiences with Jimmy, our advocacy work on the part of persons with autism, and our growing social network, including professionals at

Linwood. As the story unfolded, we connected almost immediately. It hit home, on both an intellectual and emotional level. I remember sitting toward the back of the theatre, and at certain points in the movie, laughing long and hard. Other moviegoers in front of us continually turned around to look at us, seemingly annoyed by our behavior. It didn't matter. It felt so good!

For the first time in our lives, we saw our son on the screen and in the public eye. Someone like our son was not portrayed as scary and emotionally disconnected; rather, he was endearing and even warm at times. The images we had seen in the media up to that point were generic, tragic, and stereotypical. Autistic people were shown to be nonverbal and self-abusive children who spun themselves in circles, rocked constantly, and hit their heads against the wall. They were unintelligent and largely incapable of developing meaningful relationships.

While *Rain Man* was entertainment, it sensitively and to a large degree, accurately portrayed a good deal of what we were dealing with at that time. For example, we saw many of Jimmy's mannerisms and behaviors in the lead character Raymond Babbit, a middle-aged man. Raymond spoke haltingly; had excellent recall skills, avoided eye contact and physical intimacy, and struggled with stimulus overload just like Jimmy. Fortunately, we already knew that Jimmy and most people with autism were not savants and did not possess extraordinary talents like Raymond. We later discovered that savant syndrome is not unique to people with autism.

This Academy Award-winning movie was not simply about a high-functioning person with autism who had a remarkable range of abilities and disabilities. Rather, it explored human relationships, personal growth, and change. *Rain Man* focuses on two characters - Raymond and his brother, Charlie Babbitt (Tom Cruise). As they get to know each other, their relationship grows deeper and more meaningful, especially during the course of a 6-day cross-country road trip they take together from Cincinnati to Los Angeles, with a noteworthy stopover in Las Vegas. Charlie gradually becomes much less selfish and materialistic as he comes to appreciate his brother as a person, including Raymond's needs, abilities, and feelings. Raymond becomes a bit more open to affection and more tolerant of deviations from his precious routine.

Two scenes in particular struck my wife and me as very funny. In one, we watched Raymond's singular, all-encompassing preoccupation with watching Judge Wapner and the television show *People's Court*. After all, this was part of Raymond's routine each and every week. What Charlie went through during the road trip to accommodate Raymond was no easy feat. When Raymond begins to perseverate about watching *People's Court*, Charlie takes a detour and drives miles out of his way. Charlie then stops at a house along the side of a road, knocks on the door of a complete stranger, and somehow persuades her to let them come in and watch TV. In no time, this mother and her family as well as Charlie and Raymond are all watching *People's Court*. This made perfect sense to us. We KNEW that no matter what, they would find a way to watch *People's Court*. The fact that they were driving along a deserted highway didn't matter. Raymond would get his needs met by any means necessary. This was our life.

A second scene revolves around Raymond and underwear. During the road trip, Raymond makes a random comment that he's not wearing underwear. In disbelief, Charlie asks why, noting that he gave Raymond a fresh pair of his briefs that morning. Raymond answers "Gotta get my boxer shorts at K-mart in Cincinnati, 400 Oak Street." Raymond continues, explaining that the underwear Charlie gave him are not boxer shorts. They're Hanes 32, and they're too tight. Charlie repeatedly tries to persuade Raymond that underwear is underwear; it doesn't matter where you buy it. When Raymond acts like he's not listening and repeats "K-mart…boxer shorts at K-mart," Charlie loses his cool. He stops the car, gets out, walks a few steps, and starts screaming at the top of his lungs. "What difference does it make where you buy underwear? Underwear is underwear!" Charlie continues, "You know what I think, Ray? I think this autism is a bunch of shit! Because you can't tell me that you're not in there somewhere!" After Charlie's tirade, Raymond uttered matter-of-factly, "Boxer shorts. K-mart."

Wow, did I identify with Charlie's frustration! No matter how much I tried, there were times when I couldn't get through to Jimmy about seemingly simple things, even though I was certain my point of view made perfect sense, and to my way of thinking he was fully capable of understanding me.

After seeing Rain Man, I was struck by the amazing similarities my son shared with Raymond. Yes, they were both unique, with different ages, personalities, life experiences, preferences, mannerisms, fears and joys. But it was like they shared the same "operating system." Before I watched Rain Man, I had never known anyone who was really like my son. For example, I absolutely knew ahead of time that there was no way Charlie was going to get Raymond to stop complaining about his underwear. And I knew that somehow, they would end up watching Judge

Wapner, no matter what it took.
      --the mommy

Movies like *Rain Man* and later, *Temple Grandin*, have opened doors for us and others like us. After we saw it, we suggested to our parents and friends that they see it. Once they did, we could then use *Rain Man* as a reference point when we discussed Jimmy. Can stereotypes be found in *Rain Man*? Isn't it true that Raymond, an autistic savant whose language and sensory processing skills lagged far behind his extraordinary math and memory skills, represents only a minute portion of the autism spectrum? Doesn't autism affect individuals differently? Isn't autism found in females as well as males? Might some people think they know what autism is all about once they have seen this movie? My response to all of these questions is, "Of course." But *one* movie such as *Rain Man* can only do so much. Despite its limitations, *Rain Man* provided another perspective on autism and brought about massive public awareness around the world.

Recently, I had the privilege to talk with Dr. Ruth Sullivan about *Rain Man* and her tireless and passionate advocacy for children and adults with autism and their families. Dr. Sullivan assisted in the production of *Rain Man*. And in order to prepare for his role as Raymond, Dustin Hoffman worked with a number of young men with autism, including Dr. Sullivan's son, Joseph. Dr. Sullivan credits *Rain Man* with making autism a household word. To quote Dr. Sullivan, "*Rain Man* put us a quarter of a century ahead of where we would otherwise be." Even though most people might not have known someone with autism when the movie was released, people could finally put a face on autism.[34]

Rain Man accelerated the process of making

the public more aware of autism. I feel a deep sense of gratitude to Barry Levinson, the director of *Rain Man*. No one movie, book, or storyline can begin to represent everyone on the autism spectrum. And now, with numerous and varied media portrayals of people with autism, any one representation of autism doesn't carry the same weight as *Rain Man* once did. And that is a good thing.

13 Not All Napkins Are the Same

Stimming, or self-stimulatory behavior, is a common symptom of autism. It refers to repetitive behaviors or movement of objects. For example, an autistic child might repeat commercials over and over again, constantly flap her arms, or spend hours spinning toys. Dr. Leo Kanner observed stimming in his 1943 groundbreaking study of childhood autism that appeared in the journal *Nervous Child*. Although rare, some stimming such as head banging and scratching can be so intense that it causes physical harm. Stims may vary over time, differ in intensity depending on the circumstance, and involve a variety of emotions. What's more, theories suggest stimming may provide sensory stimulation or decrease sensory overload.

At Clemson University, Dr. Jennifer Bisson and her Creative Inquiry team of students have begun to observe children in therapy sessions wearing compression clothing. Made of spandex-type material, it clings to the bodies of these autistic children. The researchers take copious notes in order to determine if this type of clothing alters their stimming and allows them to focus better. The idea of using compression clothing comes from the work of Temple Grandin, a professor with autism who at age 18 built a squeeze machine to reduce her stress. Dr. Bisson is interested in whether compression clothing can also have this calming effect and possibly complement therapy."[35] While it has a long way to go, the work of the team has gotten positive feedback from therapists and parents.

Stimming can interfere with socialization and make

learning difficult. In addition, some parents of autistic children report that dealing with a child's stimming on a daily basis disrupts family routines and results in considerable stress. Despite being described as problematic and even purposeless, stimming can be functional and have positive consequences for children and adults across the autistic spectrum. For instance, stimming can help relieve stress and anxiety; it can be fun and enjoyable. Repetitive behaviors may help keep one's mind occupied. Although information on intervention practices is limited, we know that some stimming phases out over time. New research shows that children who were later diagnosed with autism generally showed 4-8 types of repetitive behaviors as early as one year of age. Scientists emphasize that not every autistic child stims, and every child who stims is not necessarily autistic.[36]

One summer, when Jimmy was a teenager, our family was leisurely walking through stores in the heart of Virginia Beach. Suddenly, Jimmy spied a box of playing cards. This box was no ordinary box of cards; rather, it contained twelve individual decks of Bicycle playing cards, his absolute favorite when it came to stimming. I think it might have been the biggest box of Bicycle playing cards Jimmy ever saw. Immediately, he started to obsess that he *had* to buy this box. Even though we tried, there was no talking him out of it.

As Jimmy started screaming, jumping, and flapping his hands, we kept our cool, or at least we tried. After all, we had seen this behavior many times in the past. Before we left with a sobbing 19-year-old man, we saw a store that was wall-to-wall customers empty out in a matter of 30 seconds. We did not buy the cards for Jimmy. For one, we didn't want to reward this behavior. Moreover, the cost of $36 was exorbitant. Outside the store, he kept asking, "I did a

good job, didn't I?" I answered, "What do you think?"
As usual, he continued to ask whether he did a good
job for close to an hour.

We affectionately refer to whatever Jimmy is
using for the purpose of stimming as Jimmy's
"junque." Junque is a collection of odds and ends that
is considered far more valuable than it really is.
When allowed, Jimmy carries a small gym bag of his
junque around with him. Without a doubt, his junque
is one of his most valuable possessions. If I ask
Jimmy for most anything, he will willingly give it to me,
no strings attached. But if I ask teasingly for a single
piece of his junque, forget it. He will politely but firmly
decline.

His junque has a long history. When Jimmy
was around 4, he would shred towels, rugs, or
furniture. If he couldn't find anything around our
home to shred, he would tear skin off his body. Any
skin that was protruding or loose was fair game. For
instance, he would pick at the skin around his
fingernails until it bled; and the bleeding did not make
him stop. Pat and I agreed that we would rather have
him shredding towels than skin, so we gave him a
cheap, faded Florida beach towel. We let him shred it
to his "heart's content."

At this point, Judy, our occupational therapist,
suggested giving him pieces of foam to shred. She
saw this as therapeutic, since Jimmy's ability to pick
up things with his fingers and thumb was limited by
his mild cerebral palsy. Continually pulling and
picking pieces of foam would allow him to develop his
pincer grasp. So, towels gave way to foam. When
we ran out of foam one day, Pat gave him colored
construction paper that she found in my office. Jimmy
took to shredding and playing with it, along with
whatever foam he still had.

One day, when Jimmy's supply of construction

paper and foam ran out, Pat gave him some napkins. Over time, he developed an affinity for McDonald's napkins. Whenever we go on a trip, even to this day, he asks if we can stop at McDonald's. We know why. Even though he has difficulty writing and cannot use scissors, button his shirt or buckle his belt, his lack of fine motor skills fades into the background when it comes to napkins. As soon as he gets napkins, he somehow methodically tears them into seemingly identical strips about one inch wide.

Soon playing cards became part of his junque. Seemingly mesmerized, he plays with his cards for hours at a time. Interestingly, he only likes certain cards, such as Bicycle or Aviator. He loves holding a bunch of cards in two hands, as much as 5 or 6 decks. Then he will lay them out on the floor or some other hard surface, slap or wallop them, pick them up, and then gently squeeze them. Sometimes this is accompanied by humming. He repeats this process of spreading the cards out and then putting them back together so much so that the cards become worn around the edges. This routine can go on for hours at a time. Sometimes, he will decide that a certain card is no good anymore and it will end up in the wastebasket.

Figure 7 SOME OF JIMMY'S FAVORITE THINGS.

Jimmy has diversified in his old age. Recently, he shared with me that he also likes the brown, "soft" napkins from 7-Eleven, as well as wrapping tissue for packaging gifts. We limit the size of his collection; otherwise, it would quickly become a fire hazard. Finally, we have an agreement with Jimmy; once his junque get dirty, it's time to throw it out and replace.

One of Linwood's biggest gifts was helping Jimmy learn when he can play with his junque and when he cannot. For example, instead of forcing him to go "cold turkey" and give up playing with napkins and cards altogether, the Linwood staff weaned him from this activity little by little. Initially, the staff required him to go without his junque for short periods of time, gradually extending the length of time and always rewarding him when he succeeded.

While playing with his bag of junque seems to soothe him and relieve his anxiety, he is now able to work a full six-hour day without it. That's progress! And I have changed as well. First, my understanding of Jimmy's stimming has grown. I realize that many of us stim; some repeatedly tap their pencil, twirl their hair, or make a habit of biting their nails. And I appreciate that some of Jimmy's stimming enables him to communicate his feelings in a very special way. For instance, Jimmy repeatedly flaps his hands in church when he is moved by music or a message. I like to think that his emotions are spilling over as he opens his heart to the Lord. He could care less that he's the center of attention. I no longer motion to him to stop. After all, what better way to communicate his passion and love?

In her book, *Emergence: Labeled Autistic*, Dr. Temple Grandin provides insight into why she spends so much time writing and talking about how autistic people can change. "I have read enough to know that there are still many parents, and yes, professionals too, who believe that 'once autistic, always autistic.' This dictum has meant sad and sorry lives for many children diagnosed, as I was in early life, as autistic. To these people, it is incomprehensible that the characteristics of autism can be modified and controlled. However, I feel strongly that I am living proof that they can."[37]

In a recent book, Dr. Grandin encourages caregivers to "nudge with love." With Linwood's help and guidance, my wife and I have tried to push Jimmy out of his comfort zone with love. Jimmy dictates when, where, and how much we nudge and even shove. He has learned to control his obsession with his junque when he is out in the community. But this couldn't happen until Jimmy was ready to understand when this behavior is or is not okay. Equally important, we had to understand that trying to completely extinguish certain behaviors was counterproductive and not necessary. In all likelihood, Jimmy will always need some time each day for this emotional outlet.

    Months before her wedding, my youngest daughter reserved her venue. Before finalizing plans, one of her priorities was making sure the venue had a private room near the reception where Jimmy could go when needed; to get away from all the excitement of the wedding and of course, play with his bag of junque.

14   Family First

Researchers have given very little attention to the perspectives and experiences of fathers of children on the autism spectrum. When it comes to parenting, fathers remain afterthoughts. However, as gender roles change, fathers are more likely to see parenting as central to their identity. Compared to past generations, they are less likely to be the sole breadwinner and more likely to be involved in child care.[38]

Typically, each parent has unique strengths when it comes to raising a child-on the autism spectrum. For example, fathers are more apt to engage in "rough-and-tumble" type play and use more complicated words.[39] One oft-cited study found that greater early involvement of dads in reading, playing, and caring for their children on the spectrum allowed moms to do other things that lowered their stress level. And dads who frequently read to their children, told stories, and sang songs, made a significant difference in their child's socialization and communication skills.[40]

Still another study focuses attention on the psychological well-being of dads themselves. Hartley and Seltzer surveyed 91 fathers of children with disabilities, including autism. Fathers of children with autism were found to be especially susceptible to depressive symptoms. They struggled as they tried to juggle work, leisure time, and family responsibilities.[41] When fathers need support, they often lean on their partners, and vice versa. However, another in-depth study of eight fathers suggests friends may be kept in the dark when it comes to difficulties at home. "I haven't made it easy for my friends, because I have tended to become more introverted…it is a way of not wanting them to think that I am that tragic figure defined by autism." Therefore, Michael doesn't get into what's going on at home in order to pretend he has "a relatively normal life."[42]

M y goals and priorities have been strongly influenced by my mom and dad, and my wife and children. While family has always been important to me, it might not have been quite as important if my first child didn't have autism; at least not in terms of the way I budget my time, allocate my resources, and focus my energy. In a world without Jimmy, more of my life might revolve around me, and more of my attention might be on my work, my professional network, my status as a professor and author, and my leisure time activities apart from family.

Early in Jimmy's life, my weekends were consumed with taking him shopping, giving him plenty of exercise, reading, singing, and playing with him; and just as important, giving my wife some much-needed relief from childcare. We both believed we were the ultimate authorities on Jimmy, so we became our own support network.

Pat and I bring different perspectives and talents to child care. And at any time, Pat or I "pass Jimmy off" when we feel we cannot manage him for another second. While Pat tends to be more analytical and doesn't want to bother anybody unless she is sure it's really an emergency, I'm more likely to "pull the emergency cord" and seek medical care immediately. For example, Pat reminds me that I saved Jimmy's life by going with my gut instinct and pushing for emergency medical care; such as when he overdosed on his medication for seizures. There was also the time his appendix was about to rupture, or when his wisdom tooth infection showed signs of spreading dangerously. In circumstances such as these, we had to collaborate, share our opinions and make an educated guess. Even today, since Jimmy has difficulty telling us when he's in pain, we have to be fully tuned into whatever he's saying and feeling.

Ever since Jimmy was 3, shopping for groceries and other odds and ends was something "the guys" did at least once a week. It became a fun, routine part of our weekend. First of all, my wife hardly ever shopped for groceries, and when she did, she had no idea what to buy or where things were located once she got to the store. I, on the other hand, had Jimmy. He became my shopping list and "go to" person. We had the shop "down pat," especially when we went to a store called "George's." When we parked outside the store, Jimmy would ask me to go over each item on our shopping list before we got out of the car.

Once we started shopping, we went aisle by aisle, left to right. By then, Jimmy had committed as many as 30-40 items to memory after reading the list once. If I didn't know where something was, he told me what aisle and its exact location. If I missed something, he pointed that out as well. Finally, he helped me lift groceries out of the cart, put them back in the cart after we paid for them, and then unpack once we got home. He knew he was a tremendous shopper, and he took great pride in being such a big help. As an adult, he still loves to join me whenever I go shopping.

When Jimmy was about 8 years old, I found myself on a bus full of women. Two women were sitting behind me, chatting about grocery shopping. One remarked, 'Oh, I love shopping at George's too. Have you ever seen that tall man who brings his son to the store? The boy seems to have problems.' Her friend responded, 'You mean the boy who seems so hyper – brown hair? Yeah, he is something with that boy. I feel good every time I see them. It's amazing to watch the two of them shop.'"

"I almost didn't want to turn around, what they were saying made me feel so good. Truthfully, if I ever heard anyone talk about my son in the past when they didn't know I was the mom, I usually ended up feeling terrible. But I did engage them with a few questions to be certain, and then let them know they were talking about my husband and my Jimmy.

--the mommy

My job as a college professor provided my family with a steady source of income. Moreover, it was the ideal job in terms of giving me the flexibility and freedom I needed to "be there" for Jimmy and the rest of my family. My income, along with health insurance and some money in our savings, allowed us to pay our bills and made it possible for Pat to be a full-time mother.

I was raised by a wonderful father, Charles Augustus Bucher. He was a Professor of Education at New York University and the author of more than twenty texts, many of them published in numerous languages. While family was always a priority with my dad, part of the reason he accomplished so much was because he was constantly working. If he wasn't actually writing, teaching, speaking, or consulting, there was a good chance he was thinking about these activities.

Figure 8 Jimmy and Pop C (my dad)

Since Jimmy was born, my family has always come first. There were jobs I did not pursue because it would have meant uprooting my family. Perhaps more importantly, a move would have jeopardized Jimmy's education and residential placement. I had to learn to say no to professional opportunities that would have taken time away from my family. Lastly, I couldn't afford to constantly think about work. If anything, much of my time at work was spent thinking about family.

Jimmy helps me set my priorities straight, especially when I feel the urge to lose myself in my work. Furthermore, he has brought our family closer together. Part of our closeness comes from the realization that we share something unique that others may not be able to relate to or understand.

There's a lot of stuff that only the five of us know and appreciate.
--a sister (Suzy)

In my college classes, I make it very clear to my students that family comes first in their lives, not sociology. As a professor, we invariably talk about the family institution. I question whether moms, by nature, are better able to raise children. I wonder out loud whether dads lose something by not being more involved with child rearing. And I share with my students how I put family first and the difference it has made in my professional and personal life.

According to a new Pew research study, "6 Facts About American Fathers," many still think that mothers are better equipped than fathers to care for their children. 45% feel it's better if mom stays home to tend to the family, only 2% say a child's better off if dad's at home.[43]

If I had been asked, my answer would be it depends on *the* mother and *the* father. Being such a big part of my children's lives has given me a certain confidence, even cockiness, that I can do "the job." That's not to diminish the role of mothers, or my amazing wife. I feel like fatherhood is something I was born to do, an expectation that is rooted somewhere in my past. Yes, it's a responsibility that I take seriously. However, it's also a responsibility that I embrace, cherish, and work on, each and every day.

15 Peer Play

By examining research in his book, *The Power of Play*, child development expert David Elkind shows that creative, imaginative play among children fosters significant mental and social development.[44] Even though peer-play might seem like a natural occurrence for all children, requiring minimal motivation and guidance, it's not. Autistic children may find this type of play challenging, given their social skills, communication styles, and repetitive behaviors. Therefore, it comes as no surprise they tend to have fewer friendships, smaller social networks, and greater loneliness. Nevertheless, they have the same need for peer-group interaction as other children.

But peer play is relational, meaning it's not just about the social skills of *one* individual. When neurotypical peers (NT), those without autism, were shown short video clips or still images of social interaction, they rated images of autistic people as "more awkward," "less approachable," and "less likely to pursue friendship with." While these are first impressions, researchers found they have a lasting impact on attitudes and behaviors. In effect, the biases of NT children frequently lead to rejection or avoidance of those on the spectrum.[45]

Given these findings, interventions and educational approaches increasingly target those with *and* without autism. A recent landmark study, led by Dr. Kasari of UCLA's Center for Autism Research and Treatment, examined peer-play in real-life settings (56 classrooms and 30 schools). Classmates in grades 1 through 5 were taught how to engage and interact with children who struggle with social interaction. Following training of their peers, children with autism improved their social skills in the classroom and spent less time alone on the playground.

This improvement continued into the new school year after changing classmates and classrooms.[46]

When I was growing up in Port Chester, New York, I lived in a neighborhood that was swarming with kids my age. The elementary school was within walking distance for me, just across the street. And playing with other kids, going to birthday parties, and being invited over to a friend's house for a sleepover or to play was something my parents and I took for granted.

Jimmy grew up in a similar development, consisting of single-family homes with cozy yards that nestled up against each other. Most of the parents were in their 20's and 30's, raising young children who attended a nearby elementary school. Jimmy watched groups of children roam from yard to yard, playing on swing sets, choosing up sides for a game of Whiffle ball, kicking a soccer ball, or perhaps just spending time talking about most anything.

One day, when Jimmy came home from school, he saw three little boys around his age playing on a swing set in our neighbor's fenced-in backyard. Jimmy began to ask, "Mama, can I go play with them?" "Mama, can I go play with them?" "Mama, can I go play with them?" After much hesitation and thought, Pat said yes. She took Jimmy's hand and they walked to the neighbor's house, whereupon Pat asked the boys if Jimmy could play with them. Once Pat got positive vibes from the boys, Jimmy made it clear he wanted his mama to go away.

Pat returned to our house just down the road and went to our backyard where she could see Jimmy, but he could not see her. As the other boys continued playing with each other on the swings, Jimmy walked along the edge of the property, fluffing leaves that had piled up against their wire fence and humming to himself. After playing with leaves for about ten minutes, Jimmy saw an electric chain saw that our neighbor had left in his backyard.

Jimmy made a beeline for the saw, and Pat took off, remembering how Jimmy had a habit of putting himself in danger. More than once, we found him drawn to dangerous things, whether it was a hot stove, scissors, or a sharp knife. My wife caught Jimmy just before he reached the saw, and noticed that it was plugged in. As Pat took Jimmy by the hand, she told the boys thanks and waved goodbye. Jimmy was clearly happy because he got to play with the "big boys."

When Jimmy was in elementary school, I was a young college instructor. Typically, I taught one-night class each semester which would require me to arrive early at work and stay late. But on the other days of the week, by mid-afternoon I had finished teaching my classes, meeting with students, and attending meetings. And on those days, I was faced with a decision. Do I stay and put in the extra hours that are necessary to get promoted and recognized? Since I was taking graduate courses at nearby Howard University at the time, there was another consideration. Do I stay and study in my office, a place that was quiet and free of distractions; or do I go home and play with my son?

99% of the time, I went home and played with my son. My wife and I, and later my daughters, made up Jimmy's peer group. This was not by choice but by necessity. I can remember zero times in Jimmy's life that he was invited over to play at someone's house, without my wife or I accompanying him. I repeat, zero.

When I drove home from work, turned onto our street and approached our home, I knew Jimmy would be waiting for me, standing beside our green mailbox. When he recognized my car, he would jump up and down, smile, and flap his hands, gleefully and emphatically. That "welcome" never got old, and it was a simple but powerful reminder that I had made the right decision to go home early.

16   Two Sisters

My autistic brother (Philip) has "bestowed upon me empathy for all the incredible ways people are different. I developed patience, compassion…and advocacy at a very young age." As Philip's sister, "I quietly pressured myself to be without fault and to never give my parents a moment's worry. As I grew up…my awareness that I would have a bigger, fuller life than my brother was enormously guilt-producing." [47]

For the longest time, families were told to institutionalize their children with disabilities for the sake of their siblings. But then scientific data began to reveal that the effects of having a disabled brother or sister are complex and not always negative. While a relationship such as this might be challenging, it might benefit immensely.

Clearly, no two siblings adapt to each other or their family situation in exactly the same way and relationships change over time. A number of factors may come into play, such as parents' temperament and coping styles, marital stress, family size, and differences in the gender and age of siblings. Fortunately, researchers who now want to know more about brothers and sisters of children on the autism spectrum no longer simply ask their parents; rather, they ask the siblings themselves.

Through in-person interviews with siblings ages 7 to 15, one recent study found they shared a wide range of emotions. Many were thankful for the unique relationship and closeness they shared with an autistic sibling, but there were also feelings of embarrassment and frustration when their brother or sister showed socially inappropriate behavior, especially in public. Other interviewees cited a need to be by themselves when things got stressful or talk with someone who understood their situation. Finally, many felt a deep sense of responsibility, taking on a variety of roles such as 'caregivers' and 'entertainers' if their siblings needed to be redirected or kept busy, 'rescuers' if they became aggressive, and 'parents' helpers.'[48]

I don't think of Jimmy as my autistic brother. I think of Jimmy as my brother.
        --a sister (Katie)

By no means does autism define Jimmy. Autism is not what makes Jimmy Jimmy.
        --a sister (Suzy)

As our first child, Jimmy was at the center of our lives. Everything else was secondary. But once Jimmy had siblings, with their own unique needs and interests, we knew that we couldn't always put Jimmy "first." And that was a good thing, for Jimmy, my wife and me, and our entire family.

For the first ten years of his life, Jimmy was on my mind constantly. It was a luxury to think about Katie.
        --the mommy

A few years after Jimmy was born, we faced a big decision. Should we have more children? When we got married, I was leaning toward having two children and Pat wanted four; but now we weren't so sure. While it would be some time before Jimmy's autistic diagnosis, Jimmy's serious developmental issues were no longer in question. But Jimmy's doctors encouraged Pat to have another child, saying his brain injury was a fluke; an entirely chance occurrence. But we weren't completely sold. After a good deal of deliberation and prayer, we decided even if we had another "Jimmy," we could manage. We'd rather have two Jimmy's than just one child.

Once Katie was born, we put off deciding whether to have still another child. As Pat approached 40, we kept hopelessly waiting for our lives to settle down. Eventually, we came to the realization that it was now or never. We took a leap of faith, and Suzy was conceived. About three months into Pat's pregnancy, Jimmy was diagnosed with autism.

Shortly after Suzy's birth, we started hearing stories about families like ours. Studies were pointing to the possibility that having one autistic child increased the risk of having another. Pat remembers thinking how grateful she was that neither of us had heard any of this before.

It's not unusual for literature on autism to refer to siblings of a child with autism as "typically developing." I'm not quite sure what that means but I can assure you there's very little that's typical or ordinary about the maturation of Jimmy's sisters' social skills, emotional intelligence, and knowledge. Because of their upbringing and make-up, they are far from typical, in their eyes and ours.

When Jimmy was three, Katie was born; when he was ten, Suzy arrived. Unlike Pat and me, his sisters can't think of a life before Jimmy. They had no concept of a typical brother and sister relationship, if there is such a thing. Rather than seeing their relationship with Jimmy as different, they simply see it as special.

FIGURE 9   *I NEVER HAD A FEELING OF WHAT COULD HAVE BEEN* --A SISTER (KATIE)

Jimmy has had a profound influence on both Suzy and Katie.

Having a handicapped brother isn't always easy. Sometimes you're doing something you worked hard on and he messes it all up by accident. My brother likes napkins a lot; he tears them up and pounds them on the floor. He also likes to watch Muppets and game shows. Sometimes he's hard to understand. But you get used to it and you start understanding everything he says. It makes me mad when people stare at him, so I start hiding him. He gets upset easily, like when the schedule changes he starts getting all uptight. But he gets happy easily too. Once I took a piece of paper and took one of his old toys and wrapped it up and he got all excited. My brother's name is Jimmy. He's autistic. He doesn't have a wheelchair and he's not retarded. He's very, very smart too. Just because he's handicapped doesn't mean he's not smart. He memorized the

whole T.V. guide and when stores open and close.
I'm kind of glad I have a handicapped brother.[49]
    --a sister (Katie, age 10)

Jimmy has expanded his sisters' worlds. Not too long ago, I was interviewed by a journalist who was writing an article for *ParentMap*, a magazine for parents. The writer was putting together an article on how parents can help develop their children's cultural intelligence. Specifically, the writer posed this question; "How can parents help build their child's awareness and appreciation of other ways of life, especially if they live in an area without much diversity?" When I put this question to my daughter Suzy, she answered half-jokingly, "You had Jimmy."

Figure 10 JIMMY AND HIS SISTERS HAVING FUN AT THE LAKE GEORGE COTTAGE.

Suzy continued to talk about the kind of household in which she grew up, where the repercussions for saying a cussword were less than those for bullying or making fun of someone. The importance of valuing people who are different, intellectually and physically, was something she learned and lived interacting with her brother and his friends. When she sees someone who appears to have a disability, she smiles and, in her words,, "tries not to look too much." Early in life, she learned to appreciate differences in others, rather than wonder why they aren't like her.

When members of our immediate family meet someone for the first time, how that person reacts to Jimmy carries a great deal of weight. For instance, my daughters seemingly waited awhile to introduce one of their boyfriends to Jimmy. Recently, I came across a siblings' comment that referred to this encounter as a "deal breaker" for her, meaning it had everything to do with whether the relationship was worth continuing. When I asked Katie and Suzy if a boyfriend or a spouse-to-be of theirs had to get along with Jimmy, their response was a bit different.

For Suzy, she said she wouldn't have been attracted in the first place to someone who didn't embrace her brother. It was more about how that person treats people in general, not just Jimmy. Suzy went on to say this was built into her character from the day she was born. Katie said the phrase "getting along with Jimmy" wasn't quite right, it was "bigger than that." She added, "It was almost a quality I ended up not even looking for, it became subconscious; maybe better described as a level of character, goodness, and maturity in a person. I knew *before* I 'introduced' them to Jimmy, not after."

A few years ago, an article in *Time* referred to siblings of children with autism as "Autism's Invisible Victims." When I asked Suzy how she felt about being referred to as a "victim," her response was telling. "It pisses me off," and "makes me feel uncomfortable," she said. "Who are *you* to tell me I'm a victim? I've had a great life." She continued, "Jimmy is different, and sometimes that difference makes people uncomfortable. I look at Jimmy's difference as being special and unique. He doesn't stereotype, he doesn't know how to hate, and he has an innocence about him. I look at what Jimmy can do, not what he can't do. Public ignorance is the only thing I have been a victim of as the sister of someone with autism."

When Suzy applied to college, she was asked to write about a person who has changed how she views herself and the world around her. She chose to write about Jimmy. The following is an excerpt from her essay:

From age three on I knew that I had someone special and unique in my life, my brother Jimmy. From a young age, my brother has made me more mature and helped me become aware of so many things that I would have never even considered without having him in my life. It is Jimmy who has helped me so much in succeeding in life so far and is always making me a better person."

Not only have my brother's individual traits taught me and influenced me in my life; his surroundings have had an effect on me as well. Attending Special Olympics and my brother's special education activities since I was very young allowed me to be an open-minded person, accepting many people with all kinds of differences. Now more than ever the things I have learned from my family come into play. In a little less than a year I will be off to college with thousands of people I do not know at all. Many of them will be completely different from anyone that I hang out with now. Most of my friends are already scared about who their roommate will be or who they are going to have to get along with and I am as well. Yet, at the same time I am excited to again learn more things from people that are dissimilar from me or maybe have a lifestyle far different from mine. I look at college in general as an exciting challenge that will be a continuation of my learning experiences and another chance for me to grow.

Years ago, when Katie was asked to write about her life's goals, and the main inspiration behind those goals, she also wrote about her brother. To quote Katie, "When I think about my priorities and goals in life, I tend to think of Jimmy."

The relationship between Suzy and Katie is significantly different because of their brother. Not surprisingly, Suzy looked up to her older sister for guidance; what was good, what was cool, and how to carry herself. But by watching Katie, she also learned how to treat Jimmy. As Jimmy got older, Suzy learned not to treat him like a little kid. Katie respected Jimmy and his ability to make decisions for himself, and that lesson trickled down to Suzy.

When Jimmy was in his late teens, he took computer classes at nearby Mt. Hebron High School. When prom time came around, he heard everyone talking about it and hinted he'd like to go too. When we asked him who he'd like to invite, he said Denise, a friend of his with autism who we had known for some time. After the two of them attended the dance, my wife told Jimmy, "You know, you're old enough to have a girlfriend if you want one." Jimmy simply responded, "No, I don't need one of those. I'll just stick with my sisters."

Figure 11 JIMMY WITH HIS PROM DATE, DENISE.

When Jimmy was fifteen years of age, he was given a school assignment. He was asked to write about his best friends. This is what he wrote:

Katie and Suzy are my best friends. They live with me at my house. They make me laugh at all times. I think Katie and Suzy are my best friends because I like them to tell me things that are going to happen ahead of time. I like that because I get all excited. I like Katie and Suzy to eat with me at breakfast, lunch, and dinner on the weekends. I like to play

Wheel of Fortune with Katie. I like Katie because she is nice to me. I think Suzy is nice too.
    --Jimmy, age 15 (from his journal)

17   Lessons from the Street

More than one-thousand research studies have examined *Sesame Street*, according to Michael Davis, author of *Street Gang: The Complete History of Sesame Street*. Davis himself spent five years writing and researching his book. Sesame Street is the longest running children's TV program in history. Today its reach extends to more than 8 million preschoolers in over 150 countries. Its mission, "to help all children grow smarter, stronger, and kinder," speaks to empowering children and teaching them it's okay to be different. [50]   Research backs up this mission. Findings from one massive study of more than 10,000 children from 15 countries outside the U.S. reveal that watching *Sesame Street* is associated with more positive attitudes about people who are not part of one's own group and for that reason tend to be stereotyped and devalued.[51]

Julia, a little girl with autism, is *Sesame Street's* newest character. Besides being smart and curious; Julia flaps her arms when she's excited, takes a long time to answer questions, and tends to avoid eye contact. Julia is a reminder that the spectrum is very, very broad. For instance, even though the vast majority of children on the spectrum are boys, Julia is a girl. Wendy Stone, a professor whose research targets behaviors of young children with autism, is a consultant for *Sesame Street*. In addressing perceptions, Dr. Stone does not want to stereotype or sugarcoat. She explains, "People know the word 'autism,' but I think they're still scared of interacting with a parent of a kid with autism or inviting them for a play date."[52]

Stacey Gordon, Julia's puppeteer and the mother of a son with autism, wishes Julia was created years ago.

"Had my son's friends been exposed to his behaviors through something they had seen on TV before they experienced them in the classroom, they might not have been frightened. And they would have known that he plays in a different way, and that that's okay."[53] To Julia Bascom, an autism rights advocate, seeing Julia on screen made her "feel real." Describing Julia's significance is difficult for Bascom. "It's like trying to describe water to someone who has never drunk water. It's such a simple thing, and you weren't even aware that you didn't have it until you do. I had no idea that I'd been waiting to see an autistic character played on *Sesame Street*. "[54]

When Jimmy started watching *Sesame Street* in the late 1970's, awareness of autism was slowly filtering down through health care professionals, educators, parents and caregivers. Regrettably, it was virtually ignored by the media. Even in the 80's, if we told people Jimmy was autistic, it wasn't unusual for them to automatically assume we said artistic. In this environment, the Buchers and other parents of children found support hard to come by. For the most part, we learned by trial and error.

According to the U.S. Department of State, autism-related stories became front page news while *Sesame Street* became the most widely viewed children's television show in the world. In 2015, Sesame Workshop launched a new initiative, "See Amazing in All Children," to provide assistance to parents and caregivers of children with autism. Resources include a free iPad app, instructional cards, and storybooks with *Sesame Street* Characters. An online media campaign using #seeamazing encourages parents to share positive stories about their children. This initiative was due in part due to feedback from parents of children with autism, parents who repeatedly mentioned the connection their children formed with *Sesame Street* and *The Muppets*.

When Jimmy watched *Sesame Street*, he would absorb information even though it seemed like he wasn't paying attention at all. Prior to age three, he would sit in my wife's lap as she vigorously rocked back and forth in her favorite chair. When that didn't work, Pat danced around the room with Jimmy, singing along with every song. As a preschooler, Cookie Monster and Bert and Ernie segments began to catch his attention. During other segments, Jimmy would wander around the TV room, touching everything in sight. But he would stay in the room; and for Jimmy, this was highly unusual. Unlike other TV programs at that time, *Sesame Street* caught his attention; keeping his focus for any length of time would come later.

Ernie and Bert kept me alive.
    --the mommy

Figure 12 JIM WITH HIS BUDDY, BERT.

According to Malcolm Gladwell, author of *The Tipping Point*, there was one small thing about *Sesame Street* that had everything to do with its success. Its creators understood "that if you can hold the attention of children, you can educate them."[55] So how did this hour-long show manage to hold Jimmy's attention, at least intermittently?

A number of things appealed to Jimmy. First, *Sesame Street* was highly repetitious. Jimmy thrived on repetition. Second, rather than throwing too much at Jimmy in a short span of time, its creators focused on only one thing and left out irrelevant and possibly distracting content. That one thing might be the letter "C" or the number "7." Lastly, music was a key part of each episode, and Jimmy loved music. All these qualities increased what Gladwell terms the "stickiness factor" of *Sesame Street*, making it that much more appealing to Jimmy.

When Pat started to teach Jimmy numbers, she discovered that he already knew them. Pat would start to count, and he would finish. Because of *Sesame Street*, Jimmy learned to count in Spanish as well as English. He learned his alphabet in the same way. Around age five, he started reading, thanks in part to *Sesame Street*. Learning the alphabet on *Sesame Street* opened the door to reading. Once he could spell, his ability to remember words and communicate improved dramatically.

From the beginning, *Sesame Street* has used different styles of music, combined with repetition, as teaching tools. For instance, Jimmy's favorite song was "Alphabet Chat," at least that's what he told me not too long ago. Keep in mind he began to watch this show in the 1970s.

I like, I love 'Alphabet Chat' because of the characters, and the closing with Guy Smiley. He

comes out and says, 'Excuse me, excuse me, I have a commercial!' He interrupts Mr. Chatterly. I love the opening song to each letter. That's how 'Alphabet Chat' begins; and ends "And ayee, byee, ceee."
          --Jimmy, age 40

After more than three decades, Jimmy can still sing songs like "Alphabet Chat" with me. Like other *Sesame Street* numbers, "Alphabet Chat" used repetition and music to educate. This song had a catchy tune that begins and ends each sketch. The lyrics, "A b c d e, C d e f g, H i j k, L m n o p, Q r s t u, R s t u v, S t u v w x y z, and A b c," are set to classical music. Against a background of comedic chaos, a professorial-looking Muppet named Lord Chatterly explains the significance of "the letter of the day."

When we needed help, we often looked to Oscar the Grouch, Cookie Monster, Grover, or some other character on *Sesame Street*. For example, if we were waiting in line with Jimmy and he started getting anxious and difficult to control, Pat or I would ad-lib our own Bert and Ernie stories. And we would tell them again and again, all the while doing our best impersonations of their voices (she was a much better Bert and Ernie than I). As we read to him from *Ernie's Big Mess* or some other *Sesame Street* book, he would start laughing and giggling uncontrollably. Moments like that kept us going.

Sesame Street's message that "we are all different, but the same" struck a nerve with me. By educating *and* entertaining, the show sought to prepare children for school. It was my hope that *Sesame Street* might expand Jimmy's world and counterbalance the intolerance that found its way into his social world. To what degree Jimmy could relate to the idea that we're all human and worthy of respect is something I'll never know. But its multi-ethnic cast and colorful Muppet characters emphasized to their audience that we are much more alike than different. Everybody feels rejection, needs friends, and wants to be loved and respected for who we are and what we can do.

Figure 13 SESAME STREET'S ELMO GIVES JIMMY A HUG IN LAS VEGAS.

18   Using Fixations

There's a tendency to see autistic people's fixations as limiting and dysfunctional. Dr. Temple Grandin, author and autism activist, counters that we "need to use fixations to motivate instead of trying to stamp them out." She uses the example of Mme. Currie who fixated on her work and in the process, discovered radium. Dr. Grandin argues that fixation, or one's preoccupation with something, can "get things done."[56]

Jennifer Cook O'Toole, who was recently diagnosed with Asperger's Syndrome (AS), uses special interests and fixations to motivate and educate children on the spectrum. According to O'Toole, the first step is to determine the scope of the passion for the child. Then become knowledgeable about it. Lastly, look for diverse and creative ways of using the child's passion to expand opportunities for growth.[57]

When Jimmy was four and still pretty much non-verbal, Pat and I found ourselves singing in our car, which is not all that unusual for the Bucher family. We love to sing, and it kept Jimmy occupied on long road trips. A music teacher prior to becoming a full-time mommy, my wife had an extensive repertoire of children's songs. One in particular, called the "Barnyard Song," highlights the different noises animals make. While singing the last section of the chorus of the song, "Had a little rooster by the barnyard gate and that little rooster was my playmate, and that little rooster went cock-a-doodle-doo...," a rabbit jumped out in front of our car. At that instant, we both stopped singing. From the back seat, we heard Jimmy complete the verse, "doo doo do, doo doo do, doo doo do, do do." We were shocked! Much to our surprise, Jimmy had developed a passion for finishing a rhyme or a song. It was the first time we had ever heard Jimmy sing or string together so many syllables and sounds.

We then began to use this ability and Jimmy's need to finish whatever we started to say. First, it was a matter of finishing various nursery rhymes. Over time, this grew into stopping mid-sentence while reading a favorite book, to see how much he would finish. We were amazed. Finishing sentences soon became finishing paragraphs. His earliest speech consisted of memorized phrases from books and television shows, sometimes used in a way that gave us a good laugh. For example, when Jimmy was barely verbal, he uttered "No way Jose" and "No problem." Only later did we realize that he picked up each of these phrases from two of his favorite TV shows, *Full House* and *Alf*.

You take a snippet from any song that was performed in any of the 120 Muppet shows, and Jimmy can tell you the guest star of that episode.
        ---the mommy

Jimmy loves the Muppets, and so does the Bucher family. His obsessions with *The Muppet Show* and the Muppet segments that were a huge part of *Sesame Street* began at a young age and continue to this day. To maintain our sanity and satisfy his needs, my wife bought a new VCR as soon as she heard about them. She then proceeded to videotape each and every Muppet show that was produced; all 120 of them. The show, produced by puppeteer Jim Henson, stars Kermit the Frog, Miss Piggy, Gonzo, Fozzie Bear, and a host of other

Muppet characters. Each episode featured lots of singing and music, slapstick humor, and a real-life guest star. One of his favorite Muppets on *Sesame Street* was Cookie Monster and one of his favorite songs was "C is for Cookie."

When he was pre-school age, Pat and Jimmy would go outside, even during the cold winter months, and get on the swing set in our backyard. While going back and forth on a glider big enough for two, Pat would sing songs to Jimmy. Improvising, and using her best impression of Cookie Monster (which was actually pretty good), she taught Jimmy the sounds of the entire alphabet; starting with "A is for apple, that's good enough for me, B is for banana, that's good enough for me, C is for cookie…" and so on. Once she thought he knew the sounds of each letter of the alphabet, Pat would purposely make mistakes, whereupon Jimmy would giggle and correct her. Becoming an "expert" on the alphabet over time meant plenty of positive feedback and allowed him to seamlessly move on to reading. Jimmy's passion for finishing had morphed into a passion for correcting.

Later, we used the Muppets to teach Jimmy basic math facts and how to read. My wife, the techie in our family, integrated the Muppets into a computerized program. When Jimmy accessed the program, he would read. "Kermit wants to know what is 4 plus 4? Or Gonzo wants to know what is 3 times 2? Whenever Jimmy got the correct answer, Pat made sure he would see something like "YAY Jimbo!" The structure and predictability of this program was tailor-made for Jimmy. He would answer these questions for as long as we would allow.

Because of his fondness for *The Muppet Show*, Jimmy developed a love of Golden Oldies music from the 1960s as well as many other types of music. We used guest stars on *The Muppet Show* to expand Jimmy's world. For instance, stars such as Joel Grey and Ethel Merman became an opportunity to introduce Jimmy to Broadway. The guest appearance of Steve Martin segued to the movie, *Father of the Bride*, starring Steve Martin. As a result, Jimmy became enamored with movies about weddings. And so on.

Even as a middle-aged adult, Jimmy's fixations prove useful. This is particularly true of his job as a cart pusher at Walmart. Jimmy is obsessive about getting to work on time and working every minute he is supposed to be working. If he sees carts that need to be rounded up and brought back into the store, he'll do it, regardless of weather, how he's feeling, or whether his shift is about to end.

At his group home, Jimmy makes sure everyone knows his schedule, including counselors. In so doing, he holds everyone accountable and ensures his needs are met. For example, if Bernice needs to take him to a doctor's appointment or pick him up at Special Olympics practice, Jimmy persists until he is absolutely certain she knows that ahead of time. While this compulsion to stay on top of things may rub some the wrong way, it has proven to be an invaluable life skill.

Jimmy's life is ruled by his fixation on doing a good job.
        --the mommy

19 A Litmus Test

"I have gotten the distinct impression that all of the physicians I have seen have had no clue what autism means or entails or how that should change how they treat me." Another adult with ASD shared, "I thought doctors would understand my autism. I thought saying, 'well, I have autism' would be a suitable explanation for why I have age-inappropriate troubles with managing my healthcare, but it's not." Still another autistic interviewee in this study by Christina Nicolaidis, a physician and a mother of a son with autism, commented, "It is always hard for me because I don't have the words that normal people have to communicate with. I don't always know how to respond properly to questions from health care providers."[58]

Research raises serious questions about whether health care providers have both the knowledge and skills to care for people with autism. In a recent survey of more than 900 providers, the vast majority (79%) rated their knowledge and skills as "poor" or "fair" and expressed a desire for more autism training. Many providers were not even aware they had patients on the spectrum.[59]

People look to doctors like they're some kind of angel. They're just human beings, regular people.
--the podiatrist (Dr. Steven Wiener)

Jimmy can bring out the best in people. Unfortunately, in many cases, his hyperactivity can rub off on people as well, including medical professionals. Jimmy's constant questioning and extraneous movements would rattle them, wind them up, and make it difficult for all of us to focus on the reason for the visit. When this occurred, Jimmy would inevitably get extremely distressed, making it nearly impossible for him to cooperate.

It's safe to say that Jimmy is a litmus test of sorts for these professionals, in that their interaction with Jimmy tends to speak volumes about their values, background, and diversity consciousness. When I introduce Jimmy to them, or when he introduces himself, do they stare, smile, or freeze? Do they treat him as the adult he is or infantilize him? Does Jimmy move them outside their comfort zone, or are they at ease interacting with him? Do they talk directly to Jimmy, or just me?

Imagine being a child and seeing that not even the adults around you can keep you under control.
        --the neurologist (Dr. Kenton Holden)

When Jimmy was very young and extraordinarily hyperactive and difficult to handle, bringing him to a new medical professional was always a crap shoot. But then there was his podiatrist, Dr. Wiener. He had a calm, "I'm in control, I care about you" attitude. When Jimmy entered his room, he would settle in and cooperate. Dr. Wiener's clinical empathy was extraordinary. Even the scheduling of an appointment was done with Jimmy in mind. As he said, you cannot keep the same time structure with the "Jimmy Buchers of the world."

Dr. Wiener always scheduled our son last. He knew that Jimmy would take a lot more time and energy than his other patients, and he didn't want to feel rushed. When I inquired about his comfort level, he said, "I will always remember the trust and friendship Jimmy has given to me, and that he really is blessed not only by having you both as parents but in being himself a brave and kind young soul. I've learned that *all* children are given different strengths. If life were measured by the amount of joy and love one gives and receives, Jimmy would be placed in the gifted and talented class."

Nothing is more rewarding than for Jimmy to remember me.
   --the podiatrist (Dr. Steven Wiener), after
   receiving one of Jimmy's annual birthday cards

  Like Dr. Wiener, some health care providers are confident in their ability to accommodate children and adults with autism. Rather than avoid patients with autism, they welcome and engage them. Rather than simply rely on an hour-long online course or weekend conference on autism, they continually educate themselves through self-reflection and studious observation of their patient's preferences. By carefully listening to patients, caregivers, and other professionals, doctors may find it helps to avoid broad questions and be more concrete. Getting to know their individual patients better can help them realize that one's ability to speak clearly may have very little to do with comprehension. Newfound understanding might encourage them to adjust their scheduling, avoid medical terms, and tailor their waiting and exam rooms to accommodate the sensory sensitivities of their autistic patients. But regardless of their strategies, health care providers must develop an array of skills in this area. Why? Because doing so will lead to more accurate diagnoses and more effective treatments.

20   Managing Fears

Imagine you and your spouse are observing, via video, your autistic child in a virtual environment called "The Blue Room." In this 360-degree virtual world, all the surfaces are screens so your child does not have to wear a headset or goggles. The neat thing about this virtual reality room is that it feels real and it's totally safe. Your daughter Rachel has an intense fear of getting on a crowded bus. By responding to audio visual images representing the "real world," she can slowly address her fears. To make the bus less threatening, she initially boards an empty bus using iPad controls. Gradually, more and more people get on. Since Rachel is in control, she determines when she is ready to move on and board the virtual bus. While she is totally immersed in this environment, a therapist seated next to her encourages Rachel to practice relaxation exercises.[60]

Almost 75 years ago, Dr. Leo Kanner observed that children with autism had unusual fears. The children he studied feared things such as elevators, swings, and even the wind. Dr. Kanner found that what is tolerable to most children might be absolutely terrifying to a child with autism.[61] Researchers at New Castle University (UK) have used "The Blue Room" to help autistic children overcome their unusual fears. Results are promising, considering that eight of nine children in their initial study completely overcame their fears, even a year later.[62]

In a recent study of over one-thousand children with autism, nearly half of the parents reported a total of 92 intense and unusual fears, ranging from mechanical things to the weather, in addition to more common childhood fears (e.g., bugs and snakes, the dark, monsters). The number one unusual fear was toilets. [63] Researchers noted, "Children with autism perceive, experience, and react to the world differently than children without autism. What is tolerable for most children might be terrifying, distressing, or infuriating for a child with autism. But each child on the spectrum is likely to have different fears, so learning when a child is fearful and what triggers her or his fears is critical. Sparse research indicates exposure, modeling, and reinforcement may prove helpful.[64]

I t would have been all too easy to dismiss or trivialize Jimmy's fears. After all, they seemed irrational and ridiculous. He was fearful of things that didn't seem scary. But by tuning into Jimmy and acknowledging his fears, we discovered that they were very real to him. The uniqueness of his fears didn't make them any less problematic. As a child, the unbelievable anxiety that accompanied his fears often interfered with his everyday life and ours. Like me, he didn't choose his fears. And like me, his fears were a response to a world that can seem unpredictable, overwhelming, and confusing.

To help Jimmy manage his fears, we exposed, desensitized, nudged and reinforced whenever we got the chance. Modeling proved worthless. We could model how to be fearless until we were "blue in the face," but it wouldn't have made a difference. If possible, we might have avoided what was triggering his fear, at least for the moment. Professional help was always an option. But usually, we discovered that Jimmy needed to be lovingly pushed, and over time, he might develop the ability to work though his fears.

At one time, Jimmy had a long list of intense and unusual fears, such as riding in a car on partly cloudy days, listening to a new song, and walking on grass. Now, going anywhere in a car in all types of weather and listening to various types of unfamiliar music are among his favorite activities. How did he get to the point where he was able to manage his fears? To be honest, I'm not sure. Pat and I pushed him, and we did not let his anxiety or screaming stop us. But we made sure we were never mean or insulting to him; rather, we always pushed him with love and compassion.

When Jimmy had a fear, we had to stop everything and give him our full, undivided attention for however long it took to help him deal with the fear. As an example, Pat took Jimmy outside to play on our front lawn when he was about 18 months. She thought nothing of letting him go out barefoot, as it was the first warm day of spring. After helping him stand on the grass, she started walking away. Instead of following her, he started to whimper. Pat thought it was kind of cute that he seemed hesitant to walk on the grass. Knowing that Jimmy always wanted to be close to her, she walked further away, thinking that this would motivate him to walk on the grass. Instead, he let out a full blood-curdling scream. She then realized he was absolutely terrified and was now panicking.

She ran to him, picked him up, and comforted him, realizing this was still another intense and irrational fear that was brought on by his sensitivities. After waiting a day, she went outside with Jimmy. Pat sat Jimmy on her lap, and over the course of thirty minutes, helped him adjust to the feel of the lawn by gently brushing his toes along the top of blades of grass. She praised and loved him through it until he could walk on grass. Since then, walking barefoot on grass has not been an issue, although he still doesn't like it much.

As a toddler, Jimmy loved music and especially music on *Sesame Street*. However, his fondness of music was limited to certain songs. If a new song came on, he would start to cry, clap his hands, and spin, so we found ourselves listening to the same songs over and over again. Finally, Pat decided to add new songs to his repertoire. As soon as a new one began, Pat held him in her arms, enveloping him so tightly he could not move. She proceeded to dance with Jimmy, spinning and singing the song as she pulsed her arms to the beat, all the while hugging him tightly. His reaction was not immediate, but once the song was repeated enough, he began to smile. Slowly, Jimmy grew to tolerate and even enjoy more and more songs.

On car trips, Jimmy at five years of age would randomly scream and kick his legs in his booster seat. These outbursts followed no particular pattern, or so we thought. Then, on one sunny day, Pat was driving Jimmy around and doing errands. She stopped at a long stoplight. Suddenly, a dark cloud covered the sun and Jimmy started screaming and kicking. It clicked. Pat asked Jimmy, "Does it scare you when clouds cover the sun?" Jimmy replied, "Yes." Pat reasoned he knew that clouds were a sign of rain, and Jimmy hated rain because it messed with his routine. Now that Jimmy could verbalize his fear of clouds, he could talk about it. Once Pat explained that clouds don't always mean rain, Jimmy could then ask, "Clouds? Rain?" A change of weather, especially when it's unanticipated, still stresses him out. But fortunately, he has learned to voice his concerns and settle himself down.

As a child, Jimmy was overcome by fear if we lost our electricity. When he was 6, I remember losing electricity after he went to bed one night. Jimmy immediately started screaming and crying uncontrollably. When Pat went to his room to comfort him, she asked, "What's wrong?" Sobbingly, he replied, "I was floating in the dark." That was a major breakthrough for Jimmy, to be able to verbalize his sensations at that moment. Evidently, Jimmy had not developed the concept of permanence. If he could not see it, it wasn't there. So later Pat turned his lights on and off, on and off, and had Jimmy touch objects in the dark. He could then process that things didn't go away just because he couldn't see them.

As Jimmy got older, his self-esteem grew as he became extraordinarily proud of not letting his fears get the better of him. For instance, he slowly expanded his repertoire of amusement park rides. After he got off a new thrill ride, he would turn to us, beam, and repeat, "I'm brave, I'm brave." Then came ballgames, the beach, weddings, Broadway shows, fancy hotels, sightseeing, and flying cross-country. Now, doing something for the first time still causes anxiety, but not panic. With encouragement and support, he's more than able to manage lots of stimulus, waiting in long lines, and sudden changes in his schedule.

21   Micro-affirmations

"We appreciate you, we hear you, I couldn't have done this without you, I love you." We know how good it feels when a group or individual gives us positive feedback. It could be something as simple as a smile, eye contact, or someone simply taking the time to really listen. Micro-affirmations, those timely and positive acknowledgements of someone's contributions, distinctiveness, and skills, may seem minor but research shows they can have a huge impact, especially for people "who may feel isolated or invisible in an environment."[65]

Because of constant negativity, some people with autism are made to feel unworthy and unappreciated. Instead of consistent feedback that acknowledges and builds on their strengths, they may be repeatedly reminded of what they can't do. It can be very subtle and take the form of gestures, rude comments, or low expectations. For example, some autistic people feel ignored on a regular basis. Or because of messages they get from society, acquaintances, or even caregivers, they may get the impression that they don't belong, they aren't smart, and their opinion doesn't matter. Studies tell us that the effects of these negative micro-messages can be significant; in that they may be linked to lower self-esteem.[66]

Not only do micro-affirmations help us feel good about ourselves, they improve our ability to perform up to our potential. But it can't be false praise, according to The Children's Hospital of Philadelphia Center for Autism Research (CAR). "Look for things, both small and large, that your child can do, and when your child overcomes a previous challenge, celebrate your child's progress."[67] In the course of a day, we may send hundreds and even thousands of micro-affirmations to each other. Research shows that micro-affirmations can balance out or even override negative messages that make us feel as if we don't measure up.[68]

Given our family's experiences, we have learned that micro-affirmations, particularly gestures of inclusion can make a world of difference. Affirmations of this nature can take place anywhere and anytime. For example, when he walks through the doors at Walmart to begin each work day, coworkers go out of their way to greet him with big smiles and welcomes, such as "Good morning Jimmy" and "Hi Jimmy."

Trudy became an important part of Jimmy's social environment when he was a boy. As the operator of a local roller-skating rink, she arranged lessons for Jimmy and other children with disabilities, one hour before it opened. More importantly, Trudy responded to them as children, not disabled children. She laughed with them, joked with them, and played with them. And she always had a big smile on her face. The skating rink was the only place at that time where Jimmy could be more than 5 feet away from us and we weren't worried.

When we opened Liberty Skate Center, I started doing skating lessons. A mother (Pat) asked me if I'd be willing to have a class for the special needs children in the community. I thought that was an awesome idea and began a Sunday morning class that turned out to be my favorite skating class. I so enjoyed watching their smiling faces! One of these children was Jimmy. He was such a sweet little boy who liked to sit with me at the ticket window after lessons were over. Jimmy liked to rip paper into tiny

pieces, so I just kept him close to me at the window and provided him with all the paper he wanted. He would zoom out and zoom around the rink and come back and sit with me while his sister skated around. It was an awesome time in my life to watch my 'special' kids grow. To watch these children having so much fun and treated like other kids was such a joy. Pat and Rich never held Jimmy back from doing anything that gave him pleasure.
  --a friend (Trudy Glass)

Jimmy grew to love roller skating. Unfortunately, the rink shut down a few years later. Without missing a beat, we decided to give an ice rink within driving distance a try. Jimmy picked it up immediately. Having a new skill that got his family all excited did wonders for his self-esteem. When I asked Jimmy, "How are ice skating and roller skating the same," his answer said it all. "I can do both VERY WELL!"

Figure 14 WHEN HE'S SKATING, JIMMY'S ALL SMILES.

Shortly after Jimmy was born, Pat recollects holding him in her arms and thinking, "Kid, you are going to be so loved." Because of our family's affection for Jimmy and our awareness of the biases and intolerance people with disabilities encounter in the real world, he is still routinely bombarded with micro-affirmations. We make a habit of supporting him with "good job," "you're smart," smiles of approval, hugs (when he lets us), and an endless variety of genuine and heartfelt micro-affirmations.

In a way, we thought it was our role to armor him with confidence and make sure he understood that he was special, loved, intelligent, and capable of standing up for himself. Gradually, Jimmy has learned to give himself affirmations, repeatedly telling himself out loud "Good job" or asking us to say it if we forget.

Often, his self-esteem seems tied to whether he feels he has done a good job. If he thinks he hasn't done a good job, he might break into tears. Pat might say, "You have autism. It's harder for you to sit still and control yourself. You work so hard on it, and we're so proud of you." And I remind him, "We all have tough days and make mistakes. I know I make mistakes, plenty of them." Nevertheless, Jimmy continues to need lots of positive reinforcement, just like so many of us.

22   Side Effects

"I'm not thrilled with all the drugs our 10-year-old son is taking; but we need something to calm him down. He's constantly flapping his hands, grinding his teeth, and running all over the place. It seems he can't sit still and focus on anything." "My daughter's taking Ritalin. But her biting and facial tics have increased." "I don't care for Risperdal, even though my doctor pushed it. Some parents recommend Haldol, but I'm worried about the side effects."

A majority of children and teens with autism are taking one or more medications, according to the National Institute of Mental Health.[69] Some are critical of this high rate, saying parents and teachers use these "chemical straitjackets" to make it easier to manage children with challenging behaviors. There's also concern that drugs may be "short-cuts" for more appropriate treatments. In some cases, schools pressure parents, letting them know that without medication, their child cannot learn or even function in a classroom setting.

Evaluating the effectiveness of meds is often a matter of trial and error. Different children may react differently to the same med, and there is surprisingly little research on their short- and long-term effectiveness. Given their possible side effects, parents wonder whether they're worth the risk. A few years ago, researchers at Vanderbilt University conducted a thorough review of the commonly prescribed medications used to treat children with ASD.[70] These meds, including antidepressants, antipsychotic drugs, and stimulants, don't cure autism. Rather, some may be effective in treating conditions that often accompany autism, such as hyperactivity, anxiety, irritability, and aggression. For many, meds represent hope for a better life; a last resort when nothing else seems to work.

We often asked ourselves, "Is it Jimmy or is it the meds?"
    --the mommy

When Jimmy started kindergarten, it became obvious that even though he could learn, his extremely short attention span and hyperactivity were making it nearly impossible for him to learn at school. School staff strongly encouraged us to talk to our doctor about medicating Jimmy to help him focus and sit still in one place for more than a few minutes. Initially, I was very reticent to put Jimmy on anything. But after doing some research, talking with Pat, and listening to parents' stories about so-called wonder drugs, I agreed that we should at least explore this option.

After sitting down and talking with Jimmy's neurologist, we all decided it was worth the risk to put him on Ritalin, the popular drug of the day. I say risk because Ritalin had some serious potential side effects, and there was no guarantee it would slow him down or increase his attention span. Not only is Ritalin highly addictive, but we learned it can, among other things, slow a child's physical growth and cause seizures. The last thing we wanted to see was a recurrence of Jimmy's seizures.

Once we put him on Ritalin, Jimmy's anxiety became more of an issue and panic attacks became more frequent and intense. As he became more agitated and screaming episodes grew louder and longer, we were never sure how demanding we should be. Was Ritalin causing this behavior, was the dose too high or too low, or was Jimmy not even trying to control himself? Pat and I had no idea what was going on, and Jimmy couldn't tell us.

One incident stands out. While grocery shopping with Pat and his grandmother in Las Vegas, Jimmy suddenly wrapped his arms tightly around a metal pole in the middle of the store. He would not let go, even when Pat tried to get Jimmy to follow her. With a terrified look in his eyes, he started screaming. Eventually, my wife peeled him off the pole. Once again, she didn't know whether to comfort him, scold him, or both. Comfort versus discipline was always a dilemma, but medications made it worse.

After three weeks on Ritalin, Jimmy's school reported little to no improvement in his behavior. We told the doctor we were taking him off it. When Jimmy was ten, school staff, including his teachers and social worker, pressured Pat again. They asked her to talk with Jimmy's neurologist to see if another medication might work. We acquiesced. Dr. Holden mentioned Haldol, a powerful drug that was more experimental in nature. Further, he advised us against administering it at home at the start; rather, we were sent to Johns Hopkins Hospital, so Jimmy could be closely monitored as soon as he was put on Haldol.

At Hopkins, we were fully expecting that Jimmy would be admitted to the Pediatric Ward. After being directed to a particular wing, we noticed a sign over the entrance that shook us. It read, "Child Psychiatric Ward." Jimmy stayed there for a month. Even though we tried to visit whenever possible, our interaction with him was limited by the Ward's rules. After a month, Hopkins' doctors sent him home with what they determined was the right dosage of Haldol. Although they claimed "breakthroughs" now that Jimmy was on Haldol, we saw absolutely no change in his behaviors. Possible side effects, we came to find out, included irregular heartbeats, insomnia, and uncontrolled shaking.

At this time, the local school system was still looking for a suitable private educational placement for our son. Needless to say, we were growing increasingly frustrated. To make matters worse, Jimmy began to develop a nervous tic, in which he repeatedly licked his fingers and tapped his nose. When we returned to Johns Hopkins for advice, we discovered that tics are a common side effect of Haldol; and if left untreated, the tic could become permanent. Hopkins recommended still another medication to control Jimmy's tic.

When we returned home and had a chance to think and talk some more, my wife and I decided, enough is enough. With all of these side effects, there were just too many risks. And on top of all that, these medications weren't doing him any good. The risks outweighed the benefits. When we let Dr. Holden know how we felt, he encouraged us to not give up quite yet and put us in touch with another doctor.

Meanwhile, as she continued to research medications and treatment options, Pat read about a drug called Paxil. A number of studies showed it was highly effective in curbing anxiety attacks. At this point, another doctor called us at Dr. Holden's request. After informing us that he knew of no other drugs that might work for Jimmy, Pat asked him about Paxil. His answer was not what we were looking for. He simply said, "I've never heard of Paxil for this, but sure, I'd be willing to try it." When my wife turned to me and shared the doctor's response, I made my position perfectly clear. No one would be using our son as a guinea pig.

About a year later, Linwood came into our lives. Linwood wanted Jimmy on *no* medications, period. Rather, they wanted to treat our son as he was, just plain Jimmy. That was music to our ears; and since then, he has never taken any medications for behaviors.

23   Driving Through the Fog

When Jimmy was in his thirties, The Drexel Institute issued *The National Autism Indicators Report: Transition into Young Adulthood.* The highly critical report stated, "When it comes to understanding how well our nation is helping youth affected by autism, our situation is like driving a car through the fog with no dashboard. We know we're moving, but we do not have many indicators to tell us how fast we are going, whether we're getting close to our goals, or what kind of mileage we are getting from the resources fueling our trip."[71]

Each year, it is reassuring to know that billions of dollars and more and more services are available to help our autistic population. But given big gaps in our knowledge, insufficient research, and a lack of input from the autistic community, we remain in the dark when it comes to evaluating how good a job we're doing. In other words, what money is well-spent, what services are accessible and used, and what's actually working? According to Anne Roux, the lead author of Drexel's Report, many young adults with autism remain disconnected from jobs; schooling, vocational services, and social activities in their communities. Roux adds, "Many are truly dissatisfied with their quality of life and the difficulties they have finding services that could help improve their situation."[72]

From Jimmy's birth on, Pat and I often felt like we were going it alone; "driving in a fog" with few if any resources. We didn't know where we were, where we were going, and how much fuel we had left in our tank. The one thing we did have was faith in

God and faith in ourselves as a team.

As Jimmy became school-age, the fog continued. Looking for answers, we turned to professionals and so-called experts, but they were of little help much of the time. Consequently, we did our best to become experts ourselves. Some people in-the-know provided us with nuggets of wisdom that changed our lives. For example, Pat attended a workshop led by Dr. Linda Jacobs, an educator and expert on the Education for All Handicapped Children Act (Public Law 94-142). Dr. Jacobs warned participants "Don't let them wait you out and wear you out." We took her advice to heart. While she was talking about the educational system, she could just as easily be referring to any of the systems on which our son's quality of life depended.

While taking several graduate courses and attending every workshop Pat could find on Attentional Deficit Disorder (Jim's diagnosis from age 6 to 11) and behavior management, she kept looking for strategies that would help Jimmy control himself. She studied the laws and rights of parents. Pat also signed up for parent advocacy training offered by the State of Maryland; training that armed her with the language, insight, and knowledge she needed to effectively support children with disabilities, and Jimmy in particular.

Expanding and diversifying our social network helped up to a point, but the fog that enveloped us continued to obstruct our view. We tried to learn from friends, family, and others who could relate both intellectually and emotionally to our circumstances. Through it all, we made plenty of mistakes. Jimmy's future development fell squarely on us, or at least we thought. We felt very, very alone.

Sensing our need for help, our pastor introduced my wife to a member of our congregation, a mother of a 7-year-old special needs son who was a few years older than Jimmy. Once they found time to spend a few minutes together, Helen shared her simple approach with Pat. "I let go and let God. God's in charge." As Helen saw it, her job was to love her son; not to advocate for him or involve herself with his schooling or that sort of thing. Helen's advice didn't click. She was looking for a friend; someone she could relate to, someone who might help her help Jimmy be the best he could be. Not long after that, she organized her mother's group, a support group of parents with special needs children.

I found a group of very special people in my life, and that's the other mothers I've met who are in the same situation I'm in.
   --the mommy

   The Carroll County Special Parents Support Group, whose members still lean on each other for support, advice, and friendship, is a wonderfully diverse mix of mothers and fathers of different ages, interests, educational and family backgrounds, and marital status. Their diversity extends to the nature of their child's disability and their goals for each of their children. However, they shared a common goal for their special child, a goal that was addressed by Fran Allen, one of the members of the group. Fran, who recently passed, was the mother of a son with Down syndrome. She was once asked, "What do you want your son to do when he grows up?" Her straightforward, eloquent response was, "Pay taxes." Simply put, she wanted her son to be a contributing member of society.

   In advocating for her son and other students with disabilities, Fran made it known she didn't want anyone putting her on a pedestal, or assuming she had everything under control. Like the group's other mothers, she had worries about her son, both now and in the future. And like other parents, she needed help - lots of it.

I don't want anyone telling me that I have special skills and that I'm unique.
        --a friend (Fran Allen)

As they coalesced as a group, the mothers did everything in their power to help each other and create a more supportive and caring environment. They held birthday parties, holiday parties, and outings. All of their children were able to go to everybody's parties and get-togethers, an all-too-rare event for many children with disabilities. Each month, they invited speakers to their meetings, including lawyers, doctors, counselors, therapists, and educators, to help them understand their children's needs better. At other times, mothers from the group with their children in tow appeared before the local Board of Education in order to air their concerns about special education and the needs of their children. Later, they met with state and federal elected officials to make their case for strengthening public education for children with disabilities.

A recent study from Manchester, England reveals that Pat's support group and others like it provide families with much-needed knowledge, understanding, and acceptance. Jen, who joined an autism support group when her son was diagnosed with autism, comments, "…we kind of laughed about the situations we were in, in a way that you wouldn't laugh with other people." Jen continues, "It kind of put things into perspective. We were all coming through it. Also, I think you realize that there were other people who actually had far worse situations than yourself to deal with…"[73]

Like all parents of children with disabilities, there were times Pat and her support group pushed ahead without a script. In our own case, we often wondered if Jimmy was able or ready to tackle whatever his next big challenge might be. Even today, it's not unusual for us to feel underprepared and overwhelmed. Ginny, a friend and a teacher, gave us advice back then which has stayed with us through the years. "Love him through it," she said. And that's exactly what we've tried to do.

24 Questions, Questions, Questions

"Am I grounded?" "Am I grounded?" "Am I grounded?" "Am I grounded?" This example of repetitive questioning is found in Wendy's blog, "Autism and why all the repetitive questions? I am going crazy!" Even though her ten-year-old autistic daughter knows the answer, Wendy hears this question repeatedly each and every day. There are no easy answers; the therapist says her daughter "just needs confirmation and to ignore her." Her doctors can't figure it out, and they're changing her daughter's medicine yet again.[74]

Depending on the autistic individual, reasons for repetitive questioning might reflect the need for reassurance, a desire for attention and information, or the challenge of starting and maintaining a conversation. Asking the same question over and over serves to lessen the unpredictability of everyday communication, as well as the stress of taking turns speaking and discussing topics of interest to others.

In one experiment, coaching and visual cues increased the spontaneity and frequency of oral communication between autistic high school students and their classmates without disabilities. Autistic students learned to ask questions of their peers using a "communication book." Drawings in these books pointed to topics that could serve as "openers" for conversing. Questions like, "What are you doing this weekend?" or "What kind of music do you like?" got autistic students talking. They were taught to: 1) look at their conversational partner, 2) verbalize the question, 3) wait for a response, 4) expand on their partner's response, and then, 5) move on to the next question.[75]

I still remember a time early in Jimmy's life when I wondered if he would ever be able to utter a meaningful word or phrase. Once Jimmy started to verbalize around three years of age, he was incomprehensible. But as he grew and finally began to talk, it became clear he would much rather ask questions than answer questions. To this day, it's not even close. My mom once asked me, "Why don't you just answer all of his questions?" Well, that could take a while.

When Jimmy was 6, Pat remembers talking with our neurologist, Dr. Holden, about his repetitive questions. She asked, "Why does he keep asking me questions that he already knows to the answer to?" Our doctor then posed a question of his own, "Did you ever look in your purse for something you already knew was there? Well that's what he's doing." This was the first time anyone provided insight into Jimmy's questioning that made sense.

Since age 21, Jimmy has lived in an adult living unit with two other middle-aged men with autism. When he sees my wife or me on weekends, the questions begin. It's as if he saves up all of his questions during the week for our time together. Often, these questions are non-stop and last well over an hour. Many of them are rapid-fire, one after another after another. In a typical weekend visit, Jimmy asks hundreds and hundreds of questions.

It's not surprising that Suzy decided to go into the field of event planning. Indeed, all of us have become "event planners" of sorts since Jimmy was born. During a visit to Aunt Frances's house, 13-year-old Katie wanted to get some idea of the next day's schedule. "What time are we getting up?" "When are we leaving?" Frances simply answered, "Whenever." Katie wasn't sure what to do; she had never heard that response in her entire life.

Nearly all of Jimmy's questions have to do with *his* upcoming schedule; events such as birthdays, vacations, shopping trips, doctor appointments, meals, holidays, and various forms of entertainment. He wants to know when, where, who is involved, how long, and so on. In most cases, Jimmy's questions have already been answered, and yes, he remembers the answer. Ninety-nine percent of the time he knows exactly what he will be doing in the days, weeks, and if he's able to manipulate it out of us, months ahead.

If I didn't set limits, I'm not sure where this line of questioning would end. For instance, in the middle of June, he may start asking me about when he can come home for Christmas. To discourage such questions, I might simply tell him he can ask me about plans for Christmas on December 1st. Invariably, he will try to resume this line of questioning with me in the days, weeks, and months ahead. If he does, I will simply remind him that we have already talked about this and ask *him* to tell me when he can ask. Usually, this works - for a while.

My wife and I have become much better listeners because of Jimmy. We tune in when he is talking to us, others, and himself. In spite of his incessant questioning, we're hesitant to tune him out, even for a short period of time. Listening conveys our respect and our interest in Jimmy and his world. And we wonder how many other people really listen to him. Because of Jimmy's constant repetition, not many people will show the patience necessary to really listen to him. We might pick up on the smallest thing, sandwiched between a sea of mundane comments, and it might be critically important. For example, this is how we discovered that someone was routinely taking money from him.

It didn't take me long to figure out that answers to Jimmy's questions should avoid any uncertainty. For instance, a response using the words *it depends* or *it looks like* is to be avoided at all costs, even if it means fudging the answer. If he asks me about the weather, he does his best to weasel out of me what it will be like on a given date. Obviously, weather can be an iffy proposition. Once, after being bombarded with questions about the forecast, I asked Jimmy, "Who is the only one who knows exactly what the weather is going to be?" Jimmy's matter-of-fact response made me laugh; "God, and Norm Lewis" (our TV weatherman).

One day as Pat was running around getting ready to go somewhere, Jimmy was peppering her with rapid-fire questions about everything in his schedule for the next three months or so. My wife finally had it. She almost never, ever yells at him, but this time she let loose with "Jimmy would you STOP asking me so many questions!!!" Pat clearly remembers what happened next. "I can see him now, sitting on the stairs, suddenly very still, when he said, 'How?' I was completely blown away. This was so completely different from anything I ever heard come out of his mouth; I was speechless. I don't remember my answer. I just remember becoming very loving and patient at that moment."

Pat called Bill Moss, Linwood's Director, who has consistently been there for us whenever we need his advice. Pat thought he would understand the extraordinariness of Jimmy's response and hopefully provide some guidance. Bill explained that we should tell Jimmy we're trying to help him; first by how we limit his questions, and then by working with him so he can talk about other things. We took his advice to heart. Since then, we feel more comfortable setting limits when it comes to questions. For example, Jimmy and I might take a "quiet walk," or we might have a dinner with "no schedule questions."

A doctor once asked my wife if Jimmy is in a constant state of anticipation. She answered with a heartfelt, "Yes!!" I think asking questions helps Jimmy deal with a level of anticipation that I can't fully appreciate. Even when Jimmy has been asking for months about an event, his line of questioning never changes. Often, when the long-anticipated event finally arrives, Jimmy starts with the why, when, and where of the next event. Case in point; on a ride at Disney World over the summer, Jimmy started to ask me about our plans for Christmas.

In recent years, I have tried to teach Jimmy how to show interest in other people by asking certain types of open-ended questions. For instance, the question, "How are you?" or "How was your day?" is becoming a slightly more common part of our communication. Usually however, I need to prompt him to ask a question of this nature. As an example, a recent phone conversation with Jimmy went something like this. Without saying hi or identifying himself, Jimmy immediately tells me he has a question, or he needs to know something. "Is my schedule correct?" In an instant, he asks again.

Jimmy: "Is my schedule correct?"
Daddy: No answer

Jimmy: "Is my schedule correct?"
Daddy: No answer

Jimmy: "Is my schedule correct?"
Daddy: No answer

Jimmy: "Daddy, how are you?"

At that point, I begin to answer his last question the best I can and tell him all about my day. After a short while (or what must seem like an eternity to him), he will interrupt me and try to refocus the discussion on *his* schedule. I might then have some fun with him, saying, "I thought you wanted to know how *I* am." At that point, he will grudgingly say, "Oh, OKAY, how are you?" and I will continue.

Well, we're making headway. Today, Jimmy is seated at our computer writing an email. He wants to bring a number of issues to the attention of two staff members at Linwood. While composing the email, he proudly shares with us, "I asked them how they're doing before I started pumping them full of questions."

25 What's Wrong with Him?

When her son was diagnosed with autism at age three, Dr. Christina Nicolaidis was terrified. Immediately, frightening images from the movie *Rain Man* filled her mind, along with an incident in which security personnel had to constrain her 350-pound autistic patient during one of his violent meltdowns. Doctors gave Nicolaidis, a professor and physician, a number of intensive treatments to "fix" her son, encouraging her to start them as soon as possible. Looking for answers, she pored over research, met with therapists, and read books by so-called experts to address her son's impairments and limitations.[76]

Researcher and consultant Barry Prizant recounts facilitating a staff training session on special education at an elementary school. After the session, the school's principal asked to meet him in private. Once alone, the principal began to talk about his son, age nine, who had just been diagnosed with autism. The principal asked Dr. Prizant, "should I be scared to death?" According to Dr. Prizant, this type of response by parents to a diagnosis of autism is not at all unusual, given our views of autism.[77]

Explanations and acceptance of autism can be difficult at any age. One sibling states, "My friends would always ask like what's wrong with my brother. And it was very hard to describe to them. I would say he has autism but I mean at ten years old you have no idea what that means. It made it even harder to describe because he didn't look like he had a disability. He wasn't in a wheelchair or had distinct physical features like Down Syndrome, so it wasn't obvious."[78]

Perhaps my youngest daughter, Suzy, put it best when she was a child. Talking about people's reactions to Jimmy, she said, "When I let people know my brother has a disability, they sometimes ask me what's wrong with him. It hurts me when I hear this even though they don't mean to. Nothing is wrong with Jimmy; it's what is special about him. Also, it's what he's able to do that others can't do." That point of view counters the perspectives of many educators, clinicians, and parents. Even the language we use, autism spectrum *disorder*, defines Jimmy by what needs fixing.

When people meet Jimmy for the first time, they're apt to notice certain things. He talks a little too loud, stands a little too close, and can be a bit difficult to understand. Often, people assume he's mentally slow. But if you take the time to really get to know Jimmy, you'll begin to see he has strengths as well as shortcomings, just like the rest of us. Like many others with autism, Jimmy is very punctual, has an excellent memory, is unbelievably honest, is very detail-oriented, and avoids breaking rules at all costs.

While autism makes Jimmy different from his sisters in some ways, it doesn't follow that Jimmy is necessarily less competent than his sisters. Even though he has a distinctive and rather uneven skill-set, his sisters have grown to value, respect, and even emulate his talents in a number of areas. For instance, Jimmy's kindness as well as his ability to see kindness in others is extraordinary. Suzy explains, "When I see Jimmy interact with people, he responds differently than most. He doesn't judge people by the way they look but sees the person's kindness as the biggest factor. Even though he's smart at other things, he cannot tell a person's race. I look up to him when he does this and wish more people could be like Jimmy in that way."

Our family values Jimmy for who he is. Our ultimate goal is not to cure or "normalize" him or make him more like us. Yes, he has a serious disability. And with the help of many people, Jimmy has made a phenomenal effort to modify many of his behaviors so he can participate more fully in the communities in which he lives. But we want Jimmy to be Jimmy. We want Jimmy to be comfortable in his own skin.

We don't look at Jimmy in terms of what is adequate and inadequate; rather, we look at Jimmy as a work in progress, just like the rest of us. While his autism contributes to his uniqueness, people's inability to move beyond the autistic label can make it difficult for them to appreciate his many strengths. Similarly, long-held stereotypes of the autistic population keep people at a distance. The idea that someone like him must be strange, unpredictable, and have a difficult personality makes meaningful interaction much less likely. Consequently, many never take advantage of the opportunity to find out what a neat guy he is and what they have in common.

Given Jimmy's disability, it's all too easy to adopt an "Us vs. Them" mentality. We do the same thing when we fail to realize that people of different races, religions and cultures share a common humanity. While my mind works differently than Jimmy's in some ways, it also works differently than my wife's. That doesn't make one mind any healthier or better than the other; rather, we're just different. Similarly, a preoccupation with skills that each of us might not have makes it that much more difficult to see and value our strengths and hidden potential.

I have grown to appreciate all that unites my son and me. In many ways, we're not all that different. We both enjoy sports and look forward to taking long walks together. At times we're serious, and often we're crazy silly. We're both sensitive, extremely passionate, and tend to get easily distracted. We love listening to music in the car, especially music from Broadway shows and Golden Oldies from the 50s and 60s. Jimmy has difficulty adapting to change, and often, I share that trait with him. He brightens my day, and I like to think I do the same for him. Finally, family means everything to both of us.

As his father, my ability to identify and nourish Jimmy's strengths brings us closer together. I see a lot of him in me.
        --the daddy

        I find it interesting that someone who has such difficulty communicating can impact others so dramatically. Driving home from James Madison University after dropping off Katie her freshman year, Pat and I were listening to some music on the radio. My mind was wandering when Suzy, age 11, from the back seat, asks me, "Daddy, if you could get rid of Jimmy's disability (autism), would you?" I remember being caught completely off guard and trying in vain to come up with an answer. Suzy, sensing that I was struggling, gave her own answer. "People see disability as a disadvantage, as something you're stuck with. But I see it as more of a gift." At that moment, I remember being "blown away" by the depth and wisdom of her response.
        Would I get rid of Jimmy's disability? For me, the answer is clearly no; autism is an integral part of who he is. With Jimmy, it's a total package, rooted in a complex and dynamic mix of genetics and social interaction. Do I worry about him, especially when I think about the future? Absolutely. But I have

learned to worry less and rely more on my faith.

Yes, there may be times when his autism seems to hide his true talents and potential. But more often than not, it isn't autism that hides his gifts. It is our culturally bound views of autism and people with disabilities. That awareness motivates me to work on myself, my own cultural lens, and the world in which I live.

Many people act like they feel sorry for me when I tell them I have a brother with a disability. But they shouldn't feel that way. It isn't necessarily a negative thing. When I hear my friends talk about the way their brothers act, I know that having Jimmy as a brother is an advantage."
--a sister (Suzy)

Focusing on Jimmy's strengths doesn't mean ignoring his weaknesses. But as his father, I try to avoid thinking of them as deficits, much less "core deficits" of autism. Rather, they're areas in which he needs help. Occupational, speech, and physical therapists have addressed many of these areas; along with our family, the staff at Linwood, and of course, Jimmy himself. When Suzy was a teen, she referred to his weaknesses as "difficulties." She noted, "Jimmy does have difficulties with certain things, but don't we all? It's hard for him to use his hands. He can't ride a bike or drive a car even though he's an adult. He has trouble communicating and showing his feelings. He gets very upset when people he loves are hurting. He's very used to his schedule and gets very distressed when other people change it. Just like everybody else, he works on being better at things he's not good at."

In his book *Uniquely Human: A Different Way of Seeing Autism*, Dr. Prizant takes issue with the idea that autism is simply a dreadful illness, characterized by a "checklist of deficits." Rather, he suggests parents, caregivers, and professionals reexamine their own thinking, including what constitutes strengths. Based on his decades of working with adults and children with autism, Prizant argues against trying to "fix" or normalize individuals like Jimmy by eliminating their symptoms. Rather, we should try to understand their differences and the reasons behind their behaviors. Bottom line, we all have "behaviors" that help us cope one way or another.[79]

26 Challenging Behaviors

When it comes to behaviors, what we consider challenging varies. Frequently, parents, teachers, and caregivers define behaviors as challenging if they find them irritating and difficult to control. In the literature on autism, behaviors are generally not considered challenging unless they are intense, long-lasting, frequent, and undermine learning and/or pose a significant risk to one's own physical safety or the safety of others.[80]

Scientific literature on autism points to challenging behaviors that can be difficult to understand yet serve one or a number of functions or purposes. Such behaviors include destruction of property, aggression toward others such as kicking and biting, self-injurious behavior such as head banging and picking at oneself, and disruptive behavior like meltdowns or running away. For autistic people, challenging behaviors may have serious consequences, making it difficult for them to succeed in school or participate in social activities.

Understanding why challenging behaviors occur is well, challenging. And understanding a behavior is not the same as accepting it. One young woman with autism explains that for her, behaviors such as biting, hitting, and running allowed her to get away from people who made her feel uncomfortable. Since she didn't have the ability to express her wishes verbally at the time, her only option as she saw it was to act this way. It was almost an automatic response on her part. As she grew older and developed her ability to sign and use communication technology, she could express herself differently and not resort to aggression.

Our son Jimmy, like many children with autism, had his fair share of challenging behaviors, including kicking, head butting, biting, and meltdowns. Many of these behaviors surfaced well before he was diagnosed with autism. We had no idea where these behaviors were coming from or why he was acting this way. Trying to understand these behaviors didn't mean that we necessarily accepted them. Without sufficient knowledge to fall back on, we asked questions, listened, and showered him with love and all the patience we could muster as we tried to help him manage his behaviors.

As a child, I'm sure my parents considered me a challenge, especially when it came to teasing my siblings, not eating certain foods, and not doing my homework. And while my son can be a challenge to say the least, I have found that reactions to his behaviors pose significant challenges as well. They may cause people in general to not really listen to him or show empathy. People may make unwarranted assumptions about why he's acting a certain way. As a result, many are often hesitant to reach out to him.

When Jimmy was about three years-old, he started biting repeatedly. What began as kisses on the cheek turned into bites. We felt overwhelmed by the presence of a new, challenging behavior. Why in the world would he bite Pat when she asked him to give her a kiss? Maybe he didn't want to be kissed. Did biting her feel good? Was he trying to get attention or perhaps avoid something? What triggered this behavior was a mystery. And the last thing Pat wanted to do was reinforce it. The first time it happened, Pat pushed him away and tried to keep her cool.

Pat's teacher training taught her quite a bit about behavior modification. But it never occurred to her to put it to use until our pediatrician mentioned it.

Somewhere in her distant memory she remembered the importance of teaching the right behavior by reinforcing the behavior you want. Simply punishing the unwanted behavior was not going to work.

Her plan to get rid of this challenging behavior targeted Jimmy's desire to please. If Jimmy could go two minutes without biting, Pat would heap on the praise. Then, she proceeded to repeat this process. After Jimmy refrained from biting for thirty – 2-minute intervals, Pat stretched the time to 5 minutes. She continued this pattern all day. By the end of the first day, he could go a full hour without biting. By the end of the second day, he could go two hours, and now he was being rewarded with ice cream. By the end of the week, the behavior was gone, and never returned.

We only targeted certain behaviors, as he grew ready and able to modify them. Some were much more difficult to modify than others. Putting an end to biting people took days, while modifying other challenging behaviors required years. Some we continue to battle. For instance, he still eats way too fast, so fast that he often chokes on his food unless he is supervised. We have tried almost everything it seems, but nothing seems to work. We're still trying.

When he was young, and his sisters were visibly upset, Jimmy would try to forcefully calm them down, by "banging heads" or grabbing them and screaming as he jumped up and down. In moments like these, trying to explain to Jimmy that his behavior was inappropriate was nearly impossible. More often than not, we would need to send him to his room again and again for "time out." Sometimes, it would take a good part of the day for him to get his emotions under control.

If Jimmy is overcome with emotions, it's a struggle to get through to him. Before Pat and I try to teach him anything, we've learned to wait until he calms down and we calm down. If something "bad" happens and everyone is upset, he needs to be reassured it's not his fault. Teaching him how others might want to be treated can be a mammoth undertaking, but it is doable. As an example, helping Jimmy understand that sometimes people want to be left alone when they're sad or they argue is something we continue to work on. But it helps that he wants to make everybody happy. Over time, we've seen Jimmy make significant strides. Case in point, when his sisters or Pat and I are trying to work things out, he now makes a concerted effort to give us the space we need.

When he was ten, Carroll County Public Schools finally came to the conclusion that they were unable to manage Jimmy's challenging behaviors *and* meet his educational needs. While this didn't come as a shock to us, it was still hard to digest. After taking some time to familiarize ourselves with Jimmy's educational options, Pat and I began the process of applying on behalf of our son to dozens of facilities for children with disabilities. Over the summer, we searched for a place for Jimmy Buchers in nearby private schools. Twenty-three rejected him. Some places informed us that they could handle his "challenging" behaviors but couldn't teach him at his intellectual level. Others made it clear that they could teach him but couldn't deal with the severity of his behaviors.

However, there was still hope. There were a handful of places that were "maybe's;" one in Rhode Island, one in Texas, and two others in Pennsylvania and Virginia respectively. The facility in Pennsylvania provided a glimpse of what we were up against. When we arrived, they were very positive about accepting Jimmy and their ability to teach him. Toward the end of our visit, staff told us to meet

Jimmy at the main office at 1:30 p.m. They returned with him at 1:20 p.m. and we weren't there. Suddenly, Jimmy began to scream, cry, and spin. Their response was to hold him down on the floor till we arrived, which only served to escalate his panic. Needless to say, we crossed this facility of our list, and they crossed him off as well.

Another special facility in northern Virginia was next. Pat left Jimmy at home with me. First, she was taken to the indoor play area. In one corner was a pile of used building materials, including studs with nails sticking out. Even though students were ignoring the pile, Pat knew that Jimmy would be immediately drawn to it and likely hurt himself. Already, she was sensing this wasn't a place for "Jimmys." During the course of the visit, staff showed her a cement-walled room with one high window and a metal door. She was told this was the "time-out" room. Pat asked, "When could we visit him?" Their answer, "Once he had maintained appropriate behavior for one week." At this point, one hour of acceptable behavior in a classroom setting was an unbelievable accomplishment for Jimmy. Another facility off our list.

After the Virginia trip, we continued looking for viable options. Pat described some of our eye-opening visits with a member of the team that was created to help us find a placement for Jimmy. The educator's advice left us feeling even more alone and desperate. "Sometimes," she said, "we have to send our kids to a place that isn't really right because that's the only option." Pat thought to herself, "No way!"

That next fall, Jimmy went back to public school. He was placed in the class for emotionally disturbed children, the only one that could manage him, and on good days teach him. Everyone agreed that we needed to continue to explore our options.

27 The Linwood Method

Recently, I had the pleasure of talking with a student from Linwood's early years. He describes himself as successful later in life; someone who got married and became a certified public accountant. When our talk turned toward Linwood, he said, "Linwood opened up the floodgates of the real me. It basically made the rest of my life feasible. At Linwood, I was not funny in the head, I was not all twisted up. These are words my dad sometimes used to describe me."[81] Now retired, he serves on Linwood's Board of Directors.

Jeanne Simons, founder of Linwood, had a simple philosophy. She did not assume that people with autism were somehow defective and needed to be isolated and fixed. Simons believed that changes in the behavior of people with autism do not take place by manipulating, training, or constantly sedating them, but by changing their environment. Specifically, she sought to identify what in the environment influences behavior and promotes participation and cooperation. As Simons saw it, every interaction and every event in a person's life, no matter where or when it takes place, is important. In essence, the staff at Linwood "manipulates the environment, rather than manipulating the child."[82]

Throughout the day at Linwood, autistic children have opportunities to learn self-help skills, develop functional language, and experience consequences for one's actions. This type of learning might take place in class, during bath time, on outings to see the Baltimore Orioles, over lunch, or during free time. Everyone at Linwood is involved in nurturing and teaching, including volunteers, social workers, teacher aides, clerical staff, and kitchen personnel. By design, the Linwood staff keeps in constant contact with parents. Consequently, parents are that much better prepared to contribute to their child's growth at Linwood and at home.

Linwood is an extraordinary place. I feel absolutely swept over by what Ms. Simons has done for me and my family. She's given me a life. She's given my family a life. I felt like I was in the presence of greatness when I was around her. Her ability to love children with autism was extraordinary. She had the ability to see past labels, past obstructions, and embrace their inner selves.
--the mommy

I n 1950, Jeanne Simons was working at a center for emotionally disturbed children in Washington, D.C. After a while, she noticed that the center's staff refused to work with certain children whose severe behaviors required more attention; labeling them as "too retarded." Simons later discovered that these children were in fact autistic.

Simons observed these children from afar. The staff provided minimal care until these children transitioned to an institution close by. The parents of these children cared deeply but were looking for answers. Simons cared as well, and out of this experience grew a strong commitment to find a suitable place for children such as these. After a lengthy search, Simons established a school and residential haven in 1955, and named it the Linwood Center for Disturbed Children. Linwood was the first school of its kind to work solely with individuals with autism. There were 24 students in all, 14 received day care and 10 were residents. The average length of stay was three years. If it hadn't been for Linwood, these children would in all likelihood have been institutionalized.

Figure 15 JEANNE SIMONS, FOUNDER AND LONGTIME DIRECTOR OF LINWOOD CENTER

Ms. Simons was somebody I knew I could count on. I could always go see Ms. Simons and discuss anything and everything with her. I felt safe with her.
--a former Linwood student

Simons co-authored *The Hidden Child: The Linwood Method for Reaching the Autistic Child.* The foundation of this model is her belief in the "worth of the individual in all of his manifestations, and respect for the healthy potential that exists in even the most handicapped human being." [83] Additionally, she emphasizes the critical importance of prolonged, intense, and early intervention.

Shortly after the book was published in 1986, she traveled to Mexico City's Intercontinental University. Simons was invited to share her philosophy and expertise with the staff at the University's fledgling Center for Autism. After numerous return trips, Simons developed a newfound appreciation for U.S. laws that require education of people with disabilities, as well as taxes that fund education of this nature. In Mexico, help of this nature was not available to families of children with disabilities.

Simon's philosophy struck a nerve with Pat and me. Linwood was not looking to play the blame game; rather, it sought to provide a culture of support and guidance for children with autism *as well as* their parents. Given Simon's concern with the environment of children with autism, it's not surprising that she focused on reaching out to parents. As Simons once said early on, "There was no help for mothers. I was the first one who didn't blame them."[84]

The parents and families need all the support they can get.
--Bill Moss, Executive Director of Linwood Center

Visiting Linwood for the first time, as my wife and I entered the front door we encountered a little boy around age 7. He came running out of a classroom and threw himself on the floor, curled up in a ball while rolling down the hallway. All the while he was screaming at the top of his lungs. Then an adult came out of the classroom, picked the child up in a matter-of-fact kind of way, and carried him back into the room. We had a difficult time processing what took place. If we weren't so desperate to find a facility for Jimmy that met his needs, we would have turned around and left.

Even you and Rich are not enough. At any given time, we might have seven different people we can hand Jimmy off to.
--Bill Moss, Executive Director of Linwood Center

Soon after Jimmy was placed in Linwood's residential 5-day school (age 11), I remember visiting him for the first time. Upon entering, I exchanged pleasantries with some of the staff and students, and then was directed to Jimmy's classroom. When I entered through the doorway, I saw three straight lines of Linwood students, each sitting in front of a desk. The students were methodically putting a number of small objects in a small, plastic grey container. My eyes turned to my son. He was focused on following instructions, putting "x" contents in the container, and then moving on to the next one. For some reason, I wasn't prepared for this. I remember saying to myself, "This is MY son?" "Can't they think of something more productive, more meaningful? I know better than anyone what he's capable of."

The idea of my son doing this type of contract work was unsettling at first. This was beneath him. Maybe it was appropriate for other children at Linwood, but certainly not *my* son. After all, Jimmy is a Bucher. I was raised in a family in which education is highly valued and going to college is a given. As much as I hate to admit it, my hidden biases were starting to surface.

Recently, my wife and I visited one of Linwood's work sites for the first time. We were there to attend an IP (Individual Plan) meeting. Jimmy, as usual, would join us. At this meeting, we talk with a number of staff and the service coordinator to lay out and tweak Jimmy's vocational and residential plans for the coming year. One of Linwood's staff members showed us around the work site prior to the meeting. When we entered a large spacious room, my gaze focused on a familiar figure seated at one of the tables. Jimmy was doing contract work, only this time he was putting prizes in little plastic bubbles. In spite of his mild cerebral palsy and his limited attention span, he was able to do this task, which required using his pointer finger and thumb in opposition. Like twenty years ago, when I first I saw him doing contract work, he was focused on his job, for which he earned a small wage. I, on the other hand, saw something quite different now. I no longer saw this work as simply filling time or "beneath him." Rather it was important, meaningful work, teaching him life skills that carry over to his job at Walmart and his personal life.

28 A Question of Empathy

Geraldine Dawson distinctly remembers an encounter at work that gave her pause. One day, Dr. Dawson, Director of Duke University's Center for Autism and Brain Development, felt very stressed although none of her colleagues seemed to pick up on this. A young man with autism who works at the Center approached Dr. Dawson and asked how her day was going? Dr. Dawson responded by citing her schedule which was chock full of appointments. With a concerned look, the young man replied, "Dr. Dawson, I think you need a break." Dawson remembers thinking he's right, of course.[85]

In his controversial book, *Mindblindness: An Essay on Autism and Theory of the Mind*, Professor Baron-Cohen advances the idea that autistic children suffer from mindblindness. His theory suggests that unlike other children who are wired at birth to read others' mental states, children with autism are "blind" to what people are thinking, intending, or believing.[86] Questions have been raised about Baron-Cohen's theory and how he arrived at his findings. For example, his findings are based on research involving only 20 autistic children; yet he made conclusions about millions of children. In analyzing his data, Baron-Cohen glossed over significant differences in the empathy of the individuals he studied. And his study reduces empathy, a complex and wide range of human experiences, to relatively simple categories.

Assumptions of an "empathy deficit" or "empathy dysfunction" color how we view autistic people. It makes them out to be less than human; uncaring, incapable of loving, emotionless, and even pathological. It widens the chasm between *them* and *us*. Children with autism have been compared to robots, chimpanzees, and apes. Comments by professionals describe people along the spectrum as extremely aloof, selfish, and self-centered. Others assumed to be in the know are quoted in the media as saying, "autistic people are missing a core component of humanity (empathy)," [87] and "trying to teach a person with autism empathy is like trying to teach a pig to sing – it is a waste of time…"[88]

Roughly thirty years ago, I remember picking up a copy of *Newsweek*. The cover story characterized autism as a form of mindblindness. The article's byline, "Why more kids and families are facing the challenge of mindblindness," spoke to the upsurge in autism at that time. The use of the term mindblindness to describe people like my son jarred my senses and didn't sit well with me. Like many depictions of autism, it seemed stereotypical, fuzzy, and negative.

Many times, Jimmy seems to have a great deal of difficulty putting himself in someone else's shoes in order to tune into their thoughts and intentions. As a child, he insisted on getting his own emotional needs met, even at the expense of everybody else. Consequently, when our family took a vacation or just went out to eat, Jimmy's needs came first. He still seems to struggle with his own emotions versus the feelings of others.

Reacting in a socially appropriate manner when emotions are high has been a lifelong struggle for Jimmy. For example, he can't stand to see his sisters cry. Pat had a saying, "If one got cut, the other bled." Their empathy for each other was and is extraordinary. Unfortunately, there were times when Jimmy found it difficult *to show* empathy toward his sisters, especially when his emotions started to kick in. If Katie cried, Jimmy would jump in place, cry louder or scream. When his sisters accidentally broke something, Jimmy would forcefully intervene. Shouting "I'll pay for it, I'll pay it," was his way of coming up with an immediate solution and making the pain go away.

In their teens, our daughters even shared their own frustration about showing their emotions. They felt they couldn't cry, get mad or upset without their brother completely losing it. While he only made matters worse by getting involved, it was clear he felt his sisters' pain. Jimmy's neurologist once attributed reactions of this nature to "wiring in his brain that got crossed."

Since the first time I brought Suzy home, Jimmy has adored her. While Jimmy can seem detached, I loved what Suzy brought out in him. As far as I knew, Jimmy never sang. But he sang to his sister, songs I had no idea he knew the words to. Now that they're adults, he often expresses concern for Suzy and loves spending time with her.
    --the mommy

Figure 16 JIMMY READING TO SUZY

In Baron-Cohen's more recent book, *The Science of Evil: On Empathy and the Origins of Cruelty*, he theorizes that autistic people have zero degrees of empathy on a scale of 0 to 6 degrees. This diverse population's total lack of empathy is due to the malfunctioning of something he calls an "empathy circuit" that lies deep within the brain.[89] However, this is a theory, not a fact. To believe Baron-Cohen is to assume we know what Jimmy and people like Jimmy are thinking and feeling at any moment and in any situation. We do not. And portraying those with autism in this manner perpetuates the false notion that people *without* autism are naturally empathetic. The stereotypical assumption that people with autism lack empathy points to a fundamental lack of understanding and empathy on the part of people who make this assumption.

As Jimmy's father, I continually need to examine my own empathy, however uncomfortable that might be. For instance, I may mistakenly assume I know what Jimmy is dealing with when in fact I haven't a clue. Take the fact that like many people on the spectrum, he almost always eats and drinks too fast. I have struggled with this behavior for years, wondering why he doesn't try harder to pace himself and remember what I've told him.

Each meal it seems I have to remind him to slow down and eat little bites, or he will start choking on his food or even throw up. Yes, I make sure to cut up his food into small pieces and give him small portions as well as smallish utensils and glasses. Once he starts eating and drinking, he usually needs some gentle coaching. When he begins to gag or hiccup because he tries to woof down his dinner in a matter of minutes, I will instruct him to stop eating and wait a moment. I might then suggest he take some *sips* of milk in between bites and remind him to slow down. Regardless of my efforts, there is no carryover to the next meal.

I can only imagine how difficult this must be for him, especially when he senses the irritation and impatience in my voice. Jimmy is a middle-aged man, and his daddy is telling him what to eat, how to eat, and how fast to eat. It's amazing how unbelievably cooperative he is; not once has he ever told me to "go to hell" or just "leave me alone." His eating habits are challenging because of my assumptions. I forget that sitting and eating for a period of time is a social activity, one which involves a considerable amount of face-to-face interaction and communication skills. I assume if he would just try harder, he's capable of self-monitoring his eating.

When I researched this behavior, I learned that food texture, extreme hunger, anxiety, and a lack of sensory awareness may contribute to his inability to slow himself down. After all, Jimmy's emotions run high constantly. To assume that I can understand and interpret his behavior by comparing it to mine is my issue, not his. In other words, I tend to show a lack of empathy when I forget to at least try to understand motives and perspectives that don't align with mine.

For the longest time, people have not given Jimmy credit for being as capable as he is. The same thing applies to empathy. The question of how much empathy Jimmy has isn't as simple as it might seem. In some ways, it depends on how we define empathy and how we define autism. Imagine a continuum of empathy, stretching from unbelievably empathetic to totally lacking in empathy. I've taught nonautistic or neurotypical students who appear incapable of gauging what another student might be thinking or feeling. While Jimmy struggles with expressing empathy, it would be a mistake to assume he cannot identify with the thoughts and emotions of another.

There are different levels of empathy. No one fully understands another person's emotions. But Jimmy can strip away biases and make a raw assessment of someone else. He might not know the details of every situation, but sometimes details can interfere with empathy. Autism allows Jimmy to be more genuine. I can't say why.
--a sister (Suzy)

Being able to tune into and perhaps understand another person's feelings or body language is one thing but showing care or appreciation for someone's situation is altogether different. For Jimmy, it seems easier for him to express his feelings in writing rather than face-to-face or even talking on the phone. When someone is going through difficult times, he immediately wants to send a greeting card. Choosing, reading, signing and sending or giving a card to someone is a deeply personal act for Jimmy. It isn't just a matter of buying any old card and stuffing it in an envelope. Rather, Jimmy must feel that the message and the design of the card are perfectly tailored to the individual in question. For example, he might ask me if the person is religious. If so, he will choose a card with a religious theme that fits both the occasion and the person. If the card was for his grandmother, someone he knew to be visually impaired, Jimmy wanted to know if the writing was "big enough."

Recently, I found myself using a men's restroom along with Jimmy. After washing his hands, he made a point of not using the automatic dryer. Rather, he dried his hands with a paper towel. Why? Because Jimmy remembered a conversation we had not too long ago. He understands that the high-pitch noise emitted by this kind of hand-dryer hurts my ears, and he takes pride in remembering something that is important to his daddy.

For over two decades, Tai Mitchell, Jimmy's counselor, was in charge of his daily care at Linwood. Tai and Jimmy grew very close, so much so that the Buchers considered Tai "family." Toward the end of his life, Tai was dealing with some serious health issues which forced him to retire from his position at Linwood. Before Tai passed away, Jimmy got a chance to talk with his "best friend" (his words) on the phone. While I have no idea what they talked about, I do know that during the course of the conversation, a tear ran down Jimmy's cheek. Showing a deep, heartfelt emotion in a quiet, controlled manner is a rarity for Jimmy.

Kathy, a good friend of Jimmy's and a fellow coworker at Walmart, passed away during the holiday season a while back. Initially, Jimmy asked his mother if he could send Kathy a sympathy card. Pat said that would be impossible, but he could send one to his family. After buying the card, Jimmy wanted to know if he could also send her family a Christmas card. "That's not necessary," said Pat, "but it was a nice thought." "They'll miss her on Christmas," said Jimmy. When it comes to empathy, Jimmy has a way of surprising us.

Empathy comes in all shapes and sizes. A Special Olympics coach put the notion of mindblindness in perspective when he described one of Jimmy's greatest gifts; "When he interacts with you, he might avert his eyes, but he engages your heart."

29 An Autistic Bubble

My life is very closed, not a lot of people can deal with my son or are comfortable around him. I can't take him a lot of places because of crowds and noise, so we spend a lot of time at home or grandparent's house."[90] For another parent, the reactions of others put her on edge when she goes out with her autistic son. "The hardest thing, one of the hardest things I find is other people. You know that is the thing I am always bothered about. I know it is a problem more in my head and other people just say, 'I don't care what people think,' but you know from when he was little and he used to scream and head bang and people used to stare in shops...I feel uncomfortable with that."[91]

Autistic individuals and their families were given an interesting assignment by the London-based National Autistic Society (NAS). They were asked to keep a log of their encounters with the public over time. Specifically, they were to record incidents in which they experienced difficulties, such as misunderstandings or intolerance of some sort. But when participants returned their log sheets, very few contained any difficult encounters, and some were blank.

Initially, NAS researchers assumed the data point to autistic people being absorbed and accepted into society. However, further analysis revealed something quite different. Participants didn't regularly experience difficulties because they had learned to avoid them. After a while, they grew tired of being judged and misunderstood by the public. Feeling worn down, they stopped going to places they knew might be problematic, such as the movie theatre, shopping center, or church. One mother, talking about how her world became smaller and smaller over time, said "We're in a bubble, an autistic bubble."[92]

I wish that people would get to know others like my brother and ignore what they see on the outside, paying attention to what's on the inside.
        --a sister (Katie, age 9)

In her book, *The Loving Push*, Dr. Temple Grandin stresses the importance of parents giving "careful, loving pushes to get their autistic child to try new things."[93] She acknowledges that parents have to fight their inclination to be overprotective, fearing that their child may be excluded and get hurt if they "let go" too soon. Without loving pushes, autistic children will not learn the skills they need to become more independent.

As Jimmy's father, I'm very aware of what it means to be living in an autistic bubble, and why the family of a child with a serious disability might take the extreme step of retreating from society. Even though the rate of autism has increased dramatically during the last few decades, the number of "Jimmys" we see when we venture outside our home has not. For years, we never came across individuals in public places who communicated, interacted, and behaved in a way that was reminiscent of our son.

- Not at weddings.
- Not at the neighborhood pool.
- Not on the beach.
- Not at the movies.
- Not at baseball, football, or basketball games.
- Not on cruise ships or airplanes.
- Not at Broadway musicals or dinner theaters.
- Not at restaurants.
- Not at the grocery store.

- Not at church.

And today, "Jimmys" seem no more visible in public than they were decades ago. At least that's been our experience.

A parent living on the West Bank describes something as simple as walking down the street with her child. "Everyone leaves what they are looking at or doing and starts watching your kid. You feel like you are the star of a puppet show."[94] When I'm with Jimmy in public settings, I often feel as though a bright spotlight is shining on us. In situations such as these, I try to focus on Jimmy rather than the outside world, but I wonder how he feels.

When Jimmy was younger, it was not uncommon for people to look at the two of us with a critical eye during one of his meltdowns, and mistakenly assume his strange behaviors showed a lack of self-control on his part. Little did they know that Jimmy's behaviors were his way of coping with a situation that was overwhelming for him. What's more, I often sensed that others were judging me as if to say, why doesn't this father do a better job of disciplining and teaching his son how to control himself?

When Jimmy seemed out of control, my wife would get unasked-for advice in public, from acquaintances and strangers alike. People with the best of intentions would say things like, "Have you ever given him a good spanking?" or "You know you need to stop feeding that child so much sugar."

Even when we were made to feel welcome, subtle but significant barriers stood in our way. For example, when Jimmy was a young teen, I remember sitting in the back of our local church one Sunday morning. The preacher was making announcements, listing a number of upcoming church-related events.

Jimmy seemed to be in another world; I should have known better.

When the preacher began discussing an upcoming event for youth, Jimmy perked up. "Can I go?" "Can I go?" he asked. When I hesitated, he asked again with a sense of urgency, "Daddy, can I go?" I told him to be quiet since we were in the middle of the service; he could ask me later. Then, before moving on to the next announcement, the preacher stated, "Supervision will be provided." Those four words stuck with me. I had heard this message many times before, and I knew what it meant. Supervision meant that one or maybe two church members would accompany the children and maintain some semblance of order. It didn't mean one-on-one supervision, which Jimmy absolutely needed at that point in his life. If Jimmy attended the event, either Pat or I would need to accompany him. Once again, I felt as though I was trying to push Jimmy out into the community, but our community was pushing him right back at us.

For the longest time, Jimmy has found relationships to be a challenge. But relationships are a two-way street. Often, people find it all too easy to jump to conclusions and in the process, misread his behaviors, such as when he gets agitated, has a meltdown, or carries on a conversation with himself. The stares and the looks of disapproval get old. And as he ages, I wonder how much of the world around him he's processing. I'm quick to recognize his elation when people are genuinely interested in him and his endless questions and stories. But I have a more difficult time discerning what Jimmy is feeling when people don't take the time to really try to understand him; or when they feign interest but could care less.

Daily exposure to a society that prejudges and

misjudges our son can alter the lens that shapes what we see. This is true when Jimmy is with us, and even when he's not. When he was young, I remember attending a church musical program along with my wife. We left Jimmy home with a relative. Early in the performance, Pat and I could not help but notice two young people who were seated directly in front of us. For more than one-half hour, they were constantly turning their heads to look at something in our direction, and then giggling as they turned back to look at the show. On our way home, we tried to make sense of the strange looks from the teens. Only then did we realize that if Jimmy had been with us, we would have been absolutely sure they were looking at him.

We took Jimmy out of his comfort zone and shoved him into this world.
--the mommy

Our family refuses to live in a bubble. Even though it's easier to follow familiar routines when we remain inside our bubble, we've gradually developed the courage to take trips and go on vacations to places we've never been before. When you do something for the first time, it can become part of a new routine. Over time, we've found that visiting new places and doing new things have become much easier and more enjoyable for Jimmy and the rest of us. So, our routines evolve and change to some degree.

When our community tries to segregate or ignore us and other families like us, we do what we can to resist and push back. If we have the time and feel empowered, we will advocate, initiate, and educate. As an example, Pat was determined to create layers of support in our community where none existed.

During the long summer months, we were both stressed because Jimmy had nothing to do, in part because he didn't know how to play with another child for more than a minute or two. With the help of other one of Jimmy's teachers and town officials, Pat helped create Camp Fun, a YMCA camp for children with disabilities. Instead of staying inside all summer, Camp Fun gave children like Jimmy the opportunity to be outside and play with other children their age. To get it up and running, Pat approached a family who already operated a day care center, riding academy, and summer camp on their horse farm. They liked Pat's idea, and a camp for 6 to 12-year-olds became a reality. Children got the opportunity to learn how to swim, ride horses, have fun with arts and crafts, and most importantly, socialize. Articles about the camp appeared in local newspapers. In a county where summer programs for children with disabilities were nonexistent, Camp Fun made an enormous difference.

It's a wonderful, wonderful camp…and to go there is to feel just terrific, because you know these children would be spending their summer inside with nothing to do…but they're all out there – they have friends, they're out in the sun, and they learn how to swim…
*   --the mommy*

Figure 17 DISABLED CHILDREN MADE ALL KINDS OF NEW FRIENDS AT CAMP FUN.

Camp Fun and similar small-scale initiatives can only do so much. Throughout the world, individuals with ASD along with their parents and caregivers retreat to autism bubbles when they grow exceedingly weary and disillusioned in the face of social barriers. In his comments on World Autism Day, United Nations Secretary General Ban-Ki-moon addressed this global challenge. He stated, "To measure the success of our societies, we should examine how well those with different abilities, including persons with autism, are integrated as full and valued members."[95]

30   Feeling Pain?

Question: Studies show individuals on the spectrum are:

a) Oversensitive to pain (hypersensitivity).
b) Undersensitive to pain (hyposensitivity).
c) Express pain discomfort differently.

It's noteworthy that scientific data supports each of these findings. For example, case studies indicate that some autistic children may tolerate extreme heat or cold and seem impervious to pain. Research also shows that some autistic people may be unusually vulnerable to pain, but they may struggle to show discomfort. Imagine not crying or moaning after grabbing a hot frying pan or not complaining while playing without any clothes on in the snow; or not even grimacing or saying "ouch" after being repeatedly punched in the stomach.

A father, who describes his son as being "on the more extreme end of the autism spectrum," talks about the challenge of recognizing and treating pain in her child. "I have seen him walk into a concrete wall because he wasn't paying attention, and not even blink. I have also seen him shout in pain and have tears in his eyes because he scratched himself. Finding out exactly what hurts and where he is having pain can be quite difficult."[96] Noah, a middle-aged man diagnosed with Asperger's Syndrome, remembers not realizing his sensory world was not like others. He recalls, "I had no idea that what I was feeling was not what everyone felt."[97]

Clearly, recognizing and responding to pain in an autistic child or adult is serious. Evaluating the need for treatment and deciding on an intervention, medical or otherwise, may hinge on an accurate diagnosis of pain. Unfortunately, there is no one reliable pain assessment tool. What we do know, based on limited research in this area, is that the pain experience for people with autism is different. Consequently, interventions and treatments "must be tailored" to *each* specific child and adult.[98]

W hen Jimmy finally started to walk around 18 months, he'd been diagnosed with mild cerebral palsy as well as a neurological disorder known as apraxia. According to the National Institute of Neurological Disorders and Stroke; apraxia can arise from brain damage. Doctors attributed his general awkwardness and clumsiness to apraxia. All day long, he fell down, or so it seemed. It never struck us as unusual that he never cried after a fall, even a pretty hefty one. We just figured he was one "tough" dude, like his daddy.

At age 5, my wife remembers taking Jimmy to the playground. He took a pretty good tumble on the grass; then kept looking at his hand when he got up but didn't show any other reaction. Pat ran over to see if he was okay and discovered he had fallen on broken glass and his hand was cut up pretty badly. Again, he didn't cry or complain; he just looked at it. Pat rushed Jimmy to the ER, where it took 5 people to restrain him, so doctors could stitch him up. His hand then had to be wrapped so the bandage had no visible edges; otherwise he would tear off the bandage and then pull at the stitches. After that, we came to the realization that Jimmy might not feel certain types of pain, or he could not express it if he did.

A few years later, Jimmy got off the school bus following an hour-long ride home. The aide on the bus told us he had been rubbing his eye all the way home. It was highly inflamed and swollen. The aide didn't intervene since he didn't make a fuss or act like he was in pain. Within a few hours, red streaks began to appear just beneath his closed, swollen eye. We rushed to the ER, where he was diagnosed with blood poisoning in the eye and face. He was put on intravenous antibiotics and stayed in the hospital for a week before he was cleared to go home. During this entire episode, he never mentioned any discomfort or pain.

At 16, Jimmy had the flu. He was home a week and seemed to be getting worse. Pat had already taken him to the doctor, but I didn't like how lethargic he seemed. For someone who usually moved 100 mph, this was very, very rare. Not wanting to take any chances, Pat took him back. When the doctor pressed on his stomach, Jimmy said, "Ow" and squirmed a little. Pat informed the doctor she had NEVER heard him say ow before; therefore, this must be serious. The doc looked at her funny, but he had known Jimmy and his mom for a long time, and thank God took what she said to heart.

Pat recounts what happened next. "Jimmy's doctor sent us to the ER. The same thing happened. The doctor pressed his stomach, and Jimmy said, "Ow." I made it clear we needed to interpret his response as if he was screaming. The doctor wasn't impressed, but said he'd do some blood work. After a few hours of tests, the doctor came to me and said Jimmy's work-up pointed to appendicitis, but he really couldn't imagine that was the case in light of Jim's muted response. Only after I pushed and pushed did the doctor decide to open Jimmy up to see what was going on. What he found was a fully perforated appendix (he told me it had probably been perforated for at least a week) and all of Jim's insides were filling with infection. The doctor did an appendectomy and kept him on intravenous antibiotics for a full week before Jimmy was medically "out of the woods." Even after surgery, Jimmy acted as if he had no pain. When nurses first asked him if he could get up and walk the next day, he started to jump out of bed and head down the hall in his normal fashion. However, something must have registered because in an instant he started to bend over and walk VERY slowly.

At 18, Jimmy had his wisdom teeth removed. Within 48 hours, an infection appeared to set in where one tooth had been. It was Sunday when his face started to swell badly on one side. The oral surgeon who saw him that evening started to probe the infected area with a metal tool. Even though he commented on how extraordinary it was that Jimmy let him do that, it made our skin crawl. We felt the surgeon was being cruel, but then, we had no idea what Jim felt when the rest of us registered pain. Seeing Jimmy squirm a bit and wince, Pat stepped in and told the surgeon to stop. By the next day, we were once again in the ER. Jimmy had blood poisoning throughout his jaw and face. Again, he was hospitalized about a week with intravenous antibiotics before he was stable enough to leave.

In his late 20s, Jimmy developed a series of tumors in his neck. Of course, he told us nothing; we just noticed the side of his neck was visibly larger and hard. After going to several doctors who dismissed our concerns since Jimmy wasn't complaining, we got a diagnosis. Jimmy had tumors that needed to be removed at once since they were multiplying and pressing on his trachea.

Around age 30, after a few days at the beach, Jimmy seemed to be walking funny. We sat him down and looked at the bottom of his foot. A small piece of glass had become embedded in his foot, and red streaks from the infection were easy to see. Again, he had surgery and antibiotics. The doctor told us he should NEVER go barefoot for two reasons. First, if he happened to step on something sharp, Jimmy wouldn't instinctively react and pull up his foot. Secondly, if he did seriously injure his foot, he wouldn't necessarily tell anybody.

As he ages, Jimmy appears better able to express pain, although whether he is more attuned to it is tough to say. While he knows if it's cold or hot outside; I'm not sure whether he knows if *he* is cold, or if *he* is hot. We've actually heard him say, "Ouch, that hurts" when something happens that seems painful. But he's still unable to tell us if he has a sore throat, ear pain, or anything like that. Rather than tell us what he's feeling, he tries to give us the answer he thinks we want to hear.

Pat and I have gotten better at pain assessment and management. We have learned the importance of listening to Jimmy with all of our senses. We try to tune into small deviations in how he acts. If he becomes irritable, we make a note of that. To the best of our ability, we constantly monitor any changes in his appearance. As an example, I closely inspect his feet and hands when I cut his nails, or his backside before he goes swimming. When Pat shaves his head and face, she examines his scalp, neck, and ears. If I think Jimmy might have hurt himself, I will treat him as if he did, regardless of his reaction. And if I'm inclined to think that he didn't hurt himself but he's acting as if he did, I'm not going to discount it until I am sure he's okay. Given that Jimmy can seem pretty oblivious to pain, we routinely ask him a ton of questions about how he feels. While we might not assume his answers are entirely accurate, they might indicate something needs to be watched or requires immediate attention.

31 Wandering and Bolting

Recent research by the Interactive Autism Network (IAN) confirms what parents of autistic children have known for some time; wandering and elopement behaviors are common, stressful, and extremely dangerous. In this study of over one-thousand children with autism, parents report nearly half attempted to run away or went missing one or more times after age 4, often putting themselves at risk for bodily harm. Compared to their "typically developing siblings," wandering and bolting were *much more* common among children on the spectrum. These children wandered from their own home or one they were visiting, school, and stores. Approximately two-thirds of these cases involved a close call with traffic or drowning. To illustrate the magnitude of this problem, drowning has become one of the leading causes of death among autistic children. Despite the injuries and fatalities associated with wandering, parents still receive relatively little support and guidance from their doctors to help them understand and cope with this issue.[99]

Wandering and elopement continue to be significant stressors for families. Over half of the parents IAN surveyed cite it as the thing they worry about most, often keeping them up at night. Due to their autistic child's wandering, they were reluctant to take part in activities away from home. Evidence from IAN's study, however, did clear up one misconception; namely that "wandering has little to do with parenting style and more to do with the nature of a child's autism."[100]

I t comes as no surprise that parents of children with ASD would ask each other, "Is your kid a runner?"[101] As a child, Jimmy was more of a bolter than a runner. When he saw something dangerous, he would run toward it, not away from it. For example, Jimmy was drawn to hot burners on a stove, sharp knives, fire and fire alarms, and moving cars. He repeatedly tried to jump off balconies. A family trip to the Grand Canyon turned out to be a nightmare for us; and taking Jimmy to the local aquarium wasn't much better. On the aquarium's second and third floors, metal horizontal railings lined the elevated walkways surrounding the shark tank. The railings, spaced about 2 feet apart, were intended to prevent children from falling off the edge of the stairs. Despite being designed to promote safety, we knew we had to hold onto Jimmy every second. In our case, the barrier was almost worthless. For a long period of time, shopping at the local mall or just walking along the side of streets in our neighborhood presented their own dangers, so we never let go of Jimmy's hand or took our eyes off him for a second.

We had no idea why Jimmy acted this way. It seemed instinctual, triggered by an intense and irrational compulsion. Contrary to findings from a new study, Jimmy wasn't necessarily upset or agitated when he tried to put himself in harm's way.[102] We got absolutely no guidance on bolting or wandering from our pediatrician or any other doctor for that matter. And for some reason, this issue was never addressed on his IEP. Jimmy's bolting seemed aimless, but we weren't really sure. Was he drawn to something or running away? Was he bored, overcome with emotion or in "another world?" Perhaps his sensory-sensitivity was kicking in? We still don't know.

When we went to Linwood for the first time, which would become Jimmy's home away from home, one of the first things we noticed were the huge, multiple deadbolt locks on each door. They were mounted at least six feet high, out of the reach of children. While the need for that many locks made me uneasy, they also gave me peace of mind. This was just one more example of Linwood shaping the environment rather than punishing the child.

Today, parents of children with autism have numerous resources, including GPS trackers, a national child alert program similar to Amber Alert, and temporary "Tattoos with Purpose" to identify their child in case they're lost. First responders are finally beginning to get the training and tracking equipment they need to effectively conduct searches, identify signs of autism, and interact appropriately with the autistic population.

Pat and I had nothing like this at our disposal. Even if we did, I doubt it would have mattered much. Bolting presents somewhat different challenges than wandering. Our strategies were simple and straightforward.

1.   Know where Jimmy is at all times.
2.   Know who "had Jimmy."
3.   Hold on to him with an iron grip.
4.   Teach him how to be safe, constantly.

We modeled this behavior for our children. When our daughters found themselves responsible for Jimmy's safety, they were ready. Something as simple as getting him off the school bus required them to be present and fully engaged. In an interview as part of a study on wandering in Los Angeles, Geena recounts her autistic daughter (Gayle) breaking away as she got off the school bus in front of her house. "She breaks away from me and runs towards the park. She runs down the street, across the street and I pretty much know where she's going because she's run there before…she doesn't look for any cars, she runs straight out in the middle of the street and almost gets hit by a car." While Geena tried to make sense of her daughter's actions that day, I knew it could've just as easily been Jimmy.[103]

In high school, my daughter Katie missed her bus one afternoon. The timing couldn't have been worse. Jimmy attended Linwood residential school at the time and on this particular day, Katie knew she had to get home before Jimmy got off the Linwood bus. Terrified of not being home when Jim arrived, she had no recourse but to walk into the principal's office, explain her situation, and "demand" someone drive her home immediately. Thankfully, the vice-principal was able to give Katie a ride after calling my wife for permission. Katie had nightmares about this incident for years.

I hovered over Jimmy like a helicopter because he was a danger to himself. I also remember getting criticized constantly for it, mostly by friends and family.
--the mommy

We learned to tell Jimmy what to do, rather than what not to do. Often, telling him not to do something had just the opposite effect. Eventually, we found that using language from *Sesame Street*, like "Danger!" or a simple "Uh oh" would get his attention. When he was a young child, setting boundaries was extremely challenging. By age 5, we had taught him his name, address, and phone number. For as long as humanly possible, whenever we went to the store, a mall, or even an amusement park, we kept him in a stroller. If we became separated from Jimmy, we weren't sure if police and other first responders would understand him, or even if he would follow our instructions. For that reason, Pat attached plastic ID tags to his shoes.

Now, Jimmy's bolting is no longer an issue. If he feels a compulsion to do something dangerous, he might verbalize what's going through his mind and even joke or giggle about it. But fortunately, he won't act on it. That he's now a shopping cart pusher for Walmart shows just how far he's come.

32   Life Lessons

Invariably, research about the "path" or "journey" of family members living and growing with autism uncovers planned and unplanned opportunities for learning about life. These life lessons run the gamut from changed perspectives to the power of faith and increased sensitivity. It's not unusual for a parent, sibling, or grandparent to share how they've learned to be more patient and caring, and how they no longer take life for granted.[104]

Life lessons often happen by chance. In *The Accidental Teacher*, a mother writes about lessons she and the rest of her family have learned from Jonah, her largely nonverbal autistic son. Life with Jonah, for example, teaches his siblings (David and Ruth) to be more caring and tolerant. Similarly, Jonah's mother (Annie) "learned that there was something to hear in his silence." But these cumulative life lessons, which leave their mark in the course of everyday life, require time to process and understand.[105]

Interestingly, many parents come to see their lives in a new light due to experiences that exclude and dehumanize their loved ones with autism. "I admire the way my daughter gets up in the morning and faces a world that often mocks her, rejects her, belittles her..." "…I wished I had a sign on my back that said, 'don't worry this is normal, my son is autistic.' I have heard all the remarks; I have sensed the animosity from acquaintances and strangers." Yet another parent commented that when she and her child are out in public, strangers' stares and comments that were "hard at first" no longer bother her.[106] In the course of reacting to and reflecting on adversity such as this, we learn more about ourselves and our own capacity for compassion.

Both of my daughters grew up in a predominantly White, middle class, Christian, suburban community. They attended public schools in which there were only a handful of students of color. Our church membership was entirely White. However, that is not to say they grew up without the benefit of diversity, nor did they somehow escape the sting of prejudice.

As a seventh grader, my eldest daughter, Katie, wrote an essay entitled, "Prejudice: Still a Problem." She entered it in a competition sponsored by the local Lions Club, and her entry went on to become the regional winner of Western Maryland. Much of the inspiration for the essay came from her brother Jimmy. She writes, "Many people think prejudice is something of the past. They are wrong." Prejudice, she explains, means "prejudging on someone's appearance." Katie described the impact of prejudice and discrimination on a very personal level, such as when people make fun of her brother or treat him differently for no good reason.[107]

Jimmy has been a teacher to me, and one of the most important things he has taught me is to accept other people no matter how different they may be.
--a sister (Katie)

Because of her brother, Suzy learned at a very young age that life isn't necessarily easy or fair. She also learned an invaluable lesson that has helped her tremendously as an adult; that it *is* possible to get through the "real tough times." Suzy and Katie frequently witnessed Jimmy's meltdowns, as well as how hard he struggled to do seemingly simple tasks that came easy to them. They were all too aware that Jimmy didn't hang with the other kids in the neighborhood, even though he wanted to. Whether shopping, eating out, or waiting in line at an amusement park, his sisters couldn't help but notice people who felt sorry for Jimmy or looked at him as if to say, "What's wrong with you?" Both of my daughters found it difficult to understand why some people jumped to the conclusion that Jimmy was lacking in "smarts" or incapable of feeling the sting of rejection.

I learned very early that not everyone's life is the same.
--a sister (Suzy)

Katie and Suzy are much more aware of the fact that "we have no idea what's going on in someone's life," or what they consider normal or natural. Dr. Melanie Yergeau, a Professor of English at the University of Michigan, writes about autistic culture and communication. In *Loud Hands: Autistic People Speaking*, she discusses how people misjudge her silence. "My silence isn't your silence. My silence is rich and meaningful. My silence is reflection, meditation and processing. My silence is trust and comfort. My silence is a sensory carnival."[108]
Because he has proven us wrong so many times, we've gradually learned to never underestimate our son. Whenever Pat is working on anything to do with his computer, television, DVD player, cable box, or satellite radio system, Jimmy is constantly looking over her shoulder and asking her questions. If she is fixing some type of equipment, he wants to know what she's doing and why. Over the years, he has developed enough tech savvy to put his father to shame.
Suzy credits Jimmy for keeping our family young. He has a joy and innocence about him. She explains, "Because of Jimmy, we're not so caught up

in what strangers think, especially when we're out in public. It takes a lot for me to be embarrassed." Jimmy inspires Suzy to be a kid, have fun. "He doesn't worry about stuff like the rest of us," says Suzy. For instance, "he would never say, 'I shouldn't dance because people will think I dance weird.'"

Figure 18 SUZY AND JIMMY ENJOY A STROLL ON A SUMMER DAY.

Jimmy has been my mentor. His various talents, experiences, and perspectives have expanded and deepened my thinking about human differences and inclusion. Being Jimmy's father has helped me expand who I see and what I value. Before Jimmy, certain people, particularly those in low-status, repetitive, and manual jobs, were not as visible to me as they are now. Because of Jimmy, I have a better understanding of the value of diversity and all that it entails. When someone talks about making *everyone* feel included, I'm now much more prone to think of people who think, communicate, and act differently than I do.

Jimmy serves as a role model for all of us in ways too numerous to mention. By observing Jimmy, we've learned an invaluable lesson; namely, that others' prejudice toward us doesn't have to cultivate prejudice within us. Even though Jimmy has had to endure his fair share of slights and put-downs over the course of his life, I have never seen Jimmy retaliate. Rather, he responds with graciousness and kindness. His ability to rise above other people's bias is all too uncommon.

Jimmy is genuinely thankful for things that the rest of us tend to take for granted, such as being able to shop at the grocery store, taking a walk through our neighborhood, and helping out with housework or yardwork. We take note of Jimmy's contentment with life. And his contentment doesn't seem to hinge on what he's doing in any given situation, nor does it change much from day to day. He isn't someone who needs to be lectured on the importance of being happy in the moment. He gives without any expectation of getting something in return. The joy of giving fills his heart. His glass isn't half full or half empty. Clearly, it's "full."

We should all be as content with our lives as Jimmy. He's amazing.
      --the mommy

Figure 19 JIMMY'S CONTENTMENT IS INFECTIOUS

Jimmy's reach extends far beyond his family. One group in particular that's been a big part of his life is the church. Gayle, his former pastor, recounts some life lessons she learned from Jimmy.

1. *"Little things matter. Pay attention to people's needs and let them know you love them."*
2. *"A greeting card carefully chosen is a supreme gift of love."*
3. *"Enjoy time with family as often as possible."*
4. *"Make new friends and try new things."*
5. *"Don't be too cool to get excited about…well, everything!"*
6. *"Be yourself."*

7. *"Keep active and engaged."*
8. *"Do your very best at whatever you're doing."*
    --a pastor (Gayle Annis-Forder)

33   SES Can Matter

The lifetime cost of raising an autistic child ranges from $1.4 to $2.4 million; and while medical care drives up costs, it's not the primary factor. Lost wages and benefits account for much of the cost, as many family caregivers have to say no to a promotion or job, work fewer hours, or leave work entirely to care for their children. Adult care, specialty schooling, special educational equipment, hospitalizations, and ongoing medical care drive up the cost too.[109] Dr. David Mandell, the study's lead author, was taken aback by the million-dollar-plus figure. His advice to parents is that "there is hope. It can get a lot better, and it does. But it takes a whole lot of money to get there."[110]

Research on autism shows that socioeconomic status (SES); meaning income, education and occupation, can and does impact one's ability to access appropriate health and education services. For example, parents struggling to make ends meet may find it particularly difficult to meet their child's service needs, in part due to transportation issues and their work schedule. In one study, a parent explains, "I work full time and have another child and most appointments are during the day. I cannot take time off or rearrange my already full schedule to work in therapy."[111] In this same study, parents with less education repeatedly said they need more information. "The problem is that it can be extremely overwhelming trying to figure out what to try, what will work, what is covered by insurance, and where to start." [112]

Pinpointing why some families manage better than others is next to impossible. While finances may enter into the picture, there are numerous other factors that may be just as if not more important. Parent's ability to deal with stressors and the family's ability to stay positive are critically important to their sense of well-being. Age, gender, and birth order of the child with autism, the severity of autism, family size, the presence of siblings, family interrelationships, parents' physical and mental health, the involvement of grandparents, and numerous other variables make every family's situation different.

Both my wife and I are teachers. Teaching music and later computers and math was sandwiched around fourteen years at home with Jimmy. A good portion of her public-school career was spent teaching special needs students, both in the mainstream classroom and in special needs facilities. Early on, she became very familiar with the legal rights of students with disabilities as well as key special education terminology and procedures.

As a sociology major at Colgate University, New York University, and Howard University, I was trained to look at human behavior with a wide-angle lens. For example, sociology taught me to look outside my family in order to understand what was going on within my family. During my college years, I gained valuable experience working at a home for "emotionally disturbed" children and volunteering at a state mental hospital. The more I studied sociology, the more I became interested in diversity, social inequality and education. By the time I earned my Doctorate degree, I had begun teaching at an HBC (historically black college). Needless to say, I had no idea these life experiences would become invaluable assets later in life.

By law, up to age 21, an Individualized Education Plan (IEP) is drawn up for every child who receives special education services. Each year, Pat and I, along with a small group of educators and professionals, would sit down to discuss Jimmy's learning needs, the services his school would provide, and how his progress would be measured. In theory, the purpose of the IEP meeting was to come up with a plan that was designed to address his specific educational needs and increase his abilities as much as possible. While our SES should not have mattered one iota, we knew differently.

Even in those early years, when we walked into the IEP meeting, we were well-prepared to advocate for our son and communicate effectively. Because of our education and occupation, we knew what we were up against. We spent hours and hours doing our "homework." We weren't going to be intimidated or steamrolled into anything; if we didn't understand something, whether it be a law, goal, or some term, we made sure we asked the teacher, administrator, or psychologist in attendance to explain it to our satisfaction. Our educational experiences helped my wife and me to talk the same language as doctors, educators, and other professionals.

Because of our occupations as teachers, we earned a steady, middle-class income and our family had excellent insurance coverage. Often, therapy provided by Jimmy's school system wasn't sufficient. Fortunately, insurance paid for Jimmy to regularly see a speech therapist as well as an occupational therapist outside of school. Visits to the doctor, hospital stays, and prescriptions were all covered by insurance. Because of the type of coverage we had, we could find the best doctors and meet his medical needs without setting ourselves back financially. This was huge.

SES made its presence felt in a variety of other ways. Our basic needs were met, including food, shelter, transportation, and clothing. Not only did this have a positive impact on our health and emotional well-being, it was one less thing we had to worry about. Our neighborhood had excellent schools, including an excellent reputation in the area of special education. With a great deal of scrimping and saving, my job as a college professor made it possible for my wife to stay home during Jimmy's early years. If this hadn't been the case, I'm not sure what we would've done, especially considering Jimmy's severe and disruptive behaviors as a child.

Our middle-class income has helped us meet many of Jimmy's needs. Because of our extensive social network, we discovered that we needed to set up a trust fund for Jimmy so that the state of Maryland would not take all of his money once we die. Years before Jimmy's placement in a group home at 21 years of age, we relied on our education and diversified network to start laying the groundwork for this critical period in his life.

Despite its importance, SES is *only one* contributing factor to life chances or opportunities in society. Sociologists talk about something called human agency or being able to make one's own choices and act independently. Human agency allows us to be proactive given the situation in which we find ourselves. As an example, there are single parents who come from poor neighborhoods, empower themselves, overcome seemingly insurmountable barriers, and do an absolutely amazing job of raising a special needs child. They understand that while love, attitude, and commitment may not provide your child with everything he or she needs, they are the foundation.

According to research, fathers of children with autism tend to assume the role of economic provider for their families. I was the primary breadwinner when Jimmy was a child, although my wife stretched our income in untold ways, through creative cooking, sewing, gardening, and teaching piano lessons. Later, after Jimmy found a "home" at Linwood, Pat went back to school and continued with her teaching career. However, work always came in a distant second for the two of us. Social status, conspicuous consumption, and upward mobility have never been a priority; rather, our choice was to make sure our family came first.

34 Why Vegas?

Like anyone, an individual with autism has the right to travel and take enjoyable vacations; but changes in routine, medical considerations, and sensory issues are just a few of the challenges that can make this undertaking overwhelming. Very little research has been conducted on what can be done to ensure that tourists with autism receive the support and assistance they need.

Helwan University (Cairo, Egypt) professor Hend M. Hamed studied how travel agencies can help autistic tourists and caregivers plan and implement their trips. One distinguishing feature of her research is that she tapped the expertise of autistic adults, providing them with a hypothetical model of a questionnaire to help plan the trip. She encouraged these adults to critique questions dealing with the trip, such as transportation, accommodations, activities, and "strategic tips." Dr. Hamed got much of her information online from four autism communities – Wrongplanet.net, Talkaboutautism.org, Autismweb.com, and Aspiesforfreedom.com.

Questions focused on travel, eating, lodging, destinations, and recreational activities as well as individual desires, needs, capabilities, and tolerances. For example, Dr. Hamed asked the prospective autistic tourist 1) whether behaviors such as rocking, bouncing, hand-flapping, and walking on tiptoes were pleasing to him or her; 2) whether crowds, bright lights, high sounds, strong smells, car rides, high places or the feel of some textures were bothersome; and 3) whether assistive technologies, such as tablets and laptops, were useful. Input from autistic tourists helps travel agencies and tour operators choose an appropriate destination and lodging. As an example, someone may or may not opt for a trip to the beach. Sensory issues may make it difficult to tolerate the sound of waves, the bright sun, wind, and the feeling of sand. In *this* study, autistic respondents preferred staying in smaller hotels rather than big resorts.[113]

"**N**othing about us without us" is a statement that's been adopted by many marginalized groups, including those with disabilities. With regard to people with autism, this statement is about creating opportunities, fostering independence, and empowerment. It's based on the premise that people with autism should have a voice. Moreover, people without autism need to listen to them, respect their voices, and involve them as much as possible in determining their own futures.

Now that Jimmy is an adult, *he* decides where he would like to spend *his* vacation. At his annual IEP meeting, Pat and I meet with his residential and vocational service providers. Since Jimmy is the focal point of this two hour-plus meeting, he's now capable of sitting with us for the entire time and providing valuable input. In the course of going over goals for the coming year, we discuss summer plans. Within reason, Jimmy gets to decide what he'd like to do and who he'd like to accompany him. After all, the income he's saved from working at Walmart is financing the trip. He helps plan the vacation ahead of time and takes pride in the fact that he's paying his own way.

Initially, Jimmy was hesitant to discuss his preferences for a summer vacation. But as he grew older, he started to make his feelings known. One year, Jimmy and I went to Atlantic City, New Jersey. He also went to Disney World with his sisters a few times. But since we've started this tradition, his destination of choice has been Las Vegas. And the person he chooses to accompany him more often than not is his mom. Why does Jimmy choose Vegas? And why his mother?

When Jimmy goes to Vegas, Pat makes sure she involves Jimmy each step of the way. Together, they plan dates, transportation, lodging, places to eat, and activities such as sightseeing and shows. If Jimmy has concerns about the cost of the trip, the schedule, or perhaps missing work, he makes his feelings known. While Jimmy and Pat do an excellent job of planning, they leave room to try different things once they arrive. And this is Jimmy's "call." If he sees an attraction that appeals to him, they try to fit it into their schedule.

On their first trip to Vegas, Jimmy and Pat found themselves walking through the casino on the way to their room in the New York-New York Hotel. As my wife sat down to play one of the slot machines for a few minutes, Jimmy watched. Pat, who had one 1 cent left on a penny slot, asked Jimmy if he wanted to play. He initially said no, but overcame his nervousness and hesitancy. "OOOOOOOOOKay." Thereupon he sat down, pushed the button on the slot machine, and won $2 on a one cent bet. "All done," he said. Mission accomplished, and that was that. He didn't want to gamble anymore; and he never has.

Since Jimmy pays for the hotel, he naturally checks in and asks about the room when they arrive at the front desk. One year, when they went to Mandalay Bay Resort (his current favorite), an employee by the name of Katie mentioned that the penthouse suite was available. When Jimmy inquired about cost, Katie said that it would cost him $500 more for three days. Jimmy looked to Pat, and she explained that $500 is the amount he earns for about two weeks of work. "Do you want to spend it?" asked Pat. Jimmy then turned to Katie. He wanted to know what the "penthouse" meant. Katie proceeded to tell him all about the layout of the room and the amenities, including two giant flat-screen TV's, Jacuzzi, and floor to ceiling windows. Upon hearing this, Jimmy started clapping his hands excitedly and humming. He gave a "fist pump" while exclaiming, "Yes!!" In subsequent visits to Vegas, he always makes a point of asking the front desk clerk, "By the way, might you have any penthouse suites available?" When Jimmy asks, employees don't flinch. Rather, they respond respectfully. Before he leaves the hotel to go home, Jimmy makes sure to write a thank you note to the hotel staff.

Figure 20 TIME TO RELAX IN THE PENTHOUSE SUITE.

Certainly, the city's glitz and glamour have something to do with Jimmy's fondness for Las Vegas. As he sees it, the entertainment is first-rate, from riding the monorail between hotels to Broadway-type shows such as *Jersey Boys* and *Lion King*. And the accommodations aren't too shabby either. Jimmy loves to be pampered and spoiled, so lounging around a spacious suite in his hotel bathrobe and watching TV as he reclines in a warm bath is his idea of nirvana. But the number one attraction to Jimmy is the culture of Las Vegas and its people.

In Vegas, Jimmy doesn't "stop traffic" like he does elsewhere. If he acts inappropriately in public, no one looks at him and no one seems to care. As an example, Jimmy and his mom were sitting on a monorail one day, going from one hotel to another. As he's prone to do when he's overcome with excitement, Jimmy started clapping his hands, humming, and stomping his feet. Despite these behaviors, Jimmy didn't receive the usual stares and looks of disapproval. Rather, there was little if any reaction from the other passengers.

The culture of Vegas feels oblivious to difference. My wife recalls going with Jimmy to a show on the Strip. During the show, a man who looked to be about 500 pounds passed out in the front row. Six employees calmly dragged the man out and upstairs. At most, there were casual glances from the audience, but the show went on as if nothing happened.

After their first trip to Vegas, my wife expressed her thanks to the Vice-President of Hotel Operations at New York-New York Hotel and Casino.

I am writing to let you know what a spectacular vacation I had with my son at your hotel. My son is a young man with autism. He speaks and behaves in manners that are quite unusual. When we go places together, the following is the standard:

Since he appears quite "normal" until he begins to

speak, people who are there to help customers will approach him or respond to him in a normal fashion – until he starts to speak in sentences. His way of expressing himself is an intriguing mix of memorized phrases from TV, children's books, songs, and movies, and his rate of speech is very fast. After he tries to communicate, everything changes. The smiling person who wanted to be helpful immediately gets this panicked look on his/her face and starts talking to me instead of Jimmy; even when he is the one paying. Jimmy is an independent adult and quite capable but is rarely treated that way by people who don't know him. I am sure people think you get used to this, but you don't. You just cope.

So, when I arrived at your hotel with Jimmy, I pretty much hardened myself beforehand for the experiences we often have when we travel. Wow – what a surprise. I was absolutely AMAZED at the communication and interpersonal skills of absolutely EVERYONE we interacted with at your hotel. Jimmy was financing the trip and wanted to handle everything. I never thought that possible, but your people at the front desk were nothing less than spectacular. When they recognized the differences about my son, their immediate reaction was to lean in, tune in, and show even more warmth and willingness to help. As the week went on, we found this to be the way we were treated in your shops, bars, restaurants, casino, and even in the hallway when interacting with our maid.

I want to thank you for the most wonderful, relaxing, gratifying vacation Jimmy and I ever had. As we were heading to the airport to go home, Jimmy asked me how soon it would be before we could come back. This is remarkable, because he's never done that before on any of our travels. We WILL be back!!

Jimmy is not the only one who enjoys his time in Vegas. Much of this has to do with his unconditional and total acceptance of others. And this extends to how Jimmy treats his mother. Jimmy is the only one in our family who never takes issue with what Pat's wearing or eating or how she may be acting. Regardless of where he goes or what he does in Vegas, he's happy, contented, and thankful. And as my wife once said, "you don't get that too often in life."

35 Following Jimmy

In 1955, Linwood opened its doors to children with autism. If not for Linwood, many of these children would have been placed in institutions. Its founder, a gifted therapist by the name of Jeanne Simons, built Linwood on the core values of humility, adaptability, dignity, respect, individuality, and self-determination. On the walls of Linwood are words she wrote: "And that's why we walk behind the child. He feels your protection when you walk behind. If you give him a chance to go any direction, he may be wrong when he goes this way or that. Just follow him. If it's a dead end, pick him up gently and bring him to the main route. But never think that you know the answer, because you are dealing with an individual who may want to go very different routes, which for him may be better. That's why I feel more comfortable behind the children so I can see where they are going."[114]

In 1965, Dr. Charles Ferster, a behavioral psychologist, began a three-year study of the treatment and education of autistic children at Linwood. He found Linwood's approach to be distinctive. First, it focused on the *reinforcement* of certain existing behaviors rather than *punishment* for less than desirable ones. Second, rewards and reinforcers were not built around eating or drinking; rather, staff made use of natural reinforcers based on a child's own needs and interests. Finally, there was no predetermined sequence of treatment. Each child set the pace and his or her individual needs dictated priorities. Dr. Ferster concluded that the children's remarkable improvements weren't the result of some miraculous breakthrough or exceptional staff member. Instead, he discovered that therapy took the form of "carefully orchestrated steps that gradually led to observable changes in behavior."[115]

The best way to get Jimmy's needs met is whenever possible; teach him how to do it.
        --Bill Moss, Executive Director of Linwood Center

As Jimmy gets older, I learn to follow him more and more. He sets the pace. Naturally, he has his own personality, interests, values, and ways of doing things. For instance, when he's buying something with our help, online or in person, he takes the lead. When Jimmy is interacting with a store clerk, a server at a restaurant, a hotel clerk, or a grocery store cashier, I try not to intervene if at all possible. After all, Jimmy is the one who's paying, and he's fully capable of making himself understood if people will only take the time and make the effort to listen. When we're out in public, there are times when Jimmy grows frustrated and starts doubting his ability to communicate. If he looks to me to speak for him, I will usually smile and ask him to repeat himself. Pat and I encourage, verbally prod, teach, and follow him whenever possible.

One Saturday, on a visit to Jim's group home, Pat took him to a nearby bagel shop for lunch. After waiting in line to place their order, it was Jimmy's turn. The man behind the counter asked, "Can I help you?" Jimmy started to speak and the person taking the order froze. A look of panic swept across his face. Pat simply waited, while another employee perked up and offered assistance as soon as he heard Jimmy's voice. As Pat said, "You could see this other young man's antenna go up." Watching the whole time, he immediately stepped in and with a big warm smile and an air of graciousness and confidence, said, "Good morning. How are you doing? What can I do for you sir?" Enthusiasm, caring, and connection; they were all there. And his body language was markedly different from the first employee, who straightened his back and pulled away as soon as Jimmy spoke.

Recently, Jimmy and I went out for lunch at McDonalds. After waiting in line, it was Jimmy's turn. He asked, "Do you have any low-fat ice cream?" The young man working behind the counter could not understand, and asked "What do you want?" Jimmy repeated himself 2 more times. The employee, who still had no idea what Jimmy was saying, began to look at me for help. I simply smiled, hoping he would return his focus to Jimmy. Instead, he proceeded to ask his manager for help. Once he returned with the manager, Jim asked once again, "Do you have any low-fat ice cream? Finally, they understood. Then, they had to problem-solve with Jimmy in order to come up with something on McDonald's menu that was low-fat. Finally, they came up with a solution; low-fat yogurt with strawberries.

Jimmy is one of the most generous and thoughtful people I know. Recently, my wife lost a dear friend, the mother of a special needs child named Greg. When Jimmy heard that his friend Greg lost his mother, he immediately expressed a desire to buy a card for him. When we went shopping a few days later, he wanted to go to Target first. After looking carefully at more than twenty cards, he found just the right one. And when he did, his face lit up and he exclaimed, "PERFECT!" The card read, "It's so sad to lose your mom."

Let your child construct his or her own world. And then value it; whatever it might be.
*   --the daddy*

Once in a while, I ask Jimmy about current events and people in the news. One day, we found ourselves talking about the presidential election; who's running, who might win, and the importance of voting; something Jimmy knows his mommy and daddy take very seriously. While he has been a registered voter since eighteen, Jimmy had never shown an interest in voting until the 2016 election. So, I asked him, "Would you like to vote?" Jimmy's answer left little doubt. "Yes!" Before we started planning all the details, I had to assure him that he could vote for free. Well that was the clincher.

Over lunch the following week, I asked Jimmy what he would like to know about each candidate for President. When he hesitated, I rephrased the question. How should each candidate act? That triggered a number of interesting responses. "Kind, nice, polite, good behavior, and not rude or mouthing off." Weeks later, we continued this discussion. I asked Jimmy what makes a president a good president? After giving it some thought, he simply said, "a good listener." When I complimented Jimmy on his excellent answers, he smiled from ear to ear.

As the election drew closer, we discussed Donald Trump and Hillary Clinton, what they stood for and their backgrounds. Also, we talked about why it's important to vote. I contacted the Board of Elections and made plans to do a "run-through" ahead of time. If necessary, I would follow Jimmy into the voting booth. But deciding on a candidate was solely up to Jimmy, and he has never shared his choice with me. After all, that's his right as an adult.

Given all of the questions Jimmy had already asked about the process of voting, we decided to "wing it" and just show up to vote one day during the early voting period. When Jimmy walked into the early voting center location close to our new home in

Frederick, Maryland, he looked around and spied lines of voters waiting to cast their ballots inside the voting booths. His immediate reaction, "Wow!!!" spoke to the significance of what he was about to do.

Not wanting my help, he sought out election officials. After introducing himself in considerable depth and explaining why he was there and what he wanted to do, a Republican and a Democratic official escorted him to the booth. When he was done, that was it. It was time for "the guys" to go home, have lunch, and take a long walk.

Jimmy's development has been full of surprises. We've learned to respect his right and ability to follow *his own* path. Additionally, we've come to understand why Jeanne Simons taught us to follow the child, not follow the children. Even among people with autism, Jimmy is one-of-a-kind. Clearly, we don't have all the answers when it comes to determining what's in Jimmy's best interests. In many ways, he's the expert. What we can do is offer protection, support, and plenty of encouragement.

*Figure 21 STAFF HELPS, BUT THE LINWOOD
STUDENT TAKES THE LEAD.*

*At Linwood, we have in our midst real adults with real
sensibilities whose opinions and insights are
substantial and whose influence is significant. As
caregivers, we must remember this.*

> *--Bill Moss, Executive Director of Linwood
> Center*

36   Long Walks

"Get them moving. Get them swimming, get them running, get them walking, get them moving."[116] Following this advice from a parent of an autistic child can be difficult. Autistic youth may shy away from participation in sports and recreational programs due to behavioral, emotional, and attentional issues. Also, exercise in wide open areas may make it difficult to keep them from wandering. One mother says her son's sensory issues can be a barrier to sports, especially if it's "too loud or too bright." "If he's standing there with his hands over his ears, how is he going to function in a game?"[117]

In spite of these challenges, it would be wrong to assume that those on the spectrum have no interest in solo or social recreational opportunities. Tommy, diagnosed with autism at two years of age, was in constant motion as a child. As he got older, he would accompany his father on walks and in time, join him for a daily run. According to his father, it just made sense; "…take something someone is instinctively driven to do and make it into a positive, rather than try to squelch a behavior."[118] The more Tommy ran, the less his anxiety, the greater his self-confidence, and the larger his social circle. His father notes, "There aren't many places where he can just be one of the guys. Not one of the autistic guys or a different guy. Just a guy…"[119]

According to special report found in *Runner's World*, "running is a sport that fits" for many on the autism spectrum.[120] Research points to the value of aerobic exercise. For example, jogging, swimming, and water exercise have been found to decrease aggressiveness and lessen spinning, rocking and other self-stimulating behaviors that may interfere with learning and social interaction. The involvement of a coach, friend, or caregiver can enhance the social value of any physical activity, making it possible to improve one's communication skills, develop relationships, and perhaps learn something about taking turns and teamwork.[121]

M y dad, Dr. Charles Bucher, lived and loved fitness. As a college professor, he lectured and wrote extensively about the importance of health, recreation, and fitness. His 28 books on this subject were published in 13 languages. He taught me the importance of finding time each and every day to keep fit. I came to adopt this mantra and passed it on to all of my children.

For my dad, the benefits of fitness went far beyond the body. As Executive Director of the National Fitness Leaders Association, he tirelessly preached about the physical, mental, emotional, and social benefits of exercise. His extensive research corroborated what he knew all along; people generally feel better and more alive when they exercise; whether it takes the form of competitive sports or some other activity. Rather than simply being an end in itself, exercise can bring a family together and promote, in his words, a "we" feeling.

The positive effects of fitness for the general population are well-substantiated; but what about those with autism? Autism literature is full of stories about the value of surfing and skiing, horseback riding, bowling, and other forms of exercise. But many of these activities require special equipment and a considerable outlay of time and money.

Originally, walking was a survival technique for Jimmy and the rest of us. It seemed as if nothing in our arsenal would settle Jimmy down, but walking helped. As a child, walking made it possible for Jimmy to "work through" meltdowns. All the same, he seemed to hate walking with me. Hand in hand, we started off by taking little walks, sometimes as far as our neighbor's house. Each day, we would walk a tiny bit further. I'm sure our neighbors thought I was abusing my defenseless, little boy since Jimmy resisted the whole time, screaming at the top of his lungs. Now, one of Jimmy's favorite things to do is taking walks with his daddy; the longer the better. It has become a special time for just the two of us.

Figure 22 EARLY IN JIMMY'S LIFE, WALKS BECAME A DAILY ROUTINE.

Walks can vary. Usually, when asked, Jimmy tells me he wants to go on what he calls a "LW" (long walk) as opposed to a "SW" (short walk). Long walks generally take about an hour and cover about three miles. On certain occasions, he might have fun requesting a "BW" (birthday walk), or perhaps a "TW" (Thanksgiving walk). Invariably, these other walks turn out to be long.

Jimmy was born with limited motor skills, like many people with autism. However, we refuse to let that stop us. Walking is something he can do and do well, for long distances and long periods of time. We avoid areas with high-speed traffic and walk on sidewalks if possible. By and large, walking requires very little communication and interaction on his part. The only rule he needs to follow is to stay close to me.

Walking is a safe, inexpensive, lifelong skill with lifelong benefits. Our walks have done wonders for Jimmy's health as well as his fitness level and general motor function. While it does not appear to lessen the frequency of his self-stimulating behaviors, it does slow him down. After a good, brisk, aerobic walk, he seems more relaxed and more in control of his emotions just like me. Moreover, walking enables him to build up his stamina; something he definitely needed in order to be hired as a shopping-cart pusher for Walmart.

During our hour or so walking together, Jimmy talks as loudly and as often as he wants. Further, he can let it "all hang out." This usually includes flapping his hands, smiling gleefully as he repeatedly nods his head, talking to himself as he makes plans or works out some issue, and looking at the sights. He can talk nonstop, unless of course, we decide to have a "QW" (quiet walk).

After years of walking, he's "hooked" and so am I. We really enjoy our routine and our time together. He knows better than to ask my wife, because walking is not "her thing." When we get together on weekends, Jimmy wants to know ahead of time what we're doing. If I don't mention it, he'll ask me if we can take a walk around the neighborhood or do something that involves exercise, "just the two of us." Before I have a chance to respond, he adds, "If possible, weather permitting."

37 A Family Vacation: Part 1

"[After] our last commercial flying experience, we both swore off of it. Never again. I'm still there. I'm not ready….He was just inconsolable."   Another caregiver commented, "We can't go to the movies. We don't go to the circus, a play…We can't go to restaurants other than McDonalds." According to parents in this study, the needs of their autistic child had to come first. One sibling had this to say, "…it's always about [my brother with autism]" and "my needs are always secondary and unfortunately…that's the way it is."[122]

Even familiar spaces close to home pose challenges, given an autistic child's repetitive behaviors, emotional outbursts, and social skills. However, going on an extended vacation and encountering new experiences in new environments amidst strangers who do not understand requires that much more planning and monitoring. One participant in the study cited earlier stated, "There's nothing I can think of that we've ever said that we are not going to do…We do stuff just because we don't want his disability to impact our family. So we really do stuff and then just deal with it if we have to."[123]

Before going on getaways and vacations, parents shared how they spent a great deal of time planning ahead for long car rides, plane trips, hotel stays, crowds and noise, and eating in unfamiliar surroundings. Whenever possible, for example, they minimized the possibility of waiting in line, which they described as a "nightmare." They thought through auditory, visual, tactile, and other stimuli in a given environment, and if necessary, adjusted their activities. Regardless of the situation, families talked about the importance of being attentive to everyone's needs. One participant simply stated, "Flexibility is my mantra."[124]

Daniel Openden, clinical services director of the Southwest Autism Research and Resource Center in Phoenix, advises planning ahead of time before going on a vacation. "Prior to leaving, the key is to simulate the vacation as slowly as possible in as many ways as possible."[125] As an example, Openden says parents can read books, look at movies, and go on the Internet with their children to find out more about their trip and destination. Furthermore, there are numerous company-sponsored programs that make new kinds of travel experiences less threatening to individuals with autism. For instance, one cruise line offers "Seas for Autism," making it possible to experience what it's like to check in, go through security, board ship, visit cabins, try out the pool and recreational activities, and eat a meal.

A Bucher family vacation is not your normal "family trip" because of my brother. We are only limited to a certain amount of days and activities. But it's been this way all my life, so I don't know anything different. Also, on these family outings we always have someone keeping a constant eye on Jimmy for his safety and helping him with what he needs. As I get older, I realize how much of a task this is for me and the rest of the family; yet it has only helped me learn about the importance of family and sticking together.
--a sister (Suzy)

Vacations are a great time to get away as a family and forget about routine and structure. At least that's what we thought before we had a child with autism. With our family vacations, improvising from day to day didn't really work; rather, the less spontaneity the better; or as my daughter Suzy put it, "No go with the flow." On the other hand, flexibility is still important. Even though we try to plan ahead as much as possible, we cannot necessarily anticipate environmental stimuli such as crowds, noise, bright lights, and a variety of other things that might trigger sensory overload.

Before leaving on vacations, Jimmy is "hell-bent" on knowing our exact schedule each day, even the when and where and how long of rest stops. Therefore, our family vacations require intense planning. Even the car ride is planned in detail. Years ago, prior to leaving, my wife would spend hours upon hours making Jimmy tapes of his favorite music, including songs by Barney, the Muppets, Marlo Thomas, and a bunch of "goldie oldies" from the 50's and 60's. Once in the car, Jimmy would ask for the tape recorder. As he listened to the tapes in the back seat, which would usually keep him occupied for two to three hours, he smiled incessantly and let out squeals of joy when he heard one of his favorite songs. Those tapes, which made all the difference in the world, have now given way to new playlists Pat creates on Jimmy's Kindle before trips.

No matter how much we planned before taking vacations as a family, it seemed as if there were always surprises along the way. These surprises could make a Bucher family vacation that much more enjoyable or extremely difficult. For instance, in Virginia Beach, we were taken aback by intolerance, coming from a stranger standing on a street corner.

One night, on vacation in Virginia Beach, my family and I went out to eat. On the way home there was a man professing Christianity on a street corner – criticizing people for their dress or behavior in a funny but caustic way. Being a Christian, I supported his

cause; although I did not necessarily agree with the way he was presenting Christianity. As we got closer to him I just began to ignore what he was doing and stopped thinking about it. As my family and I crossed the street by his corner, my brother grabbed my father's hand as he usually does before crossing. Not noticing that Jimmy was disabled this man yelled out to Jimmy and my dad, 'Hey look. We've got us a couple of Homo's. You know what God thinks about them. This is a straight zone.' I was in complete shock at what I had heard and was hurt so much by the comment. When we got back to our hotel room, I talked to my sister and mom about it for a long time that night. It was that night that reminded me once again how much my brother taught me.
--a sister (Suzy)

As I think back to that incident, all five of us were relaxed, enjoying the sights, and having a great time. Even as we walked by this man on the street corner, we found ourselves listening to his comments as he reminded passers-by in no uncertain terms to remember Christ at all times, including on vacation. Then, all of a sudden, we were blindsided. My daughters were very upset and sobbing. It took a long while for us to move beyond this uncomfortable, unsettling encounter with intolerance.

Reflecting back on this incident and others, Suzy homed in on her brother and what she learned from him.

My brother has helped me look at other people in a way that I would never have done without him. My brother had no idea that the man was speaking to him and it did not offend him in any way whatsoever. Jimmy is able to do some things that are almost inhuman. He seems to never see the bad in anyone.

He's always able to care for others no matter how they treat him. He looks for the good in everybody and can be the most helpful person you could ever imagine. In looking inside of Jimmy, I see everything that almost every human strives to be, a completely unselfish, caring, loving, and a happily helpful person.
--a sister (Suzy)

Before our vacation at Virginia Beach, we started small, with day trips to nearby places such as the beach, a night at a nearby Embassy Suites Hotel, and stays with relatives. As our children got older, we started thinking about Disney World, a more distant destination which would require much more planning. Jimmy's needs factored into our thinking about hotel stays, sightseeing, plane trips, car rides, amusement parks, and other unfamiliar spaces. In retrospect, there are things we would have done with our daughters that never happened because of Jimmy's needs.

Flying, by itself, was a huge undertaking. Then, we didn't have the benefit of programs such as The Arc's "Wings for Autism," an "airport rehearsal" designed for people with ASD, their families, and airline professionals. So, we started planning each step – how would we go about getting boarding passes, passing the time if our plane was late, going through security, boarding and seating, occupying Jimmy on the plane, going to the bathroom, deplaning, obtaining our luggage, and then leaving the airport.

In spite of our intensive planning, the first time we flew as a family did not go smoothly. We managed to board the plane and sit in our seats while Jimmy perseverated loudly over our vacation schedule; asking question after question and creating a scene. The airline attendant offered her assistance, but I explained that we had everything well in hand. While passengers were still getting themselves settled, Jimmy continued his nonstop, increasingly intense monologue. Again, the attendant returned to our seats and asked if she could help. I could sense the agitation in her voice.

I told the attendant that Jimmy was autistic, and this kind of behavior was not that unusual. Autism meant nothing to her, so I asked if she had seen the movie *Rain Man*. She had, and all of a sudden it clicked. However, instead of using this information to help us, she immediately called the captain for help. I think the attendant had visions of Jimmy having a "major meltdown," as did Raymond in *Rain Man*. As the saying goes, a little knowledge can be a dangerous thing. After educating the attendant and putting the captain's fears to rest, we got in our seats and took off on a relatively uneventful flight.

Prior to our first vacation at Disney World, we could not wait. Going to Disney World with our children had always been a dream of ours. Pat and Jimmy repeatedly watched a video she had bought, "Planning Your Trip to Disney World." Once we got there, she was hoping the video would make Disney World less overwhelming.

Once we entered Disney's Magic Kingdom, I remember Jimmy crying almost the entire time. At one point, Jimmy and Katie were riding on Dumbo as Pat and I looked on. He seemed miserable. I looked at my wife, and said, "I can't believe we spent so much money for *this*. Instead of coming to Disney World, it would have been a whole lot easier and cheaper to stay at home."

In his journal that night, Jimmy recounted his day.

We went to the airport.

We got on an airplane.
We flew to Florida.
We went swimming at The Day's Lodge.
We went to The Tasty World for dinner and
McDonald's for dessert.
   --Jimmy (from his journal)

When we woke up the next day, Pat and I along with Jimmy and Katie walked to the restaurant at the Days Inn Lodge where we were staying. As we were eating breakfast, a lady walked by our table with a tray of food. On her tray were a donut and a grapefruit. In an instant, Jimmy reached for her tray and started perseverating. As we gently admonished Jimmy, who was 6 years-old at the time, the lady stopped dead in her tracks. She "consoled" us by saying, "Please, he can have a piece of my donut if that would make him happy." Knowing Jimmy's food preferences, my wife smiled and said, "I hate to tell you, but it's not the donut he's after." The lady looked at my wife incredulously, and then walked way. To this day, grapefruit is still a favorite of his.

The night before we returned home, exhausted and wondering if it had been worth it, Jimmy recalled some of his happiest moments at Disney World.

We rode on It's A Small World, Peter Pan, and
a fast boat ride outside.
We went to a parade.
We saw Donald Duck, Mickey and Minnie
Mouse, and Goofy.
We rode a boat to pick up our car.
We had grapefruit for breakfast.
Today is the last day of May.
   --Jimmy (from his journal)

38 A Family Vacation: Part 2

Children's sensory sensitivities can impact their everyday lives. This is particularly true of autistic children, who often experience things differently because of the way their brains are wired. For instance, they may have a heightened sensitivity to taste, smell, touch, sight, sound, and even pain. Molly Bagby, an occupational therapist, decided to interview parents of children with and without autism in order to take a closer look at the impact of a family member's sensory sensitivities. One key area of questioning had to do with the degree to which the *entire* family shared special events and activities in the community.[126]

Bagby found parents of children *without* autism were more apt to go ahead with family outings to "stimulating sensory environments." It's worth noting that *some* families of children with autism did the same, trying not to let their child's disability dictate what they did and didn't do. However, families of children on the spectrum spent much more time planning and preparing ahead of time, and split up once they got to these events. And just in case, they had elaborate exit strategies if the stimulation proved too much for their child to handle. As one parent of a child with autism said, "*Everything* is affected. Where we go, how we prepare to go there, what we do once we get there is affected."[127] Both groups of parents, those with and without children on the spectrum, noted that family outings were particularly beneficial in terms of helping their children burn up their excess energy.

S ome of our fondest memories date back to Jimmy's childhood and summer vacations spent at a family-owned cottage in Lake George, New York. Going on boat rides was one of Jimmy's favorite things to do; especially aboard Uncle Bob's boat, the "Honeybear." Seated in very front, Jimmy would grin from ear to ear when Bob took us for rides up and down the Lake. And it was at Lake George that Jimmy oh so slowly but surely learned to overcome his fear of being in the water.

Figure 23 SPECIAL FAMILY TIME ON VACATION AT LAKE GEORGE.

The highlight of our yearly Lake George vacation was a short trip to an amusement park by the name of Storytown. After a few days at the cottage, we woke up our children with the question, "Who wants to go to Storytown?" Needless to say, their reaction was a resounding, "Me!" "Me!" and "Me!" In part, what made Storytown so much fun was that it was one of the few places we could go as a family and "get lost" in the crowd. However, because Jimmy has a hidden disability, there was always a chance that people would not understand when they saw him having a meltdown. For that reason, we wore Special Olympics shirts whenever we went to Storytown or any amusement park for that matter.

Over breakfast, we'd decide the first ride we would run to as soon as the park opened. Typically, Jimmy's favorite ride, the "Magical Mystery Tour, won out. When there was a line at this ride, I would have to take Jimmy for a walk until the rest of our family was at the front of the line. Waiting in lines often triggered meltdowns, and unfortunately Storytown didn't make it easy on us by providing special accommodations for people with disabilities. We had to wait in long lines just like everybody else.

The Magical Mystery Tour was a scrambler that spun you around inside a dome with very loud music. It was virtually pitch black except for the strobe lights that came on once the ride began. There was room for three people in each "car." When I sat with Jimmy and his sister, we convinced him to sit on the outside since we knew that he would be the one to get squished. Full of anticipation, Jimmy could have cared less. As soon as the ride began, the Beatles song "The Magical Mystery Tour" blared "The Magical Mystery Tour is waiting to take you away, waiting to take you away…"

Figure 24 STORYTOWN WAS MAGICAL.

In her case history, "My Experiences as an Autistic Child," Temple Grandin describes her feelings about some of her favorite carnival rides. In particular, she mentions the ride Round Up, which uses centrifugal force to restrain riders. In that sense, the ride is similar to The Magical Mystery Tour. When Grandin is on the ride, she can relax and enjoy the movement as long as it's a smooth ride and its structure does not flex or shake.[128]

In her blog, "Musings of an Aspie: One Woman's Thoughts About Life on the Spectrum," an autistic writer describes the sensation of her first amusement park ride aboard the Himalaya, another one of Jimmy's favorite rides at Storytown. She observes, "…we started to move, slowly at first, gaining speed, a little more and a little more until the wind was whipping my hair across my face and the three of us were pressed in a bone-crunching heap against the outside of the car and I was screaming right along with everyone else through 90 seconds of pure, unadulterated joy."[129]

While the Magical Mystery Tour was fun, it was

not a so-called thrill ride. When Pat and I took Jimmy on a thrill ride called "The Wild Mouse" for the first time, he was 4 and only spoke in phrases. But that was enough. During the entire ride, all we heard was "Momma down please," momma down please," "momma down please." To our surprise, as soon as we got off The Wild Mouse, he wanted to get on it again, and again and again. The roller coaster was a similar experience. Once the ride began, he spoke in short phrases. As we went up each steep incline, Jimmy uttered the words "Too slow, too slow, too slow." Going down, all we heard was "Too fast, too fast, too fast."

When Jimmy was a teen, he was fascinated by the looks of The Steamin' Demon, perhaps the biggest thrill ride at Storytown. It was an inversion roller coaster with twists made of tubular steel track. From afar, it looked pretty scary. It turned you upside down as it twisted and changed directions. One year, with his Katie by his side, Jimmy found the courage to step into The Steamin' Demon. As the attendant buckled him in, he started whining and flapping his hands. All this time, the attendant looked at us as if to say, "Are you sure this is a good idea?" My wife, Katie, and I assured the attendant that Jimmy would be fine. Once the ride started, Jimmy was all smiles.

Like so many other activities in his life, Jimmy initially resisted going on rides at amusement parks. But we were determined to bring him along since this was a family event. Like going swimming, attending church, sitting through an entire movie, and taking in an entire sporting event, these challenging, sensory stimulating events have become some of the greatest joys for him and the rest of our family. Splitting the family up was a last resort. How did we know when to nudge and even push? I'm not sure. But we prayed a lot and followed our hearts.

39 Together We Were Strong

"Eighty percent of parents of children with autism get a divorce." Years ago, I remember hearing this statistic, from professionals and media alike. We now know that the 80% divorce rate is an "urban legend," meaning there is no hard proof to support it. Recently, Dr. Freedman of the Kennedy Krieger Institute, said, "In the work I've done with children with autism, I've come across many couples who quote this 80% divorce rate to me. They don't know what the future holds for their child and feel a sense of hopelessness about the future of their marriage as well – almost like getting a diagnosis of autism and a diagnosis of divorce at the same time."[130]

Marital satisfaction is one of the best predictors of parents' ability to deal with the unique challenges of raising a son or daughter with autism. Poor marital relations, besides being an added source of stress, can make it harder to maintain a positive perspective. On the other hand, a strong marriage appears to be an important source of support for parents who encounter unique and significant demands as they try to make sense of autism and meet their child's needs during infancy, adolescence, *and* adulthood. But it isn't easy. For example, parents need to somehow find time just for themselves and effectively communicate their needs and wants.[131]

New research funded by the U.S. National Institute of Mental Health sheds more light on the experiences of couples raising children on the spectrum and those whose children aren't disabled. The biggest difference was the time couples set aside "to connect, to just share thoughts and feelings," according to Sigan Hartley, the study's lead author. Over the course of a year, 174 couples of a child with autism spent significantly less time (128 hours) with their partner. Dr. Hartley adds, "Whether they're discussing weekend plans, joking around or engaging in sex, that one-on-one time is 'so important' for maintaining intimacy." Couples raising children with autism reported feeling less closeness with their partners, and this was especially true of fathers. Dr. Hartley speculates this may be due in part to the "'wear and tear' over time that leaves couples feeling emotionally drained."[132]

I have a special closeness with my husband for having gone through all this together.
*   --the mommy*

Different studies reveal conflicting data on the divorce rate of parents of kids with autism. For example, a study published about a few years ago shows that children with ASD are at no greater risk of living in a home without both parents.[133] Two years earlier, University of Wisconsin researchers found that the likelihood of divorce among parents of autistic children was almost twice as great as the rate for couples of children without ASD. But the divorce rate was nowhere near 80%; rather, these couples had a better than three-in-four chance of staying married.[134]

In our own social circle, divorce amongst parents of children with disabilities is not uncommon. Certainly, it's reasonable to assume that stress might be a factor. And yet we know many parents of special needs children who somehow make it work and even thrive. Pat and I would joke that we would never get a divorce because neither one of us could ever go it alone and take care of Jimmy. And while we said it jokingly, there was a lot of truth to it.

Whenever I hear one of my favorite songs, *Through the Years* by Kenny Rogers, tears of gratitude begin to well up in my eyes. I think of my wife and our forty-plus years of marriage. The song brings back a flood of memories. When we got married, we had no idea what the future would hold or how it would test our commitment to each other. The song's lyrics capture the belief we had in each other that somehow "we'd always work things out" regardless of what happened along the way.

As the author of this book, I labored over those parts that seem to focus too much on me and ignored the central role played by my wife. While I could go to work each day and "lean in" without society criticizing me for shirking my duties as a father, my wife didn't really have a choice. Given our circumstances, Jimmy absolutely needed supervision 24/7 throughout his infancy and childhood. As my daughter Katie explained, Jimmy needed someone to stay home and "lay it on the line" each and every day. Fortunately, Pat willingly and lovingly embraced this role from the start, no questions asked.

Over the years, Pat and I have leaned heavily on each other for physical and emotional support, advice, and relief at a moment's notice. I can only imagine how difficult it must be to have multiple children with autism, to raise "a Jimmy" as a single parent, or to have a spouse or partner who didn't consider family a priority. And yet, there are parents and partners who find themselves in this very situation. The stress and challenges, which are significant, can drive a wedge between you and your spouse or solidify and strengthen your relationship. In our case it did both; that wedge frequently pushed us apart, but in the long run it also made us mindful of the need to stay strong and work through things together.

As Jimmy's parents, we developed an attitude of "you and me against the world." Only the two of us could really know and appreciate what it was like to raise Jimmy; the battles we fought, the effort we put forth, and the deep appreciation we felt for each other's support. When Pat had a rough day fighting for our son with doctors, educators, or with insurance companies, I was one of the few and often the only one who really understood.

Together, we found the strength we needed just days after Jimmy was born. I distinctly remember a conversation we had at the hospital with Jimmy's doctor. He let us know some tests were being run on Jimmy's brain to see if he had any brain cells or to use the medical term, gray matter. Before we left Jimmy's side, he suggested in a cavalier manner, "Why don't the two of you go and get some dinner; and we should have some answers by the time you get back?" With each other's support, we managed to rise above a doctor's insensitivity and get through that evening.

It didn't take long for Pat and me to realize that we *had* to engage in positive and effective interaction every day. We *had* to be at full speed, ready to work things out and work them out fast. If angry, we couldn't let it fester or linger. Sometimes, I would walk out of a room during a spat. But fortunately, my wife would follow me and make sure we heard each other out, and vice versa. Eventually, we would reach some sort of agreement. Conflict-resolution was not a nicety, it was an absolute necessity. In spite of this realization, we had some pretty intense squabbles, especially Sunday nights.

After Pat and I cleaned up after dinner and put the kids to sleep at the end of a long weekend, invariably we would get into a heated argument. Lots of times, the arguments were superfluous. After a while, we noticed this trend and came to the realization that our arguments weren't a reflection of different agendas, values, or priorities. Both of us knew they had nothing to do with how we felt about each other. Rather, we were "fried" and exhausted from caring for Jimmy. We had absolutely no patience left. Rather than take our pent-up frustration out on Jimmy or our daughters, we would engage in stupid arguments and yell a bit. From then on, more often than not, when we did start to argue on Sunday night we knew it was time to collect ourselves, say we're sorry, smile, and start over.

This is a classic example of "daily spillover," a phenomenon described in the literature on autism. Marital interactions may feel the effect of fatigue and disagreements that carry over from parenting experiences. Likewise, the reverse is also possible; tension found in marital relations can contribute to high levels of stressful parenting. In effect, the family is a system made up of integrated parts. Priorities and behaviors in one part can have positive or negative effects on other parts.

My close relationship with my son is due in large part to my wife. Pat's been willing to step aside and let me take the lead, especially when it's in our family's best interests to do so. I don't take this for granted, especially given society's assumptions that "mother knows best" when it comes to childrearing and decision-making. At times, my wife defers to my skill-set and interests and vice versa. Our division of labor is fluid when it comes to housework, finances, schooling, and virtually every decision that impacts our family. As a matter of fact, our children would joke about how we were so different from other parents they knew. I did the shopping with Jimmy while Pat fixed the cars; I made breakfast and lunch for our daughters on school days while Pat was the go-to person when it came to math, finances, computers, or anything technical. Regardless of what we were doing, my wife had complete faith in my parenting.

Jimmy helped us recognize and value each other's abilities and gifts. For instance, when Jimmy finally got to the point where he finally wanted his mother to read to him, the only book in which he had any interest was *The Foot Book*. To fuel that interest, Pat would read *The Foot Book* at least twenty times a day; and each time I marveled at how she read it with such feeling. By the same token, Pat loved watching me play outside with our children, and still fondly remembers the pure joy I would get from making Jimmy giggle.

Seeing him care for Jimmy made me love my husband that much more.
    --the mommy

During Jimmy's childhood, Pat felt a desperate need to get out of the house, unwind, and "do good work." Years later, she still thanks me for encouraging her to immerse herself in community volunteer work, church outreach, and teaching aerobics. She recalls, "When I felt stymied helping my own child, at least I was helping someone else."

There's no doubt in my mind that dealing with the challenges of autism has strengthened our marriage. In the course of trying to be good parents, we constantly worked on ourselves and our relationship with each other. As much as humanly possible, we didn't let Jimmy's autism consume us. *Through the Years* resonates with both of us because, to paraphrase Kenny Rogers, "through all the good and bad, we knew how much we had." And equally important, we know that together we're a strong, high performance team that's capable of meeting our childen's needs far better than either of us could alone.

Figure 25 WE'VE ALWAYS KNOWN HOW MUCH WE HAD.

40 Celebrate! Celebrate!

As a child, Scott Robertson didn't understand why he had such difficulty making friends and why other children made fun of him. It wasn't until he wrote a paper about autism in college that he realized he had autism. As an adult, one of his goals in life is to "spread awareness of the challenges adults with autism face in higher education and the workforce." One challenge, according to Dr. Robertson, is the way we think about autism. He says, "If you ask people on the street about autism, they'll think of children, as though we must disappear as adults."[135]

In 1998, a team of researchers began a massive, long-term study that focused on autism throughout the life course. The study, titled "Adolescents and Adults with Autism," involved over 400 individuals with autism and their families. Every eighteen months, the team examined changes in variables that contribute to the quality of life of autistic individuals, such as daily living skills and independence. Researchers discovered on average some autistic symptoms such as specific communication and social skills changed a great deal, while others did not. For example, an individual's ability to speak in phrases of three words or more improved a great deal, as did spontaneous gestures to offer comfort to someone who was hurting or sad. On the other hand, asking inappropriate questions not related to the topic of conversation or making statements that might be too personal changed very little. Also, making or maintaining friendships continued to be a significant challenge as autistic individuals got older.[136]

Becoming an adult is no easy feat in today's society. For a young person with autism, the prospects of adulthood can seem daunting and full of challenges. In the literature on autism, the phrase "services cliff" is often used to describe the hurdles of transitioning into adulthood. Once Jimmy became an adult at 21 years of age, we knew that Jimmy would enter the adult disability system. There would be new rules, new laws, extremely long waiting lists for services, and a lack of funding. By the time Jimmy turned 12, we had already started planning Jimmy's future, even though we knew there were no guarantees.

Like other parents in our situation, we were in dire need of direction, so we educated ourselves whenever we got the chance, read voraciously, and broadened and diversified our social networks. We knew full-well that just because Jimmy would need help when he became an adult, he wouldn't automatically get it. We heard horror stories, for example, about parents who were shell-shocked upon discovering that waiting lists for residential services numbered in the thousands. With this in mind, we started planning very early; filing official paperwork a full seven years prior to his twenty-first birthday.

Support for families like ours was and is a hit-and-miss proposition. One professional, diagnosed with Asperger's Syndrome at age 31, sees this dilemma first-hand in his work with autistic adults. He says, "When you get to be 18 or 21, it's like falling off a cliff. We don't do a great job of educating parents about what's going to happen after school ends."[137]

A few years before Jimmy turned twenty-one, we heard that Linwood was opening up a new "adult living unit." There was an opening in one of the units and *they wanted Jimmy*. After years of doing everything in our power to secure an appropriate residential placement in the state of Maryland, it's difficult to describe the massive relief and deep thankfulness we felt at this moment. If we had not secured this placement, we knew that Jimmy would be living with us; perhaps for the rest of our lives. By no means were we severing the cord that connected us to Jimmy, but we felt that Jimmy needed to take this next step to expand his world and develop his independence. We also knew that we alone couldn't possibly meet his needs.

As strange as it might seem, we decided to celebrate a few months after Jimmy moved into his new home at Linwood. Jimmy had just turned 21, and Pat and I realized that in all likelihood, Jimmy would never get married or graduate from college. However, he had just completed his "education," so why not throw a party and invite people who were instrumental in helping him reach this milestone? We knew how much he liked a good party, so we rented a hall at a local hotel, ordered a lunch, and hired a DJ.

We never dreamed that more than 90 people would say "yes" to our invitation. Relatives came from out of state. It was truly like a wedding. Everyone enjoyed themselves immensely, and no one was happier than Jimmy. We all danced together – including relatives, friends, coworkers, and those with disabilities. A friend of ours videotaped every moment. Did Jimmy understand that this celebration was in his honor? You bet. And did he understand how special we all think he is? Absolutely!

Celebrations involving Jimmy are something we continue to enjoy whenever possible. As is the case with many people with autism, Jim has his "favorite things." Family get-togethers and weddings in particular are right at the top of his list. It started with *Father of the Bride*, a movie that revolves around all of the trials, tribulations, and craziness leading up to a big, elaborate wedding. Then came *Muppets Take Manhattan*, which culminates with Miss Piggy and Kermit exchanging marriage vows. Jimmy continues to watch each of these movies over and over again.

Once he became an adult, Jimmy served as an usher at my oldest daughter's wedding and more recently, my brother invited him to do the same at his wedding. Initially, my wife and I were concerned about Jimmy, and whether he would draw attention to himself. We worried unnecessarily; he loved being a part of these weddings as well as the receptions that followed, and it was obvious that he was trying his best to do his best. Moreover, we came to realize that family and friends coming together at a wedding was in all likelihood one of Jimmy's favorite things in the whole world.

I have wonderful memories of Katie's wedding. Jimmy was a groomsman and endured many of his least favorite things; such as wearing formal clothes, posing for one group photo after another, standing still, and walking slowly. But he also exuded joy that day, proudly walking his mother and grandmother down the aisle, albeit a bit hurriedly, waving happily to friends in the church, dancing at the reception, and smiling for endless photos. He donned that tux and stretched beyond his comfort zone out of love for his sister on her special day. That's Jimmy. He adores his family and friends and shows it.
--a pastor (Gayle Annis-Forder)

Figure 26 AFTER KATIE'S WEDDING, JIMMY
POSES FOR A PHOTO.

When Jimmy got a formal invite to be part of his sister Suzy's wedding on New Year's Eve, 2017, he immediately wanted to know details. Being older and wiser, Pat and I were ready. We asked Jimmy if he'd like a companion for the weekend, someone who could offer assistance whenever he needed it, settle him down, answer his questions, and give him some space. Jimmy asked if Linda, a professional from Linwood, could be that person. We knew Linda well, so it was just a matter of making sure she could do it. Looking back, she was a tremendous help, especially during the rehearsal dinner and before, during, and after the wedding. Once again, Jimmy looked super spiffy in his new suit. He was an usher but so much more; he was the bride's brother. Dancing *all* night in his own unique way with his sisters and bridesmaids, he made the wedding that much more fun and meaningful.

Figure 27 JIM AND THE BRIDE "DANCE UP A STORM" AT SUZY'S WEDDING.

41 Say Something

Living with a child on the spectrum can open the minds and hearts of family members to worlds that they never knew existed. In one in-depth study, parents discuss their greater awareness and understanding of people with special needs. They talked about new worlds opening up and seeing life differently.[138] Often, these parents were consumed by activism. "I have read and advocated and searched until I have no brains left." Another parent states, "I have become an advocate not only for my child, but for the other parents who have children with disabilities (not just those with autism)."[139] Having a child with autism sensitized these parents to the world of disabilities; and encouraged them to become advocates, do volunteer work, and even change careers in order to bring about change in their communities and beyond.

Elena Delle Donne, a professional basketball player and perennial WNBA all-star, has a sister named Lizzie who has autism and cerebral palsy. Further, Lizzie was born blind and deaf. Even though her sister has never said a word, Elena explains that Lizzie has changed her perspective and taught her more than anyone in her life. "She's my constant perspective...I often see people not sure of how to interact with Lizzie when they meet her for the first time. *She can't see me. She can't hear me. How do I even say "hi" to her?* Elena tries to lead by example as others watch her, hoping that "as they get comfortable, they'll do the same." She says, "It's important to remember that {Lizzie's} communication is based on the remaining senses she does have; she might sniff your hair, she might even grab you and pull your hair, she might lick your head." [140]

According to Elena, "Lizzie's gift to me was opening my heart to embrace our differences and inspiring me to make the world a more inclusive and respectful place." A few years ago, Elena created a charitable foundation in her own name to raise funds and awareness for those with special needs. She advances opportunities for those with intellectual disabilities worldwide as a Global Ambassador for Special Olympics. And because of Lizzie, she's very open about the power and hurtfulness of the "r-word" and other offensive language. "My sister doesn't have a voice to defend herself [when someone uses the "r-word"], so I take a lot of pride in doing that…Whenever that happens, I speak out and say it was wrong and unfair."[141]

Advocacy takes a variety of forms in our family. Pat has met with federal and state lawmakers and appeared before our county school board to press for laws and educational services that insure equal opportunity. As he gets older, we are working on helping Jimmy to advocate or speak out for himself, especially when his parents aren't around. In many ways, Jimmy's sisters have long fought against the "r-word" and other forms of intolerance directed at their brother and others who are treated as outsiders. My activism found its way into the school where I taught and the communities where I've lived. For example, much of my writing, teaching, and preaching represents my commitment to promote awareness, understanding, and inclusion of people like Jimmy. It's our family's strong belief that advocating for those with disabilities, who may be invisible to some or lacking in power, can unite our world and make it a better place for all.

Because of our family's strong commitment to advocacy, we try to take advantage of teachable moments. As educators, Pat and I are well aware of the value of learning through real-life experiences. Katie and Suzy have also taken it upon themselves to capitalize on unplanned opportunities to educate others, each in their own way. Both have used writing as an effective means of sharing lessons learned from growing up with their brother.

While sitting on our front stoop with some of the young children in our neighborhood one day, I remember the discussion turned to Jimmy, who was somewhere else at the time. They were full of questions about Jimmy. "Why doesn't Jimmy do this?" and "Why doesn't he do that?" As a professor, I was used to being asked tough questions like this. Since Christmas was a few weeks away, my mind turned to the story of Rudolph the Red-Nosed Reindeer. We not only talked about how Rudolph was different, but also how he was the same as the other reindeer. With a little nudging on my part, the children shared their thoughts about how the other reindeer treated Rudolph, and how they learned to appreciate Rudolph's nose. Finally, I asked them what this story had to do with Jimmy. While I don't remember their exact answers, they made the connection; Rudolph reminded them of Jimmy.

Both of my daughters, Katie and Suzy, attended James Madison University (JMU) in Harrisonburg, Virginia. During her junior year, Katie called us about a fellow student's movie review of "I Am Sam," a movie she had recently seen. The review appeared in the school's weekly student newspaper. She was extremely upset. Talking about it was helpful, but she felt a need to do more. With our strong encouragement, she decided to write a letter to the newspaper's editor. Her letter was published the following week:

I was blessed to be born into a very special family

with an older autistic brother. I get extremely frustrated with the way the world reacts to him sometimes, and quite often I feel like nobody understands the pain I feel. I anxiously await movies like "Rain Man" and "I Am Sam," that show not only the pain and hurt that come along with having a disabled family member, but the kind of unique and wonderful things that go along with it as well.

Many of the comments made in regard to the movie were harsh reminders of the way our society really is. The reviewer's quote, which refers to Sam's friends as a "posse of Rainmen and Gumps," was not only extremely insensitive, but incredibly ignorant. Our society does a very good job of grouping people with differences into categories like these and neglecting to see them as individuals. Each person in that movie, regardless of ability, was different. They had different lives, struggles, strengths, and personalities. A writer would never think of referring to a group of Asians in a movie as a "posse of Jackie Chans" simply because they were all Asian, because that would be offensive.

One of the most painful things for me to read was the line referring to Sam and his friends. "Their mussed-up hair and curling fingers will be humorous to some not because they have any great one-liners, but because they deliver average lines with their childlike linguistics." Obviously, the author of this review has never spent any good amount of time with someone with mental differences.

What's amazing about my brother is the fact that he doesn't try to be funny, but quite often is. It can be very entertaining to hold a conversation with him. Since he's limited in what he will talk about, something out of the ordinary – but very ordinary for a 'normal' person – can be very funny in a loving way. The fact that he called these "average lines with childlike linguistics" shows me that he has never seen the special side of a person with a disability. I didn't see this as "poking fun" or a "desperate attempt at comic relief" as he so eloquently put it, but rather as insight into how humorous a disabled person can be.

The movie is a wonderful story that shows how uniquely compassionate and insightful somebody like Sam can be. I urge you to not only enjoy the story but pay attention to the way Sam is treated on a daily basis at restaurants, at work, and on the street. Pay attention to the cruelness somebody like him encounters and how horrible it feels to watch it. The next time you find yourself wanting to stare or laugh, remember that person is somebody's Sam and smile.

Katie's letter became a teachable moment for thousands of students. Because of her closeness with Jimmy and his friends, she recognizes how people with autism are stereotyped and stigmatized. She understands how social encapsulation and a lack of knowledge can give rise to misconceptions about people with disabilities. More importantly, she used this personal insight to educate others in the JMU community.

When the first edition of my book *Diversity Consciousness* came out in 2000, I was interviewed by a reporter from *The Baltimore Sun*. During our conversation, I could see he was trying to understand why a middle-aged white male like myself was so passionate about diversity. I mentioned going to a historically black college for my doctorate degree, teaching at a historically black community college, and even attending a women's college for a semester as an undergraduate student. Lastly, I mentioned my son Jimmy as a driving force behind this book. He looked perplexed.

Once my son was born, I saw things I had never seen before.
--the daddy

For me, Jimmy brought diversity "home." Because of my son, diversity became interwoven into my personal life, 24/7. When I introduce myself to my students at the beginning of the semester, I talk a bit about being a father, my family, and how Jimmy has transformed who I am, what I see, and what I'm about. Later on in the semester, when we address concepts such as stereotype, prejudice, and discrimination, I talk about the worlds in which Jimmy and the rest of my family find themselves.

Because of Jimmy, it was impossible for me to compartmentalize work and family. As soon as he was born, family and work became interconnected. For example, being Jimmy's dad changed the way I teach and relate to my students. I'm much more patient and empathetic, especially to students of mine who are struggling for one reason or another. I work harder at connecting with *all* of my students, and am more aware when I don't. Jimmy has become such an integral part of my teaching that former students stop me in the hallway and ask, "How's your son?" or "What's Jimmy up to?"

At the end of each semester, I administer a student evaluation in each of my classes. One question asks each of my students, "What is ONE thing you will remember most about this class in the future?" I emphasize it can be anything. The following three responses aren't uncommon.

I will remember when Dr. Bucher first told the class about his son and his family situation. I enjoyed listening and I felt that I understood Dr. Bucher more as a person than just as a teacher.

I have learned that it's easier to love everyone rather than pick and choose who you dislike. You (Dr. Bucher) opened my eyes to a totally different world, especially on the topics about your son Jimmy.

I will remember Jimmy. I feel like he was, in so many ways, a part of our class.

42   The Napkin Trivia Game

"…My sister's autism pulled us apart and brought us together many times in the past and will probably continue to do so in the future." "…I have an extraordinary family. My brother is an integral part of it." "…The one thing I've learned is that no matter what happens, that if something were to happen to my sibling or vice versa, we would be there for each other, no questions asked."[142] It's a mistake to ignore the strength, resilience, and closeness of families with an autistic son or daughter, as shown by these comments from adult siblings.

In interviews from this same study, parents repeatedly emphasized the intimate, sometimes unpredictable interrelationships among family members. A mother says, "She is part of our family. We all give and take with each other...We're richer for her being here." A father says, "She is a very important part of our family. She and her sister are very close. We enjoy her sense of humor and the everyday joys of being her parent." In this same study, another father observes, "…Because of her disability, there is constant stress in our family. She is very obsessive-compulsive. Everything must be just right; if not, she can make us miserable. It's like walking on egg shells at times."[143]

One Christmas a few years ago our entire family got together just like we always do. A truly special gift was something my daughter Suzy made for Jimmy; called "The Napkin Trivia Game." Each of the trivia questions revolved around Jimmy's amazing memory and some of his favorite passions. Because this trivia is part of Bucher family lore, many of us knew at least some of the answers. However, Jimmy knew them all. But the answers were not nearly as important as what the game signified. For us, this game was quite simply an act of love. It was a way of celebrating Jimmy and his differences.

When Jimmy opened the box containing the game, Suzy instructed him to read the directions:
Directions: Read the questions on the notecards. For every question you get right, you will win a McDonald's napkin. GOOD LUCK!
I thought to myself, this is what Christmas is all about. Suzy then asked Jimmy if he was ready. After Jimmy gave it some thought and hesitated for a brief moment, he smiled and acknowledged that yes, he was ready to start answering the questions.
Following are ten of the Trivia Game's questions and answers:

Question 1. What day of the week will Katie's birthday be next year?
Answer: *Tuesday*

Question 2. Who is Marty's favorite NFL football team? (Marty was a contestant on *Name That Tune*, a television show Jimmy watched in the 1980s)
Answer: *Miami Dolphins*

Question 3. Who is the Muppet guest star who participated in the "Dueling Banjos" skit?
Answer: *Steve Martin*

Question 4. In the Mary-Kate and Ashley sing-along, how much do they try to sell their brother for at the start of the song?
Answer: *50 cents*

Question 5. In what year did the men's University of

Maryland basketball team win the NCAA national championship?
Answer: 2002

Question 6. What song does Alf sing with a pickle?
Answer: "Old Time Rock-and-Roll"

Question 7. What does Grandma use to spike the sausage gravy in the *Garfield Christmas Movie*?
Answer: Chili powder

Question 8. Who was the original host of Family Feud?
Answer: Richard Dawson

Question 9. What is Fred Flintstone's bowling name?
Answer: Twinkle-toes

Question 10. What is the name of the amusement park we went to in Lake George (New York)?
Answer: Storytown

Each of the questions brought back special memories for our entire family. Among the memories are Jimmy's favorite television shows and movies, family vacations, cheering and having all sorts of fun attending Maryland basketball games, and of course, Jimmy's passion for napkins and penchant for remembering trivia.

To me, the Napkin Trivia Game symbolizes where we are and how much we have grown and come together as a family. Over the years, our priorities have shifted, we have become less judgmental and more accepting of people who seem different, our spirituality has strengthened, and we have become more aware of the preciousness of life.

According to the scientific literature, family growth and transformation in the face of challenging life circumstances involves pulling resources together, feeling a closeness that can weather any storm, and appreciating each day more fully. Families that find ways to cope and change find and value the positives in their unique circumstances, whatever they might be. I feel we have tried to do that as a family. Certainly, the process has not always been linear or clear to us. Like any family, we've had our share of "ups" and "downs," both individually and collectively. Hope, clarity, and confidence have been mixed with despair, confusion, and doubt. But through it all, we never take for granted that which unites us and makes us stronger; our family.

43 An Uncommon Compassion

"How has your child on the autism spectrum affected your life and your family's life?" Close to 500 parents' responses to this question were grouped into positive, negative, and mixed themes. Many focused on siblings' feelings of embarrassment, hurt, and neglect; while positive themes revolved around siblings' feelings of love and empathy. Also, parents made mention of siblings' increased understanding and tolerance for people who are different.[144]

In another study of autism and its impact, siblings of brothers and sisters with autism were instructed to describe themselves. Compassionate was one of the most frequently mentioned traits. For instance, a sibling by the name of Martha shared, "I'm almost overly compassionate, I just feel hard. I think it started with my brother, like when he was feeling hurt, I was feeling hurt. I think I'm naturally drawn to people who are feeling sad or disenfranchised or lonely." In describing herself, Jess said, "I'm just in tune to others and have a deep feeling of compassion like if I see a little kid at a store walking on their tiptoes, I know that it's not an unruly toddler. I just know their home is a little bit different."[145]

Compassion is not simply sensing how someone feels; it moves people to take action. For example, if we understand that everyone wants to be treated with love and respect, and then compassion allows us to respond to another person that way, no matter how they look, talk or act.

In recent years, science has begun to explore various ways of cultivating compassion. For example, we know that compassion is not fixed. It can be enhanced through practice, training, and education in the classroom in addition to real-life experiences. New research shows that immersion in a virtual environment holds promise for building compassion towards others as well.

Many siblings of children with autism undergo informal training every day. Everyday experiences teach them the value of being kind, patient, and connected. "These siblings have seen what it's like to have a hard time in life," says Dr. Sandra Harris, clinical psychologist and author of *Siblings of Children with Autism*. Also, these siblings know that an act of compassion can make a huge difference, because they have witnessed this time and time again.[146]

Jordan Spieth, one of the top professional golf players in the world, is a case in point. When Jordan was eight, his sister Ellie was born. For months, Ellie was hospitalized. According to his mother Chris, they almost lost Ellie two or three times. Ellie was diagnosed with autism. His mother comments, "We all live in Ellie's world." Jordan adds, "With Ellie and how we grew up with her and her struggles and her triumphs, I think it just put life a little more in perspective than maybe it would have had we not experienced it."

During his senior year in high school, Jordan volunteered one day a week at his sister's school. It was one of many experiences that provided round-the-clock lessons in patience, humility, and compassion. In his yearbook, Jordan wrote, "Ellie, I know every day presents its fair share of struggles, but the fight that you show everyday inspires everyone who knows you." Because of Ellie, Jordan sees the bigger picture. His awareness of the needs of youth with special needs led to the establishment of the Jordan Spieth Family Foundation.[147]

Jimmy has touched our lives in much the same way as Ellie has transformed the Spieth family. When she was a high school senior, Katie shared these thoughts in writing.

Growing up with my brother Jimmy, I discovered more and more about myself and other people. When someone so different is so close to you, you develop an uncommon compassion for others. I have seen the difference it makes when someone reaches out to Jimmy. I know what it feels like when another person does something little to make a difference in his life.

Even though I have many goals, the most important one is to make a difference in the world. Jimmy may not realize it, but he has changed my life. He has shown me that not everything wonderful seems wonderful at first sight.

Compassion in action changes people's lives and it takes many forms. It doesn't have to be a dramatic or life-altering event; rather, it can simply mean being fully engaged and listening actively, treating someone with kindness, displaying sincere gratitude, or perhaps just giving a warm, loving smile. Jimmy has made it possible for Katie and our entire family to widen our circle of compassion. As an example, Katie once wrote about how her relationship with Jimmy inspires her.

I have a bond with Jimmy that gives me this sense of closeness with people who are seen as different. I feel that with this compassion, I can have an effect on others' lives. I went through a lot of emotional pain when we were young, pain that many never see. Living through that, I know that no matter how tough life seems, you can get through it.

--a sister (Katie)

Because of Jimmy, we experienced many things as a family that might seem clearly negative. Case in point, there were many restrictions on where we could go and what we could do as a family. Since Jimmy was often at the center of what we did, we all had to adjust. I'm sure there were times when Katie and Suzy tired of Jimmy's behavior issues and the exhaustion and stress we all felt as a result of his meltdowns. But these experiences were also positive. They gave us insight into his world. We grew closer as a family and leaned on each other to survive and grow. We slowed down and became more compassionate. Lastly, our compassion gave us strength, and moved us to action.

44 Persistent Friendliness

When it comes to autism, the work and insight of researchers and professionals is "no match" for the damaging and demeaning stereotypes the public encounters in our media-saturated culture. Portrayals found in films, novels, plays, newspapers, magazines, and all sorts of electronic media "shape and determine public perception," according to Dr. Jennifer Sarrett.[148] Equally important, misrepresentations can impact how we behave toward those with autism and other disabilities.

While our thinking about autism has changed to some degree over the years, media depictions have not kept pace. For example, an autistic child is still portrayed as incomplete or not fully human, while a family with such a child is emotionally shattered. Savant-like traits are often on display, although in real life they are rare. Images in the 1960s put the blame for autism on broken and defective families. These days, the media gives the impression that the reverse is true; the stress of raising a child with autism tears a family apart. Or in some cases, there are stories of super parents who seemingly balance careers, family responsibilities, and autistic children with ease.

"Imprisonment" is another overriding image of autism. In the media, these children are "normal," but their autism imprisons them in spite of their cries for help. The underlying message of these images is that intense intervention from professionals and parents is necessary so that children can be freed from ASD. Years ago, psychoanalysis was seen as the answer. Now, it's all about the latest miracle cure.[149]

Another recent analysis in the field of disability studies examines autism coverage over four decades in *The*

New York Times, starting with the first article on this topic in 1973. While researchers found some mention of positive abilities, articles were more apt to emphasize abilities autistic individuals did *not* have; such as the absence of "any apparent emotion," being withdrawn and "virtually trapped" in their own world, and "frighteningly inaccessible." The study's authors suggest that images of this nature, particularly when found in a highly respected newspaper, stereotype people with autism as fundamentally "impaired," "not able enough," or "not able in the right way."[150]

As the rate of autism increases, the media shows greater interest. It's worth noting that a preponderance of negative images of autism can be found in print media around the world. For instance, elite newspapers in China foster the stereotype that autism has tragic consequences for families; in that it results in a lifetime of pain, anxiety, and suffering.[151] Similarly, analysis of Australian and British print media points to portrayals of autistic people as dangerous or unstable.[152]

By highlighting relatively few images of people on the spectrum, mass media in this country and elsewhere creates characters that tend to be extraordinarily gifted or extraordinarily impaired; there isn't a whole lot of in-between. In other words, the tremendous diversity of the autistic population gets lost. Consider that each of us has unique talents and learns in different ways. Our talents or skills might relate to our creativity, careers, sense of humor, or hobbies. In this respect, Jimmy and other autistic individuals are very ordinary.

Temple Grandin, perhaps the most universally recognized autistic person in the world elaborates, "Often, skills are uneven in autism, and a child may be good at one thing and poor at another." She adds, "Too often, there is too much emphasis on deficits and not enough emphasis on talents."[153] As Grandin sees it, we may need to change our perspective in order to see someone's uniqueness in a different light. For example, Grandin says she didn't succeed "*despite* her unique learning abilities," rather she "succeeded because of them."[154]

People across the autism spectrum show amazing abilities. While media tend to focus on savant skills, such as rare and exceptional talents in fields such as music, art, or math, our experiences with Jimmy have made us aware of other talents that may be harder to see and categorize. Two of Jimmy's most remarkable gifts are friendliness and kindness. Both help Jimmy brighten people's day.

Jimmy knocks down walls through persistent friendliness. Prior to his older sister's wedding, Jimmy and I visited a local mall so he could get fitted for a tuxedo and shoes. When we entered the store, it was crowded. The employees looked frazzled from being overworked and customers looked stressed from waiting. But by the time we left, everybody was feeling better. And their mood swing had everything to do with Jimmy's persistent friendliness.

Once Jimmy's been in a room a while, everyone feels better.
      --the daddy

Jimmy makes a habit of remembering peoples' birthdays. And once he discovers someone's birthday, that individual is almost certain to receive a birthday card from Jimmy every year. It follows that Jimmy buys a voluminous number of cards that increases every year. When I go shopping with Jimmy on weekends, he makes sure that during our time together, he buys the necessary cards. And these are not the 99-cent variety. Rather, these are full-size cards that are fancy, colorful, and most importantly, include a message to Jimmy's liking.

Figure 28 FINDING JUST THE RIGHT GREETING CARD TAKES TIME AND LOTS OF THOUGHT.

When Jimmy finds a possible card, one of us will read it out loud. Once he hears the entire message, his reaction varies from a simple, quiet "No" to an energetic and definitive, "BINGO!!!" accompanied by sounds of sheer delight and a big, big smile. Selecting just the right cards can take as long as fifteen to twenty minutes, depending on how many he needs to buy. Sometimes, the total cost of the cards can be as much as forty dollars. With his hard-earned money from Walmart, Jimmy gladly pays for these cards. Then, he signs each of them "Love James B" or simply "Jimmy," and makes sure that we get them in the mail.

Jimmy likes to get greeting cards and hear from people, especially on holidays and his birthday or when he's sick. He often keeps them on his dresser and reads them from time to time. Hearing from family, friends, or acquaintances means a lot to him. Jimmy sends far more cards than he receives. However, it's worth noting that his kindness is unconditional. In spite of his keen memory, who sends a card to Jimmy has absolutely no bearing on who gets a card from him.

Jimmy doesn't judge others by their looks. Instead he sees a person's kindness. I wish more people could be that way.
--a sister (Suzy)

In order to write this chapter, I thought it might be interesting to google "persistence" and "autism." What I found was a litany of symptoms associated with autism, such as self-injurious behavior, tip-toe walking, skin coloration, and depression. The search also took me to persistent deficits associated with ASD, such as communication and repetitive interests and behaviors. Certainly, these domains or characteristics of autism cannot be ignored when it comes to diagnosing or treating autism. But it's noteworthy that persistent talents and skills were extremely hard to find; and nowhere on the world's most used search engine could I find any mention of the persistent kindness and friendliness that distinguishes Jimmy and many others with autism.

45   The Energizer Bunny

Nearly 5 million athletes from 170 countries participate in Special Olympics (SO), supported by hundreds of thousands of coaches and volunteers. Since its inception some 50 years ago, the ability of SO to "transform lives through the joy of sports" has been documented by considerable research. Findings show that involvement of athletes with intellectual disabilities in SO has far-reaching outcomes, including the development of sports *and* social skills along with health and psychological benefits.[155]

The impact of Special Olympics (SO) extends far beyond the athletes, as parents in one study attest. SO "has been another way for us to have a family activity. It's hard sometimes to find things to do as a family." Another parent credits SO with helping her realize there are things her son can do that she didn't think he was capable of.[156] SO, to quote one more mom, "introduced me to three other families, and it's like a group. On Saturdays when the athletes bowl, it is our time to sit and talk and cry on each other's shoulders or be proud and happy. It's brought us together. I've made a lot of friends."[157]

Parents see Special Olympics as an opportunity for their disabled child to spend time with peers and develop a sense of self away from family. These opportunities can be all too rare. For many, Special Olympics is the only "game in town" when it comes to sports.[158] Said one parent, "That's one thing I love about Special Olympics, the way everybody gets a chance. Not just the top guys." Finally, SO transforms awareness and attitudes in the larger society, challenging our views of athletes, athletic competition, and the disabled.[159] An athlete's sister, who has seen first-hand the difference SO makes, says, "Don't hide them; show them how incredible they are and what an asset to society they are."[160]

I love Special Olympics. I do Special Olympics swimming and Special Olympics kayaking. It is very fun. I like to be with my friends.
    --Jimmy

L ike many athletes, once Jimmy started participating in SO, he stayed involved. For more than thirty years, Jimmy has participated in a wide variety of local and state Special Olympics competitions.

Figure 29 JIMMY'S JUMP EARNS HIM A MEDAL AT SPECIAL OLYMPICS.

As he got older, track, soccer, and basketball gave way to golf, swimming, and most recently, kayaking. As a middle-aged adult, he still enjoys Special Olympics as much as ever. No matter what the event, he trains hard and takes great pride in doing his best.

When Jimmy competes at Special Olympics, it's a family event. While all of his competitions have been memorable, his first Special Olympics in track stands out the most.

If you want to witness love, just go to a Special Olympics competition and watch the parents and athletes interact.
--the mommy

Jimmy was eight and Katie had just turned four. As he was approaching the starting line of his first-ever race, the fifty-yard dash, Jimmy was psyched and focused. Katie had heard that Special Olympics participants had "huggers" who helped them at the Games, and she had been pestering her mom because she wanted to be Jimmy's hugger. But she was too young. As Pat was standing with her movie camera fixated on Jimmy waiting for the race to start, Katie stood directly in front of her and once again let her know how she wanted to be his hugger.

At the start, Jimmy dashed out ahead, looking like the clear winner. Between the thrill of seeing her son actually winning something and her preoccupation with the camera, Pat didn't notice that Katie had darted out on the track and was headed toward her brother. Katie stood still on the track, between her sprinting brother and the finish line. Once he saw his sister with her arms open wide, Jimmy stopped in his tracks. Jimmy bent down and gave his sister the big hug she had been waiting for, as all of the other athletes passed him by. Pat and her friends all had tears in their eyes as they took in what just happened.

Jimmy spent so many hours watching his sisters compete in everything from talent shows to swim meets. He would be their biggest fan, cheering them on alongside of us. Special Olympics give Jimmy his turn to be the center of attention in a positive way, as his family cheers him on.

--the mommy

Each year, Jimmy receives an award from his Special Olympics swim team in Howard County, Maryland. Actually, every swimmer gets an award, a certificate signed by his coach. Not surprising, the award that Jimmy seems to receive more than any other is the "Energizer Bunny Award," for the swimmer who "keeps on going, and going, and going, and never gives up." He has a motor that rarely slows down. Instead of simply viewing his endless energy as a problem to overcome, his Special Olympics coaches recognize it as one of Jimmy's strengths.

Figure 30 A VOLUNTEER CONGRATULATES JIMMY ON HIS GOLD MEDAL IN THE 200 METER BACKSTROKE.

About 30 plus years ago, when I was around 13, I

went and stayed at my aunt's house for a few days. Her daughter/my cousin ran a camp for kids with special needs and I helped out a few days. One of the campers used to eat his food really fast, so we would take turns sitting with him at lunch to talk with him and make sure he ate a little slower. He was maybe 7 or 8, and his name was Jimmy.

Fast forward about 20 years; I'm coaching Special Olympics swimming. A young man named James joined our team, and we were all thrilled by his work ethic. He would ask how many laps to swim and we would start with 2 or 4. Once those were done, he'd call out to us, 'I did my 4 laps. Now what do you want me to do?' We realized quickly to tell him a higher number! [Since then, his endurance and skills have improved to the point where he now competes in some of the longest events at SO meets].

I would also sometimes spot James at our local Walmart, and I saw how his strong work ethic came into play there, too. I'd see him working non-stop collecting and pushing carts on the lot, whether it was 90 plus degrees or snow on the ground.

One time after a SO State Games weekend had ended, I was at a party with my aunt, and somehow the subject of the little boy named Jimmy from camp came up. She said, 'You mean, Jimmy Bucher?' When I heard his full name, a look of shock came over my face because it dawned on me that the fine young man who I coached at SO swimming was the same little guy I'd met at camp all those years ago. Helping out at that camp and meeting kids like Jimmy was one of the reasons I decided to get involved in Special Olympics years later."

--a Special Olympics Coach (Joanne Gales)

Special Olympics isn't without its critics. The biggest criticism is that it's a segregated event that promotes ableism, or discrimination against people with disabilities. Unfortunately, our family is all too familiar with segregation and discrimination; in fact, we encounter it almost daily. Special Olympics fill a big void in our lives. It levels the playing field to some degree and provides opportunities that are all too rare in the larger society. While Special Olympics provide Jimmy with a chance to compete athletically, it also does wonders for his social capabilities, independence, and confidence. Best of all, he clearly feels good about competing, going to practice, and attending social activities with his team. After each race, he's a picture of pride and joy. Yes, he enjoys collecting his gold, silver, and bronze medals, which go into a tote bag in his room. But more than that, he derives tremendous satisfaction from being "brave in the attempt" in a supportive and loving environment.

Special Olympics is well, special. When he competes, our family experiences something unique. There's unconditional acceptance and an outpouring of love for our son and all athletes. Their age, race, gender, looks, speech, abilities, disabilities, and body types are totally irrelevant. Coaches, athletes, family members, friends, and volunteers are non-judgmental. They understand, and they get it; no awkward stares and no explanations necessary.

Figure 31 PLAYING SPECIAL OLYMPICS SOCCER AS A TEEN,
JIMMY'S NONSTOP MOTOR WAS AN ASSET.

As a participant in Special Olympics, Jimmy's joy overflows in physical exertion.
--a pastor (Gayle Annis-Forder)

46   Angels in Our Midst

During worship one day, Melinda Ault looked around. For the first time, it dawned on her that people with disabilities were missing from her congregation. As she said, "I knew they were out there." That realization prompted Professor Ault to study faith communities, and the experiences of parents who have children with disabilities, including autism. Her survey of over 400 parents generated some surprises, namely that one third of the parents reported changing their place of worship due to the fact that their child was not welcomed or included. If parents did stay, more than half reported they had to be with their child so he or she could participate in a religious activity. One mother of a teen told Ault, "There is either fear or resistance because of my child's behavior. We are just not welcome." Another mother of a preschooler remarked, "I brought my son to a cookout, and nobody knew how to come up to me. I felt like I was making them uncomfortable."

What sets faith communities apart are the supports they have in place as well as their welcoming attitude. When supports are not available, it's likely that parents will fill that void even though they may feel overstressed and exhausted. Furthermore, when individuals on the spectrum engage in disruptive and distracting behaviors, such as hitting themselves, wandering away, and making repetitive noises, a family member may have to intervene since others may not understand these behaviors.[161]

However, strong support from clergy and members can lead to much more positive experiences.[162] Disability philosophy, or how a faith community views disability, is critical. Rather than viewing it as a sin or deficit, many faiths focus on disability as simply one more way in which we are different and believe each of us has unique talents and each of us is a gift from God. Or, to quote one mother, "I believe God has a plan for every individual He put on earth. I want people to see a child with autism as a gift, not as someone who is damaged."[163]

I've always believed in Jesus. I feel fine going to church. I like my pastors and they like me.
--Jimmy

Even with Jimmy's special needs and challenging behaviors, my wife and I were determined that he would have a strong Christian education. Furthermore, we strongly felt that church "should" be the one place that welcomed Jimmy with open arms, no questions asked. Church could significantly expand and diversify Jimmy's social world, making it possible for him to interact with other children who by and large did not have disabilities. We chose to join a church within walking distance of our home, Wesley Freedom United Methodist in Eldersburg, Maryland.

Figure 32 READY FOR CHURCH.

Sunday school was a significant challenge for

Jimmy and his teachers. He had an attention span of less than a second, normal intelligence, intense hyperactivity, and severely delayed social and emotional skills. Moreover, he had very little use of his hands from the brain damage he sustained at birth. Panic attacks were frequent and scary.

An angel by the name of Anita Straub took Jimmy under her wing when he was in kindergarten. Even though we weren't sure how much he could learn in a Sunday school setting, we knew he was in a loving and supportive environment. Anita made it possible for us to go to church as a family, as Jimmy was way too disruptive to bring with us into the sanctuary.

However, the challenge became more difficult as Jimmy moved from one grade to another. Each year, we had to convince a new group of teachers that they could manage Jimmy and our son was capable of learning. Teachers would say, "He won't be able to do this, and he sure won't be able to do that." Our mantra was, "Yes he can. Let us show you." Then, staff would share a new concern. "He needs an aide, and we can't find one." While we understood their dilemma, our response was firm. "I'm sure there is somebody from our church who is willing to work with Jimmy one-on-one." Eventually, staff always found someone. Given that we were talking about church, our expectations were higher. We both felt this is one place where Jimmy could and should be included. Even though his autistic behaviors were still severe, he could understand and retell certain Bible stories and read passages from the Bible.

Another angel by the name of Lynn Clarke came into Jimmy's life when he became a teen. I don't remember if she was the teacher or an assistant at the beginning, but we will never forget how she made it her mission to make it possible for Jim to attend Sunday school at Wesley Freedom. Every year Jim moved up, so did Lynn. On Sunday mornings we knew Jim was in a good place and learning about the Lord. What that meant to us is hard to express, but Lynn made an enormous difference in our entire family's life those years. To this day, Jimmy sends his good friend Lynn a birthday and Christmas card every year, without fail.

How blessed I was to have been one of Jimmy's Sunday School teachers for 9-12 grades and work with him one-on-one during class time. Yes, Jimmy was special and not always easy but he and I both jelled and I think a lot of it was because I figured out when to proceed or when to back off.

Jim could read a lot of our literature but got frustrated when he couldn't write, so we would share the tasks. I would help him read (only when asked) and I would do his writing for him. I knew pretty quickly that any touching or hugging was off bounds with him, but the smiles and laughter were just as rewarding. Now, if Jimmy didn't like something we were doing, he made it clearly known. One of the best examples I remember is we were having a canned food drive where all the Sunday school classes were part of the church service. Our class, being the senior high class, was one of the last ones to enter the sanctuary. We were standing in line and I was beside Jim, waiting to walk in with him, when he decided he didn't want to go in and proceeded to have a tantrum on the floor outside the sanctuary door. So, I turned to Jim and said, 'Fine, we are going in without you.' As we walked down the aisle and presented our canned goods, I turned around and sure enough, there was Jimmy coming down the aisle with his cans. I was so proud of him.

The other very fond memory I had was once a month our class would sit in church for the service. Jim loved the organ music and to hear the choir sing. Our organist used to get the biggest kick watching him as he was playing the organ, since Jim left little doubt that he thoroughly enjoyed the music. One Sunday, as the choir director got up to direct the choir to stand up to sing, Jimmy pops up from the pew where he was sitting, turns around to face the congregation, and gestures like the music director. He says, "Everybody up!" Before I could get him to sit back down, he drew quite a few laughs.

And most of all, I remember Jim as an adult sitting in church on Christmas Eve and looking at me and smiling, while I was sitting up in the choir.

--a friend (Lynn Clarke)

For the most part, the leadership and congregation of Wesley Freedom embraced the Bucher family. Nevertheless, I fully understood that in some ways our church was not all that different from the surrounding community. For instance, when Jimmy would come to the sanctuary with his Sunday school class, he and his class would sit in pews reserved for them. The children who filed in naturally sat next to each other. But when it came to Jimmy, there was usually an empty seat or two on either side of him.

When Jimmy was 6, Pat gave a sermon in which she shared intimate details of her journey with Jimmy and her struggles with faith during that time. And as a member of the Pastor Parish Relations Committee, I tried to make inclusion of all people, regardless of their abilities or disabilities, a priority.

At age 16, Jimmy was finally able to join us for the worship service. One Sunday morning, with Jimmy seated between the two of us, we heard a sermon from the pastor that began with two rhetorical questions. To Jimmy, there is no such thing as a rhetorical question. First, the pastor asked, "Have you ever felt like you were worthless?" Jimmy immediately answered emphatically and loudly, "No!" The pastor smiled, and then asked, "Have you ever felt like your life had no meaning and other people didn't care about you?" This time, Jimmy waited a few seconds before giving a loud, thoughtful response, "No, to tell you the truth." This time, Pat and I smiled.

When our son was in his twenties, we moved to a nearby town and found a new church. Again, Jimmy developed a close relationship with the pastors and congregation of our new church, Ebenezer United Methodist Church. Our comfort level at this church has always been phenomenal. Jimmy can be Jimmy; he can clap his hands, yell "Alf" 10 times, talk to himself, pepper complete strangers with a battery of questions, and everyone takes it in stride.

One of my favorite memories of Jimmy is watching him sing hymns during worship. I was the only one with a front row seat for watching him demonstrate what it means to truly praise the Lord with your whole being! His parents always seemed a bit worried that he was bothering others. However, it always brought a smile to my face, and to those around him, to watch Jimmy jump, clap, shout and sing his praises to the Lord without holding back!!! I wish we all had that part of Jimmy in us during worship!
--a pastor (Judy Emerson)

We've recently moved again, so Pat, Jimmy and I became members of still another church. I talked to my wife about whether she thought Jimmy might want to light the advent candle or read a short prayer at the Christmas Eve service. At our former church, Jimmy and I took turns reading scripture in front of our entire congregation during this service. But this was a new church and Pat was a bit unsure. Before we went any further, we decided to ask Jimmy. Jimmy gave his OK and we notified Pastor Wade. Prior to the service, we practiced reading the prayer together. Using my finger under each word helped Jimmy keep track of where he was and slowed him down. Also, I helped him with pronunciation when necessary. After practicing a number of times, I felt we were ready.

I do greatly appreciate Jimmy's passion as it is genuine and inspiring. More of us would do well to be so expressive in our joy in the Lord.
        ---a pastor (Wade Martin)

        At the service that night, Pastor Wade approached Pat, Jimmy, and me. He showed us where we would stand as we read the prayer, how to position ourselves in front of the mike, and how to go about lighting and blowing out the candle. Jimmy seemed to understand, so we took our seats. A few minutes into the service, it was our turn. Jimmy and I stood before the podium while Pat stood to one side. Jimmy took the lead and started reading the prayer. I placed my finger under the text and helped him when he paused a bit. After we read a few words together, Jimmy informed me and the entire congregation that he was starting over and reading the prayer all by himself. I smiled, backed off, and Jimmy proceeded to read the prayer as we had rehearsed, slowly and deliberately. At that point, I followed Jimmy to one side and he lit the candle as Pat read her part of the prayer. Once we finished, our 40 year-old son relaxed a bit, and returned to his seat skipping, clapping his hands, and repeating, "I did a good job! I did a good job!"

Every time I think of Jimmy, I smile a big smile, and am inspired again to be a better person.
--a pastor (Gayle Annis-Forder)

47 Staying Positive

"...I am a stronger, deeper, better developed person. I learned the truest meaning of unconditional love and support because of my autistic brother. My perspective on life is bright and hopeful, and mostly optimistic." "...Through her I have learned tolerance, patience and to be thankful for all that I have." "I am very open to different people or situations...I always choose to work with the 'black sheep' of the group. I am also very sensitive to others' feelings." Over 200 adult siblings in this study were asked how their lives have been affected by having a brother or sister with ASD. Siblings talked about growing up, relationships, community acceptance, and the future; and many reflected on the positive things they learned.[164]

For some, the positives are hard to come by. One sibling recalls being bitten on the cheek by her autistic brother, and once hiding him in a closet when her boyfriend picked her up from home. Understandably, she experienced a wide range of emotions growing up; "feeling resentful and then feeling guilty about feeling resentful, feeling responsible and then maybe overcompensating when you're being responsible," feeling embarrassed and then grappling with why you feel this way. She continues, sometimes you don't know "when to be angry at your parents or when to be angry at your brother or sister and when to be angry at yourself." She says it's complicated, and it is.[165]

According to research conducted by Dr. Barbara Fredrickson, our ability to change how we perceive a situation can provide us with hope and optimism and allow us to fight off negative emotions such as fear, anxiety, and anger. Fredrickson argues that negativity is inevitable, but it's important to not let it outweigh the positive. Positive emotions such as hope, inspiration, love, and joy can enable us to change our outlook and show more resilience, even in the face of extremely difficult circumstances. Staying positive can mean the difference between "languishing" and "flourishing," but Fredrickson warns it's not easy by any means.[166]

My wife is a naturally positive, "silver-lining" kind of person. I think she gets this from her mother, who had a habit of looking on the bright side of things. Pat tries to find the best in everything. When informed of Jimmy's health issues soon after birth, her positivity kicked in. As she said at the time, "I have a baby, he's adorable, and he loves me."

Jimmy's first developmental evaluation was brutal for Pat and me. Looking over the test results, the doctor informed us that because Jimmy was "severely delayed" educating him was not a realistic goal. I remember being floored by the evaluation. Pat was skeptical and raised some questions about the test. For some reason, the doctor felt it necessary to then say, "I'm going to be your wet blanket," meaning he didn't want us getting our hopes up. With my wife sobbing uncontrollably, I simply said, "He's our son. We'll love him and take care of him just as we've always done." From that moment on, we continued to do our best to stay positive, "loving him to pieces."

When he was little, we worked especially hard at keeping our cool and catching Jimmy at being good. Tackling one thing at a time and finding something positive to pull out of his behavior increased his motivation as well as his ability to "bounce back." I think it also made us feel better. While we made a point of not suffocating Jimmy with "Don't!" and "Bad Job!" we also had to moderate our positivity. Too much of any type of emotion on our part could trigger negative behaviors from him.

Nowadays, if we don't maintain a high positivity-negativity ratio in our interactions with our son, he has a funny way of reminding us. For example, after effectively handling a change in schedule, he often says to me, "Dad, I did a good job?" And if I don't respond right away, he'll ask this same question again and again, or repeat the word "Right?" until he gets a positive response from me. When I finally do acknowledge him and let him know that yes, he did a good job, his face lights up. While that is good to see, it simply reaffirms what I already know; his self-esteem is fragile. As many times as I've commended him on "doing a good job," he still feels the need to continually seek approval from me. But the good news is that he's driven to do his best.

Jimmy's positive self-talk is extraordinary. He'll say to himself, "I did a good job." He "pats himself on the back" constantly."
--the mommy

One of the ways in which I try to stay positive is to work on continually giving thanks for all of the blessings in my life. When it comes to Jimmy, the blessings haven't always been obvious, especially early in his life. His autism scared "the hell out of us" and limited what we could do as a family. Everyday challenges aside; I felt extremely fortunate to have a child like Jimmy.

Prior to Jimmy's birth, I was much more focused on productivity rather than positivity. I valued work and took pride in my work ethic. When Jimmy came into my world, my priorities began to change. Moreover, I experienced a wide range of positive and negative emotions. These emotions, which were often seemingly contradictory and nuanced, were difficult if not impossible to label as simply positive or negative.

For example, there were moments I felt frustration, particularly when I was overcome by Jimmy's inability to express himself, slow down, or pick up a new skill. On the surface, this seemed like a "negative" for both Jimmy and me. However, over time I learned to examine my own ignorance and feelings as I tried to make sense of Jimmy's inabilities. Do *I* need to work harder on *my* listening and change what *I* do? Perhaps I need to be more patient and understanding. Maybe I need to ask myself why Jimmy acts this way and try harder to put myself in Jimmy's shoes. When I manage to do these things, I find myself being much more appreciative of my son, and just how hard he's trying.

Jimmy regularly interacts with people of various races. Unlike those of us who say we don't see the color of a person's skin when we actually do, Jimmy really doesn't. With Jimmy, everything has to be taught. Because we made a conscious decision not to teach him about this concept we call race, it never became part of his thinking. For example, at the beginning of a new school year at Linwood, I happened to ask Jimmy about his African-American teacher. Out of curiosity, I asked him, "Is she Black? Jimmy answered, "Yes." Then I asked, "Is she White?" Jimmy again answered, "Yes." The fact that Jimmy could not identify a person's race was actually refreshing.

I never expected Jimmy to follow in my professional footsteps. Actually, my expectations for him were pretty basic; namely be responsible, humble and kind, do your best, and leave the world a better place than you found it. I remember being so thankful that God blessed my wife and me with this child. As I look back, Jimmy has fulfilled all of my expectations, and then some.

Prior to the birth of Jimmy, I was hoping for a boy…
A boy with whom I could play and just have fun.
A boy who would love sports as much as I do.
A boy who would turn into a young man that would make me proud.
A boy who might love me as much as I love him.
A boy who would value family and love children.
A boy who'd be willing to work hard to achieve whatever he wanted to achieve.
In Jimmy, I got all I was hoping for.

But I also got so much more…

I got to watch TV shows such as Lawrence Welk, Barney, and Andy Williams, again and again and again.
I got to read books until I almost knew them by heart, books like Pat the Bunny, Curious George, and Green Eggs and Ham.
I got to listen to Christmas music in the middle of the summer.
I have a son who whenever I ask, wants to go shopping with me.
I have a son who whenever I ask, wants to go for a walk with me.
I have a son who's always ready and willing to help me, even when I don't ask.
I have a son who makes me a better father - more patient, more understanding, and more aware of what's really important in life.
I have a son who's transformed our family and brought us closer together.
Jimmy isn't what I expected. He's so much more.
      --the daddy

Just like negativity breeds negativity, research in the workplace reveals that positive emotions are contagious. I've found this principle applies to family life as well. When anyone in our family shows joy and love, those emotions rub off on the rest of us. But, as Dr. Fredrickson found in her research, the positivity has to be genuine and appropriate, rather than overdone or forced. All of us take pride in who Jimmy is and his many accomplishments, both big and small. We work on keeping our focus on what he can do, not what he can't do.

48   Terrapin Ties

Donald, a retiree who lives by himself, has a bunch of friends. He enjoys driving, playing golf, and traveling throughout the U.S. and abroad. Germany, Hungary, Dubai, Columbia and Tunisia are just some of the 36 foreign countries he's visited. Also, Donald's travel portfolio includes an African safari, a few cruises, and numerous PGA tournaments. The trips tend to be rather short; six days is the maximum. He always travels by himself. Once he gets home, Donald does not maintain contact with any of the people he met on his travels. He puts the snapshots he took into albums, and then starts planning his next trip as soon as he calls his travel agent.[167]

When he was a child, Donald was identified as "Case 1…Donald T" in a medical article published in 1943. Donald T. (Donald Triplett) was the first person ever diagnosed with autism. As a boy, his interests were focused and included number patterns, letters of the alphabet, and pictures of U.S. presidents. He spent a good deal of time spinning himself, spinning objects, and uttering words that didn't seem to make much sense.[168]

Donald's interests much later in life seem at odds with much research that would have us believe those on the spectrum are only interested in activities that have a limited and narrow focus. However, a recent study suggests otherwise. Almost 400 adults with autism, ranging from 21 to 73 years of age, were asked to list their top five interests or hobbies. 99 percent had at least one hobby, while 75 percent had two or more hobbies. Hobbies included music and theatre, sports, video gaming, reading, and watching TV. In reporting these findings, Dr. Andrew Adesman observed, "Adults with an autism spectrum disorder expressed an interest in many of the same hobbies and activities that non-ASD adults enjoy."[169]

The beauty of sports is that it presents opportunities for everyone's involvement in some fashion or another. When it comes to people with disabilities, we tend to think of participation in Special Olympics and The Paralympic Games. Sports are also a diversion, which according to Andy Billings, Director of University of Alabama's Program in Sports Communication, can promote meaningful conversations. When Billings gave a TED talk on this subject, he discussed how sports can promote open and honest discussions about race, gender, ethnicity, and gender identity. And while that's certainly true, sports can also become a vehicle for life-changing dialogues between a father and his autistic son.

For over three decades, Jimmy and I have attended a University of Maryland basketball game every year. Following the Maryland's Terrapins, better known as the "Terps," has become a special part of our yearly routine; something we look forward to and begin to talk about once the season's schedule comes out. In recent years, Jimmy also expressed an interest in attending a Maryland football game, so that's now part of our routine as well.

Before the Terps came into the picture, Jimmy knew hardly anything about the college sports scene. Maryland basketball provided us with an *entirely different realm* of conversation. After each game, I would look for a short write-up of the game in our local newspapers. I sent this information to Jimmy at Linwood, including a summary of the game, who they played, where it took place, the box score, attendance, and a brief analysis of how Maryland played. Then, I'd call and "quiz" him with the following questions:

1. Did Maryland win or lose?
2. What is the name of the team the Terps played? What is the name of their mascot?
3. What was the score of the game?
4. Was the game played at Maryland (College Park)? If it was an away game, where was it played?
5. How many people attended the game?
6. How many games have the Terps won and how many games have they lost so far?
7. Who was the leading scorer for the Terps? How many points did he score?
8. Who was the leading rebounder for the Terps?
9. Why do you think Maryland won or lost? (he would need a bit of help with this question)
10. What team does Maryland play next?

Following Maryland athletics gave us something to talk about other than his schedule for the next week, month, or year. After quizzing him after each game and talking about the Terps during the entire basketball season, his reading, comprehension, and conversational skills improved. Jimmy even started picking up the lingo. For example, he now asks me if a particular game is going to be "tough," and whether it's a "must win." Most importantly, talking Terp basketball was fun; it was something "the guys" could do whenever we spent time together or talked on the phone.

After following this routine for less than a year, Jimmy became a sports fan. He started watching a few minutes of one or two Terp basketball games on TV, and then began asking me about their chances of going to the "Big Dance." Going to a game was the next step. At age 13, Jimmy entered Cole Field House, surrounded by about 16,000 noisy, rambunctious fans. If I had known more about autism at the time, I would have been very hesitant to bring him into such a chaotic atmosphere. There were no quiet zones or noise-cancelling headphones, like there are now in a growing number of sports arenas. Fortunately, ignorance worked in our favor. Unlike many autistic individuals who would have been overwhelmed by all of this stimulus, Jimmy loved it; the crowd, the lights, and the deafening noise from the PA system. As far as Jimmy was concerned, the louder and crazier, the better.

One year, we arranged for legendary Terp basketball coach Gary Williams to meet Jimmy after the game. Coach Williams posed for a picture with Jimmy and signed a photo of himself; which is now framed and hanging in Jim's bedroom. Every year, Jimmy asks if we can stay till the game's over, so he can spend some time with his "good buddy," Johnny Holliday, long-time radio announcer for Terrapin football and basketball. After Johnny wraps up his broadcast, we ask a security guard to let Johnny know that Jimmy would like to speak with him. As soon as he gets a chance, Johnny walks over to see Jimmy and embraces him like a long-lost friend. I have absolutely no idea what the two of them talk about, but Jimmy has Johnny's undivided attention for a good five minutes as they "catch up." For the better part of two decades, they have intermittently corresponded and developed a relationship with each other.

Anytime I get the opportunity to visit with Jimmy he lifts me up and brightens my day! In Jimmy's presence, you can feel the love he has for people and I always consider it such a privilege to spend time with him.
--a friend (Johnny Holliday)

*Figure 33 JIMMY AND JOHNNY AFTER A MARYLAND
BASKETBALL GAME.*

A while back, the Terp football team beat Penn State University for the first time in years. Jimmy was watching the game at his group home with his counselor. The Terps won a "nail biter" (Jimmy's words) on a last second field goal and as soon as the game was over, Jimmy gave me a call and wanted to talk about the game. What made this phone call so extraordinary was that when he called, he *only* wanted to talk about the game. He didn't move on to his usual barrage of schedule questions, nor did he talk about anything that wasn't related to the game. That phone call was something I will remember for the rest of my life.

Jimmy shares another intimate connection with the University of Maryland. Jim Henson, creator of the Muppets and a driving force behind television's *Sesame Street* and *The Muppet Show*, is a 1960 graduate of the University of Maryland. Throughout this book, I have referenced the Muppets because these shows and characters are such a big part of our lives, and that's still the case even though Jimmy is now a middle-aged adult. Last year, Jimmy asked me to drive him around our neighborhood, so he could see all of the fancy Christmas decorations, including Grover, Elmo, and Cookie Monster. And each time we visit Maryland's campus, we make a point of stopping and spending some time with the statue of Jim Henson and Kermit the Frog.

Figure 34 JIMMY TAKES A SEAT WITH HIS MUPPET FRIENDS AT THE UNIVERSITY OF MARYLAND

We are deeply indebted to the Terp family. They've gone out of their way to accommodate Jimmy and have been instrumental in bringing Jimmy out from under his shell. I think that's one of the reasons we

are such big fans of the University of Maryland.
       --the daddy

49 It Takes a Grandparent

"Did you play a role in identifying your grandchild's autism? How much do you worry about your adult child? How well are you coping?" Of the 2,600 grandparents surveyed by the Interactive Autism Network (IAN), 83 percent were grandmothers and 17 percent grandfathers. Their involvement ranged a great deal, from those living with their grandchild with autism to grandparents living thousands of miles away.[170]

The role of grandparents is typically an afterthought in research on the development of autistic children. IAN's study reveals that this is a big mistake. Dr. Paul Law, IAN's Director, described grandparents as an "incredible asset" for autistic children and their parents, considering their resources and the time they can give. Moreover, they tend to be so involved that many in the study (nearly one in three) played a pivotal role in initially identifying autism in their grandchildren.[171]

A majority of grandparents worry "a great deal" about what the future holds for their grandchild with ASD, his or her siblings, and their adult children. One grandparent shared, "The greatest challenge is knowing I will not be on this earth to help my son cope as his son grows to be a teenager and faces all the problems he is going to have." In spite of their many concerns, 90 percent of grandparents indicated that they have grown closer to their adult child (the grandchild's parent) as the entire family deals with the challenges of autism. Grandparents spoke of how they've grown. A grandmother said, "My granddaughter has given me a greater insight into who I am and my capacity to love. She is my heart's delight."[172]

R aising "a Jimmy" has been a communal effort, extending far beyond my wife and I and our two daughters. Our extended family and Jimmy's grandparents in particular, have broadened his social world and helped him become the man he is today. Without a doubt, Jimmy has left an indelible mark on extended family members who've had the chance to get to know and appreciate him.

Figure 35 PAT'S MOM AND JIMMY ENJOY SOME QUIET TIME.

Early on, it was difficult for our extended family to understand what we were going through. This was largely due to how far apart we lived, and the fact that our relatives knew very little about autism when we received Jimmy's diagnosis. When the media picked up on a story about an autistic savant graduating from Harvard University, my father-in-law intimated that Jimmy would be the next genius to graduate from a top-notch college. Even though he had the best of intentions, my father-in-law's comment showed just how far removed he was from our reality.

In a sense, Jimmy's grandparents were "hurt twice" by the diagnosis of autism, initially for their adult child and then for their grandchild. Out of necessity, we were totally focused on surviving from one day to the next. Educating members of our extended family would have to wait.

Both sets of Jimmy's grandparents spent a long time in denial. My parents thought we were withholding information because we didn't have answers. On the other hand, Pat's parents thought we were overreacting. After all, they reminded us of the fact that Pat was a late talker and walker. Nevertheless, our parents were very supportive of us and what we were going through. Early on, we leaned heavily on Pat's mother. At a time when we felt like we were drowning but were hesitant to ask for help, she willingly spent weeks living with us shortly after Jimmy's birth and later during one of Jimmy's prolonged hospitalizations.

Generally, both sets of grandparents were reluctant to take care of Jimmy without us. Their hesitancy, I think, stemmed from the fact that they weren't sure what might set him off or whether they could manage him if he started to suddenly lose control of his emotions. However, that changed over time.

When Jimmy was seven and Katie was three, Pat's parents pushed us to get away and spend some time together. I had just completed my doctorate degree at Howard University and we were both exhausted. Even though we were hesitant at first, her parents sealed the deal by offering to take care of our children. This was an incredible gesture on their part, especially considering they were both in their mid-60s. Thinking of leaving Jimmy for just a few days was terrifying. But we knew Gramma and Grandpa loved Jimmy just as much as we did. Pat made plans; and for four days, just the two of us did nothing but play and have fun in Florida. Looking back, it was one of the best things we ever did for our marriage.

When Jimmy was about ten, I remember taking him to his first baseball game with my dad. The three of us saw a minor league professional baseball team called the Las Vegas Stars (now the Las Vegas 51s). It was a beautiful night for a game, and a chance for "the guys" to spend some quality time together, relax, and talk baseball. After my dad bought Jimmy a souvenir, we took our seats along the first-base line.

From that moment on, it was a struggle. Jimmy could not sit still. His constant crying, mood swings, and monologue about things that had absolutely nothing to do with baseball made it impossible for us to follow or enjoy the game. As I found myself looking around at other young boys his age, sitting peacefully with their fathers and ready to pounce on the next foul ball that came their way, I fought some negative emotions. After two innings, I was exhausted. I can only imagine how my dad felt. We got up and left. I wondered to myself, why did I ever think that Jimmy could sit and watch a baseball game? When I got home that night, I put Jimmy to bed. In my heart, I knew he'd done the best he could. I was hopeful there might come a time when we could go to the park and enjoy a game, like my dad and I used to do.

Years later, when Jimmy attended Linwood, staff asked for our permission to take him to see a major league baseball game along with a small group of other autistic children. We said okay. Interestingly, they stayed for two innings. Then, each time they went back to the ballpark, they stayed a little longer. A few years ago, Jimmy and I went to see our second minor league baseball game. During the game, I wouldn't have been surprised if Jimmy had asked to leave early; however, that was not the case. Now Jimmy takes pride in being able to stay for the full nine innings.

Close relatives live quite a distance from us. Therefore, there were limited opportunities for them to provide us with some of the support and relief we desperately needed. While annual family reunions were one such opportunity, family members such as aunts, uncles, and cousins rarely found time to occupy Jimmy so Pat and I could go out by ourselves. And that was understandable, considering they were busy with their own families and enjoying some precious downtime.

In many ways, family reunions were stressful for our family. Jimmy had to adjust to an unfamiliar environment and a random schedule. The entire family was the focus; not Jimmy. Three days was usually the maximum. By the fourth day, Jimmy found it almost impossible to "hold it together" and our patience was wearing thin. At that point, we typically headed home to a more familiar, manageable routine.

Phone calls and kind words have always been extremely important. This type of support was that much more helpful since members of our extended family have always been nonjudgmental. We don't take that for granted, since we've heard horror stories from other parents in our situation who were constantly told what to do and how to do it. Rather than offer advice, they simply listened and offered encouragement.

As our family grows with autism, each new generation has been touched and transformed by Jimmy. Many family members have a deeper understanding of what it means to have autism, and what it doesn't mean. They're clearly at ease with Jimmy, more aware of his abilities and feelings, and more appreciative of his unique personality. He's one of us.

This is particularly true of our grandchildren. "Uncle Jimmy" sees them frequently, so it's not unusual when he visits. Whether it's taking in a movie, going out to eat, attending church, or just plain "chillin", Jimmy fits right in. Sometimes they ask us pointed questions, like "Why does Jimmy play with napkins?" or "Why can't Jimmy ride a bike?" We answer honestly and lovingly, just like we did for his sisters.

Figure 36   UNCLE JIMMY TAKES IN A MOVIE WITH HIS NIECE AND NEPHEW.

Our grandkids have discovered how much fun Uncle Jimmy can be. Just recently, Katie's kids went to see the movie *Hotel Transylvania 3: Summer Vacation* with Jimmy. When we asked them if Jimmy liked it, Tommy could hardly contain himself. "You should've seen Jimmy," he said. "Jimmy was cracking up; he couldn't stop laughing and clapping his hands."

Right before our Thanksgiving meal, we have a tradition of sharing something for which we are grateful. One year, after everyone was seated, we started with Jimmy and worked our way around the table. When we got to my granddaughter Tay-Tay, who was three at the time, she smiled and said, "I'm thankful for Jimmy."

Growing up, my mom and I had a great relationship. I always felt that I could talk with her about absolutely anything. The closeness of our relationship carried over to conversations we had about Jimmy. A strong, stubborn Frenchwoman, she had a soft place in her heart for Jimmy; and her relationship with him grew stronger and closer over the years. Jimmy frequently sent "Ma J" cookies and other gifts, visited her whenever he could, and he was the *only* family member who remembered to send her a special greeting card every St. Patrick's Day, Valentine's Day, Halloween, Thanksgiving, and Easter. Clearly, in his own way, Jimmy was a big part of MaJ's life.

Jimmy's grandparents and other family members grew to appreciate Jimmy, and his subtle sense of humor. For example, prior to Christmas, Jimmy knows it's impolite to ask family members, "Am I getting lots of presents?" But whenever he can, he tries to use the words "thank you" as a gentle reminder. For example, weeks before Christmas, he would say, "Thank you for getting me lots of presents."

Jimmy is very adept at manipulating people, and his grandparents were no exception. Onetime, Jimmy cornered his grandpa and handed him a piece of paper and pencil. Then, Jimmy proceeded to ask him to write down each of the following words, one by one:

"We"
"are"

"going"
"to"
"McDonalds"
"today"
"for"
"lunch"

Once Grandpa wrote down each word, Jimmy asked for the paper. He then ran into the kitchen to share his excitement with his gramma and mother. Waving the paper in his hands, Jimmy blurted out, "Look, we're going to McDonalds!"

50 Seeing Privilege

When her husband was diagnosed as a "high functioning autistic," Dr. Marlo Hode, a critical communication scholar at the University of Missouri, became interested in neurological issues for the first time. She asked herself why we assume certain ways of communication are normal while other ways are somehow deficient? Why is there a "right" way to communicate? In Hode's exhaustive research on communication, she noticed a pattern. Individuals on the spectrum tend to be characterized as anti-social and lacking in communication skills.

Dr. Hode thought of her husband. Like many with autism, he experiences difficulty with nonverbal communication. Why is her husband's communication style negative rather than just different? And isn't it true that people who don't have autism, sometimes referred to as neurotypicals, can have serious problems communicating as well? Until her husband's diagnosis, she never thought about these things.[173]

Amy Sequenzia describes herself as a proud, intelligent, non-speaking autistic activist and writer. In her words, she is someone who looks and is very disabled, and needs a great deal of help.[174] Consequently, it's not unusual for people to describe her and other non-speaking autistics as "low-functioning," "mentally retarded," "severe," or "needy." Amy says, "I am a self-advocate and I can type my thoughts. But at the moment I show up with my communication device and an aide, my credibility in the eyes of most neurotypical people is diminished. This is a constant battle…"[175]

Twenty years ago, Jimmy moved into a group home at the same time Katie went off to college. After her first few months at James Madison University, she came back home for a few days. Something was bothering her. She was enjoying all of the independence and excitement that come with being a college student, but she found it difficult to reconcile all of the opportunities she now had compared to those of her older brother. As she saw it, she had privileges he would never experience. The inequality between their lives seemed very real and painful to her. Pat did her best to remind Katie of just how content and happy Jimmy is the vast majority of the time. He didn't feel cheated at all; at least he's never expressed that to us. Pat wasn't sure she got through to Katie, and her heart hurt for her.

As Jimmy's father, I've become increasingly aware of privileges I have simply because I'm not autistic. I didn't earn these privileges, nor am I tuned into them as a general rule. Rather, I have these privileges simply because of genetics and the worlds I inhabit. For example, I had nothing to do with how my brain was wired at birth. Similarly, I live in a society and work in organizations that reward people who think, act, and talk like me.

Jimmy has made our entire family much more aware of certain privileges or assets we have and enjoy. For example, as someone who doesn't have autism and is not disabled like Jimmy, I:

1. Rarely have to wrestle with labels that stigmatize me because of how I look and act.
2. Rarely encounter people who readily assume that I'm incapable of understanding or feeling.
3. Rarely have to deal with people who stare at me for all the wrong reasons.

4. Never have to be reminded to stop talking to myself in a public setting.
5. Can readily change my body language, once I understand how it can interfere with making myself clear.
6. Can easily make friends.
7. Can adjust to new acquaintances and new situations pretty easily.
8. Can easily block out noises, lighting, and other stimuli.
9. Am never treated like a child.
10. Am rarely ignored when trying to get my needs met.

Daily, I take privileges such as the ten I just mentioned for granted. Usually, I don't see or think about them; but when I'm with my son that can change.

Outside our home, people relate easily to my communication style. Jimmy does not share this privilege. At times, the public responds to him as if he's speaking a foreign language, in part because he engages in "irrelevant speech" that many people cannot understand. Some clinicians refer to this as idiosyncratic language, meaning language that's only understood by those familiar with its origins. For instance, while conversing with a friend of mine, Jimmy might allude to something seemingly irrelevant, like "Dr. Teeth," a Muppet character. In Jimmy's mind, there's a connection but my friend is clueless.

Also, Jimmy engages in something called "movie talk." He uses chunks of speech, repeating what he's heard elsewhere. It might be something recent or long ago, such as a script from a movie, a game show, or perhaps a comment he heard from a member of our extended family. To discount his movie talk as meaningless would be a mistake. While it might sound random or irrelevant, it usually makes sense to Pat and me once we figure out how it "fits." Equally important, we know it has allowed Jimmy's language to develop. As Jimmy grows older, his language has become more creative and spontaneous.

In the eyes of many, the way Jimmy talks and acts is often seen as strange, anti-social, bizarre, and nonsensical. Like me, Jimmy carries on conversations with himself, only he does it out loud. As he walks on a crowded sidewalk or waits in line at a store, he tends to say what he's imagining at that moment. It might be calling the airport to arrange a flight, booking a room at a hotel, calling his supervisor at work, or being the game show host on *Jeopardy*.

There are other privileges that are harder to see when we venture out into the community. Institutional privileges are built into the way our society operates or conducts "business." As an example, the design of buildings, noises and lighting in stores and other public venues, rules governing how to behave at work, and the allocation of school resources can all discriminate or put autistic people at a distinct disadvantage. One blogger who describes herself as "30 years-old, female, and autistic," recounts some of her daily experiences with discrimination of this nature. In her blog, "Ableism/Disablism – What it is and how it feels," she writes, "Stores are too loud. Shops are too bright…I cannot attend concerts… The crowds are impossible for me to bear. I could certainly go, if I was allowed to stand in a little secluded area in the front or off to the side. Like those places I sometimes see for people in wheelchairs. But my disability does not seem to qualify me for those."[176]

My growing awareness of privileges, whether they are interpersonal or institutional, enables me to look at my son differently. What Jimmy says and how he behaves are simply different. For instance, Jimmy's answers to my questions are brief and to the point. During a recent conversation, I asked him:

> Daddy: "*What's your favorite meal?*"
> Jimmy: "*Everything.*"
> Daddy: "*Would you rather work or stay at home?*"
> Jimmy: "*Both.*"

I started to probe a bit and asked him these questions again, thinking to myself that Jimmy *has* to have a favorite meal. After all, I do. And like me, I'm sure there *must* be times he prefers to stay home. I then realized I was judging Jimmy by my world, my standards. Maybe his answers reveal he simply wanted to end the conversation, or perhaps he had no preferences. As Jimmy has taught me, there's more than one right answer.

51 Finding Benefit

"Maybe it made me a stronger person because I think I had family members saying things like…'he's just manipulating you…let me have him for a week and we'll sort him out.' …I didn't believe that he needed sorting out, I think he needed understanding." (Jessica) "…you always think you try fairly hard, but we've always got another, I don't know, 10, 20, 30 percent worth of something inside of us. You think 'I'm at my limit right now' and then you rarely are…so it stretches you that way." (Maddie) "It's changed even friendships and relationships too, because some friendships hang on and others don't through times like that and the ones that do are very, very worthwhile." (Danielle)

Jessica, Maddie and Danielle, mothers of children diagnosed with ASD, were part of a study by Nicole Caruso that took place in Australia.[177] Caruso wanted to provide balance, after reading study after study that showed parents of autistic children coping with stress, brought on by being "stretched beyond their limits" and wrestling with social isolation and chronic weariness.[178] Knowing that this was only part of the story, she explored positive changes stemming from raising a child on the spectrum. What she found was evidence of growth in areas such as appreciating life, relating to others, and uncovering personal strength.

Can caregivers lessen their high levels of stress by tuning into benefits that may be linked to raising autistic children? According to Dr. Mark Wetherell, the "Finding Benefit" intervention can help.[179] Each day, Dr. Wetherell and fellow researchers at North Umbria University (London U.K.) instructed participants to take a moment to jot down something positive that goes along with the stress of caregiving. After doing this for a while, caregivers showed significant improvement in their psychological well-being as well as their physical health. Most, but not all, found positives amidst the stress, such as a greater appreciation of the job done by other caregivers.

When Jimmy was about 5, he still had a very difficult time eating in a way that *I thought was appropriate*. Some meals were particularly memorable. For instance, when he ate spaghetti, it seemed as though most of the spaghetti wound up on his lap, face, shirt, pants, table and floor. This grated on my nerves and made meal times a challenge to say the least.

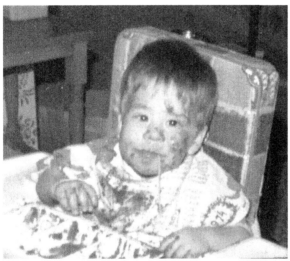

Figure 37 EATING SPAGHETTI WAS A CHALLENGE FOR JIMMY AS WELL AS HIS DADDY.

Fast forward thirty-plus years: I'm still learning to adjust to Jimmy's eating habits. Although vastly improved, he's still learning to monitor himself. Even now, someone has to be present when he's eating to remind him to eat and drink more slowly and chew his food since he has choking issues. When I assume this role, I think it's difficult on both of us. Imagine if you will a middle-aged man (Jimmy) being constantly reminded to eat slowly. After a while, I'm sure he senses the irritation in my voice although I try to hide it. While some meals seem easier than others, I feel for my son. Recently, he ate so fast that he threw up on two separate occasions over the course of a weekend. However, when I remind him to slow down, he never complains. Never. His only response, if he has one, might take the form of a question, "I'm doing a good job?" At that point, he waits for me to respond affirmatively. But he will not stop asking, "I'm doing a good job?" until I answer. If I respond, "Jimmy, I know you're doing the best you can," which he is, that's not sufficient. Rather he needs to hear that he's doing a good job, period.

Using the "Finding Benefit" intervention, I asked myself what positives could be drawn from this experience:

1. I have a greater appreciation for just how difficult it is for Jimmy to eat slowly, *and* how easy it is for me.
2. I'm more aware of stress and my ability to deal with stress. In any situation, I have some say in how much stress I feel and whether I let it affect my interaction with Jimmy or ruin part of my day.
3. I have a newfound realization that sometimes I set the bar too high for Jimmy. When it comes to eating habits, he might very well be doing the best he can, even when it seems to me, he's not.
4. I have a newfound realization that sometimes I set the bar too high for *myself*, especially when it comes to parenting. Like anyone else, there are times when I get stressed out and that's okay. I'm human.

5. I know that if I can hold up and even thrive when trying my best to be a supportive daddy, I can handle anything life might throw at me. Sometimes, I draw on this feeling of empowerment when I encounter bureaucracies that feel like they are designed to "wait me out" and "wear me out." They don't have a chance.

Over the years, I've discovered an inner strength that I didn't know I had.

After a serious fall at 66 years of age, I was looking at a year-long recovery. My pelvis was shattered, held together by an assortment of screws, and I needed help to do most anything. But I never doubted I could do what I had to do in order to walk again. As I began to tackle hours and hours of physical therapy 7 days a week, I said to myself, "With God's help I can do this, and I did." Almost 40 years of raising Jimmy had toughened me physically and mentally.
          --the daddy

Regardless of stress, the "Finding Benefit" intervention allows me to see how my relationship with Jimmy benefits me in other ways. For instance,

- I'm more careful about jumping to conclusions when I see people exhibit behavior that seems illogical or strange to me.
- I've learned that physical appearance and first impressions don't mean much.
- When I'm alone with Jimmy, I'm completely focused. Because passive parenting is *not* an option, my relationship with Jimmy and my other children is stronger.

- Jimmy's communication style makes me a better communicator. For example, I've become a much better listener. And when I'm in a room full of people, I'm more aware of my own body language and more able to shift perspectives.
- Jimmy has become a role model for me. Each day he ventures out into a world that requires him to move outside his comfort zone. When I feel hesitant to try something new, I simply think of my son.
- If it wasn't for Jimmy, I wouldn't be as physically fit as I am. When I'm with him, we exercise constantly. Moreover, maintaining my fitness helps me to deal with the rigors of caring for him along with the rest of our family.
- He's taught me the value of patience. I've learned to remain calm in the midst of chaos, almost to a bizarre degree.
- Constantly trying to tune into Jimmy's needs and feelings has increased the range and depth of my empathy.
- I've discovered it helps to put a different spin on challenges; keeping in mind they're opportunities for personal growth.

When I asked Pat to find what benefit, if any, goes along with the stress of caring for Jimmy, she had to think a while, just like I did. The first two benefits out of her mouth were patience and persistence. She has developed patience "way beyond what she thought possible" in order to survive. Even when she's "dying inside," she's learned to respond with total calmness, at least most of time.

Secondly, the stress of being Jimmy's caregiver has made her much more persistent. His needs, especially as a child, were so profound that she could not and would not accept "No" for an answer.

Now people support me much more than other mothers. I have a lot of people tell me what a good job I'm doing. I know there are a lot of mothers doing a terrific job who don't get to hear that, and I appreciate the fact that I do get to hear it.
        --the mommy

52   Otherization

For Sheri, school times were the hardest. Starting in preschool, she recalls being singled out and "treated badly" because she's autistic. "I was made fun of because I was in my own little world where I'd play with the toys on my own, eat by myself at a lunch table…I was bullied by boys in dodgeball and I was called an easy target because I wasn't good at running from the ball. I would freak out and clutch my head and be all like 'NO DON'T HIT ME BALL' and people would look at me like 'wha?'…I'd come home crying every night because I wanted to be normal, I wanted to have a zillion friends like everyone else…but I just wouldn't speak up even though people DID try to talk to me."[180]

Dr. Paul Sterzing, lead author of a major study on bullying and victimization among autistic adolescents, describes it as a "profound public health problem." Dr. Sterzing, using data from a ten year study of more than 11,000 special education students, found that students with autism are much more likely to be bullied than their non-autistic peers. The data revealed that autistic students in mainstream classes were at greatest risk where their social awkwardness, difficulty communicating, and unusual mannerisms made them stand out.[181]

Tito Mukhopadhyay, born in India in 1989, was diagnosed with autism at a young age. Tito's mother, Soma, is highly critical of something she calls "otherization," meaning "this is us and those are others." To Soma, otherization creates this idea that people with autism aren't like the rest of us. Tito is "just one of us," she says.[182] In his book *The Mind Tree*, Tito shares his dream that one day nobody will "be 'normal or abnormal'

but just human beings, accepting any other human being –
ready to grow together."[183]

I n the summer of 2016, a number of Florida State
University (FSU) football players visited nearby
Montford Middle School in Tallahassee. Because
of the actions of one FSU player, Travis Rudolph, this
visit made national news. When he entered the
school's cafeteria, Travis noticed a boy seated at a
table all by himself. After he introduced himself,
Travis joined Bo for lunch and the two of them
conversed about all sorts of things. After seeing a
picture of Travis eating lunch with her son, Bo's
mother wrote on Facebook, "I'm not sure what exactly
made this incredibly kind man share a lunch table with
my son, but I'm happy to say that it will not soon be
forgotten." Why was Bo's mother, Leah, overcome
with gratitude? After all, a college student merely ate
lunch with her son. But this was different. Leah's
reaction had everything to do with Bo's autism, and
the otherization he encounters on a regular basis.

When children like Bo and Jimmy encounter
social isolation, there's a tendency to attribute it to
cognitive or neurological differences. However, social
interaction is relational, meaning it involves others.
We know that children, such as those in Bo's
cafeteria, tend to form relationships based on "thin
slices of information" or first impressions.[184] Attitudes
persist along with avoidance and rejection simply
because children don't take the time or make the
effort to move beyond negative judgements that arise
almost instantaneously. At age 13, my daughter Katie
shared this very thought in her own words. "I wish
people would get to know others and ignore what they
see on the outside, paying attention to what's on the
inside."

With Jimmy, social difficulties and a feeling of

otherization can also be triggered by the mental states of other adults who rush to judge. To this day, we remember boarding a plane for the first time with seven-year-old Jimmy. A passenger about four rows behind us called for the stewardess. The stewardess asked, "Do you need anything?" "Yes," the passenger replied loudly, "a sedative for that kid up there."

In elementary school, Jimmy knew he was different. As a young child, he was trying to make sense of what was open to him and what wasn't. One day, we happened to drive by an athletic field where youngsters wearing uniforms were playing organized baseball. Out of the blue, Jimmy asked Pat "Is there a team like that for kids like me?" Jimmy didn't ask questions like this. Even though she was momentarily taken aback, Pat gave a straightforward response. "I don't know but I'll look." After asking around, she discovered a local program called "Challenger Baseball," which was open to children with disabilities. Jimmy joined the following spring.

The language we use can bring people together and lessen fear of the "other" or do just the opposite. As the father of a son with autism, I cringe whenever I hear the word "retard." Language such as this shapes how we think and feel about certain people who seem different, including those with autism. To me, the R word is never funny or amusing.

When people call something or someone 'retarded,' what they usually mean is stupid, worthless, or even slightly disgusting. Every time I hear that word it's a hurtful reminder of how some people still view the value of people like my son.
--the mommy

Otherization can invade our reality at times when we least expect it. Especially when he was younger, Jimmy's looks and behaviors triggered smiles, open-mouthed stares, and judgmental looks. The wide variety of reactions from people who didn't know him stems in part from the nature of his disability.

When Jimmy was 6, Pat and I took Jimmy to the World Trade Center in Baltimore. We got off the elevator on the top floor and went through the metal gate to enter the viewing area. Jimmy stayed at the gate for a moment, swinging it back and forth over and over as we paid the admission price and kept our eye on Katie. The noise of metal on metal soon got the attention of the guard who was stationed by the gate. With a scowl on his face and his finger pointed at Jimmy, he issued a sharp reprimand. As we moved Jimmy away from the gate, a family with a young girl in a wheelchair, about Jimmy's age, got off the same elevator on the other side. The guard, who seconds earlier had admonished Jimmy, completely changed his persona. With a big smile, he assisted the family into the viewing area. Yes, our families had children with different disabilities and different needs. But once again, assumptions were made because our child has a hidden disability.

I may feel otherization when Jimmy isn't present. At work, I attended a faculty presentation on cloning. The presenter, who was a biology professor, began talking about the dangers and benefits of cloning. For some reason, he felt a need to reference the comedy film, "Multiplicity," starring actor Michael Keaton. Briefly, the movie revolves around Keaton, who plays a construction worker by the name of Doug Kinney. With the help of a friendly doctor, Kinney clones himself so he can spend more time with his family. To Kinney's dismay, the procedure doesn't work as planned, creating a clone with a low IQ and a child-like persona. As my colleague explains all this, he tries to inject a little humor by sticking out his tongue as far as it would go, crunching his face, and uttering "duh." While those around me laughed or smiled, I was blindsided; totally unprepared for what I just saw and heard. For the next thirty minutes, I remained in my seat but did not process a single word. I knew I had to say something, but I wrestled with what to say, and how to say it.

As the father of an autistic child, responding to otherization is something I do quite often. But at times I second-guess myself and wonder if I should handle what I perceive as a slight or discriminatory act differently. After the presentation, feeling numb and searching for closure, I approached the professor. I shared with him how I felt and why. He was extremely apologetic. It was clear his awareness of other realities did not include mine. Yet, I left wondering if I should have interrupted the presentation, so this could have been a learning experience for students and others in the audience as well.

There are times when my daughters experience otherization, even if people act toward their brother with the best of intentions.

When I'm with my brother in public, people look at him and treat us differently. They often go out of their way to be extra kind to him. But sometimes I think they'd show more respect if they didn't treat him like a little boy but be as kind to him as they would to anyone else his age.
--a sister (Suzy)

I remember playing water polo with a group of teens from our church. Every time Jimmy would swim to get

the ball, they'd back off. They wouldn't even try to get it from him. And whenever he tried to get the ball from them, they'd just give it to him.
--a sister (Katie)

When our son became a teen, his pediatric dentist told us that Jimmy had "outgrown" him. It was time to find another excellent dentist. After asking around and making some calls, Pat selected a dentist who sounded like a good fit. When she and Jimmy arrived at the office, she noticed a big sign on the front door. It read, "Adult and Children's Dentistry – Handicapped Welcome." Yes, this seemed to confirm her choice of *this* dentist.

Upon entering, Pat and Jimmy found themselves in a waiting room. Immediately, they were ushered down a hallway and past an open room full of dentist chairs, most of which were empty. The hygienist led them to a small room in the back. She sat Jimmy down and closed the door. After the hygienist checked and cleaned his teeth, the dentist came in, carefully closing the door behind him. First he looked at Jimmy and then started chatting with my wife. As the dentist discussed Jimmy's oral health, he said, "We don't have the same dental standards for someone like your son as we do for other children."

Pat never went back. And when she got a flyer from Linwood asking what dentists she recommended, she wrote a scathing indictment of this dentist. She also shared this information with her special parents' support group. Clearly, this dentist had a double standard of care for children with and without disabilities. Instead of embracing Jimmy and treating him and his mother with respect, he treated them as others.

Interestingly, Jimmy had his first cavity some thirty years later. Once again, finding a dentist willing to fill the cavity wasn't easy. One after another were distinctly unenthusiastic. Then Pat talked to a dentist who had no experience working with someone like Jimmy, but he was willing to try, listen, and learn. With some coaching from my wife, the dentist did just fine and in the process, expanded his skill-set and developed a new-found appreciation for my son and people like him.

53 Will He Marry?

"Why can't she talk? Why are you only kind to him? Why does he jump so often? Why does she go to a different school? Why does he need help to do this? Why does he act differently?" Tanaka's study, which took place in Japan, found these are some of the most common questions siblings asked about their brother or sister with ASD. Parents who completed Tanaka's questionnaire had one child on the spectrum and one child referred to as "typically developing" (TD). In most cases, TD children found out about their siblings' ASD diagnosis when they were around 9 to 12 years of age, although what parents shared and when it was shared depended on birth order, the total number of children, and the child's age and sex. Most of the time, it was the mother who informed the TD child of the diagnosis.[185]

Before being told, most siblings in this study had already suspected something. As an example, questions about their autistic brother or sister's communication problems, odd behaviors, or need for special education were not uncommon. Discussing the diagnosis with siblings led to other topics such as symptoms and struggles (e.g. s(he) can't talk), causes of autism (e.g. the brain), and positive aspects (e.g. s(he) is honest). Reactions of TD siblings varied a great deal, from "no particular reaction" to "more positive than expected," "sadness," and a "desire to learn more."[186]

In putting together *Brothers, Sisters, and Autism: A Parent's Guide to Supporting Siblings*, the Organization for Autism Research (OAR) asked siblings what they *wish* they had known about their autistic brother or sister growing up. Included in the list are some eye-opening responses, such as "Autism is not contagious," "The way he acted was not my fault," "Some of the things my brother does, he doesn't do on purpose," and "My brother is not the only one who has autism."[187]

Katie, three years younger than Jimmy, was exposed to people who were physically and mentally different very early in life. From birth, Katie would tag along as her mother took Jimmy to special doctors, therapists, programs and activities of all kinds for children with disabilities. Katie ran very deep for a child and was extremely sensitive to people who looked and acted differently.

Recently, my wife Pat recounted an exchange she had with Katie, who was four at the time.

> Katie: *"Mommy, why can't he (Jimmy) use scissors? Why can't he talk like other people? Why won't he play with me?"*
> Mommy: *"Jimmy is handicapped (note: handicapped was an acceptable term at that time). He was born this way. Because he's different; he can do some wonderful things, but not other things."*
> Katie: *"My friend's big brother locked her in a closet and called her names. But Jimmy would never do that to me."*
> Mommy: *"You're right, he wouldn't."*
> Katie: *"He's nicer than other big brothers."*

Discussions with our daughters about their big brother flowed pretty naturally. When they had a question, we made a conscious effort to try to stop everything we were doing, sit down, and talk. As parents, we tried to be as open and honest as possible when our daughters asked us about Jimmy's differences. We didn't "pull any punches" with Katie or with our younger daughter Suzy, who's 11 years younger than Jimmy.

As Suzy got older, she had questions too.

Suzy: *"Will Jimmy ever get married?"*
Mommy: *"Probably not, but you never know."*
Suzy: *"Will he ever drive a car?"*
Mommy: *"I don't think so."*

Clearly, Suzy as well as Katie didn't want to hear that Jimmy would in all likelihood, not get married or drive a car. Both would ask Pat and me these same two questions again and again, hoping for a different answer.

Our daughters found themselves at odds with their mom on yet another subject. Both got around to asking her, "Would you 'fix' Jimmy if you could?" When Pat said "Yes," it made them both angry because they wanted him to stay just the way he was. When they asked for clarification, Pat explained she felt this way because Jimmy couldn't care for himself and therefore needed to depend on the kindness of others for the rest of his life. This conversation continued over the years, and it grew even more complex.

As they asked more questions, we filled in more blanks. Our answers took both their age and development into consideration. For example, when our girls were in elementary school, they asked why Jimmy was "handicapped." We explained that when Jimmy was born, he got stuck coming out of mommy. Because he had such a hard time being born, his brain was hurt. A few years later, we discussed mom's labor and elaborated a bit on the difficulty she experienced giving birth. When we responded, we were very matter-of-fact and unemotional. Typically, Katie and Suzy responded in kind.

At the time Suzy began asking more detailed questions, we had better answers, in part because we knew more. By then, Jimmy had been diagnosed as autistic, so we had much more insight into the reasons for his behavior and what his future might hold. Regardless of how we responded, we tried to emphasize Jimmy's strengths and his ability to understand much more than people might think. Now, our grandchildren are beginning to ask the same kinds of questions. "Why can't Jimmy do this? Why can't Jimmy do that?" Since we talk all the time, questions of this nature are no big deal. We address them openly and matter-of-factly; and in the process, hopefully help our grandchildren remember what makes their Uncle Jimmy so special.

The open lines of communication in our family are no accident. I was raised in a family where I felt I could ask my mom anything, and I did. Both Pat and I work hard at modeling acceptance and love of Jimmy. Growing up, my girls learned about human differences along with the three "R's." As an author, trainer, and professor, I write and teach about understanding and valuing our differences and recognizing all that we share in common. Each day, I brought my work in this field, my principles, and my passion home with me. Over dinner and right before I put my girls down to bed, we talked openly and honestly about anything that was on their minds, including their brother.

54 A Unique Skill-Set

E. described his years in high school as "floating around," academically and socially. One day, his class got a visit from representatives of Ro'im Rachok (Hebrew for "seeing into the future"), a program that helps autistic students prepare to enlist in the Israeli Defense Forces (IDF). To his surprise, E. discovered that two groups of autistic Israelis had already served as IDF image analysts. Even though the selection process was rigorous and the training intense, E. was hooked.

E. is now a corporal in Unit 9900, joining dozens of other autistic soldiers. Per army protocol, he didn't divulge his last name. His job is to look for anything suspicious as he sits in front of a computer screen for eight hours a day, and scans satellite images. Like many with autism, E.'s concentration, attention to detail, memory, and ability to see complex patterns make him an ideal fit for this job. According to a growing body of research, "autistics out-perform neurologically typical children and adults in a wide range of perception tasks, such as spotting a pattern in a distracting environment."[188]

For E. and other autistic members of Unit 9900, communication and getting along with peers is often harder to master than the technical aspects of the job. But the good news is that the Israeli army has an extensive support system in place. During training, autistic candidates meet with therapists to learn how to deal with new responsibilities, stress, and the expectations of serving in the army's highly structured, hierarchal environment. Equally important, they learn to develop basic living skills to allow them to become more independent and self-sufficient. For instance, they are taught how to navigate

Israel's transportation system and what to do when buses to and from the army base aren't running on schedule.[189]

J ob prospects for young adults with autism are not encouraging. In comparison to young adults with other disabilities, those with autism have a lower employment rate. Only slightly more than half of young adults on the spectrum manage to find jobs, and when they do, their pay is less.[190] Without a job, they're more likely to experience financial hardships and less likely to experience much independence.

Unfortunately, the skill-set of autistic adults is underappreciated, despite the fact they may be some of the best workers around. While some employers overlook autistic workers or view them as too much of a gamble, others are well aware of their value. Imagine if you will an employee who:

- *Has an unbelievable work ethic.* If it was up to him, he wouldn't take breaks. If someone tells him he has to miss a day of work or leave early, he gets upset. Working over Christmas, Thanksgiving, and New Year's is no big deal, especially if he's surrounded by holiday music and decorations. He always works extremely hard, regardless of whether someone is watching, and stays focused right up to the end of his shift.
- *Has a great attitude.* Once he's hired, he's not looking to move on for a better job that pays more and provides more benefits. He never criticizes his boss and his constant smile and pleasant demeanor lifts the morale of his coworkers. What's more, he never complains.
- *Is punctual and dependable.* If his employer needs him, he's there; no questions asked. He's someone who takes great pride in always being on

time and makes sure his social life and other commitments do not interfere with work.

- *Is driven to do his job well.* When he's given a task, he's intrinsically motivated. He takes it upon himself to do any task to the best of his ability, no matter what's being asked of him.
- *Doesn't slack off.* He never uses his cell phone at work. He doesn't engage in gossip or small talk. As a matter of fact, he finds it difficult to engage in small talk.
- *Displays honesty and follows rules "to a T."* It is not in his DNA to tell a lie, stretch the truth, or deviate from the rules, as long as he knows the rules.
- *Doesn't mind doing the same thing over and over and over again.* Actually, he likes it.

The person I just described happens to be my son. In an economy in which we desperately need workers who are highly motivated, trustworthy, and possess a wide range of talents, adults with autism are all too often ignored or pigeonholed. And their talents, contrary to popular opinion, are exceptionally diverse. Increasingly, people in the know are proving that hiring people like Jimmy makes good business sense.

When he was an infant, doctors told us Jimmy would never walk normally. Yet, we did not let their prognosis define Jimmy or his future. Jimmy's progress has been remarkable. For the last twenty years he has been walking; pushing shopping carts for a living, five days a week and 6 hours a day. This is the same individual, who as a child was tempted to dart out into traffic if we didn't have a firm grip on him.

Figure 38 JIMMY'S SKILL-SET SERVES HIM WELL AT WALMART.

  As a middle-aged adult, Jimmy is now a taxpayer who has seen his salary and job benefits steadily rise. In Jimmy's words, "I have worked at Walmart for twenty years without getting fired." Actually, he's being far too modest. He's a super employee who has been recognized as Walmart's "Employee of the Month" by his coworkers. At the end of each year, he receives a certificate in recognition of his excellent, hard work.

  I shudder to think what Jimmy's life would be like if he was unemployed.

1. He would be far more agitated. Over time, we've learned that one of Jimmy's greatest allies is regular exercise that is both prolonged and demanding. Jimmy, who is supercharged much of the time, burns up considerable energy pushing shopping carts in all kinds of weather. When Jimmy was much younger, his neurologist remarked, "To ask Jimmy to stay still for a prolonged period of time would be like asking Pat to sit still while someone pricks her with pins all over her body."

2. He would be far more socially isolated. At Walmart, he has friends who know him by name and greet him warmly. He's part of a team that depends on him. In this setting, interaction comes easier for Jimmy because coworkers are constantly reaching out to him or have information that he needs or wants.

3. He wouldn't be earning a salary that makes it possible him to do things *he* wants to do; like take vacations, spoil his sisters, and buy his growing list of friend's expensive birthday cards. As an adult, he manages his money with Pat's help and he decides how it's spent. Jimmy knows that losing his job would greatly change his lifestyle.

4. His confidence and self-esteem would suffer. Walmart provides him with the opportunity to be respected, included, and supported outside of his family and Linwood. He knows his job is important. We have asked him, "If there weren't carts, what would shoppers do?" Jimmy knows the answer without any help from us. "Shoppers couldn't shop." He feels immense pride in helping customers.

5. Certain life skills, such as his ability to follow professional norms and manage social interactions, wouldn't be nearly as well developed as they are.

Matching Jimmy's skills to a specific job was no easy task. He started working in the warehouse at a Caldor department store, emptying trucks and stacking boxes. He would inadvertently drop things, largely due to his lack of motor skills. When Caldor stores shut down, he found work at Wendy's. For some strange reason, he was hired to slice tomatoes. Again, this job wasn't a good fit to say the least. Then, for a period of time, he worked in a sheltered workshop that required long periods of sitting. Finally, Linwood found him a job at Walmart that provided him with a steady source of income and a certain measure of independence.

Jimmy has a unique skill-set. His fitness and strength are assets; so is his preference for routine. If directions are clear and understandable, he will try his darndest to follow them. Like all workers, Jimmy needs someone to remind him of certain things, help him adjust to changes, and lend a helping hand to enable him to learn from mistakes and improve his performance.

Jimmy understands his own limitations. Last year, he was offered the opportunity to work two hours more each day. Even though it would have meant a significant increase in salary, he thought better of it. It was too much for him to handle given the demands of his job. Doing his work and doing it well is a priority for Jimmy. As a matter of fact, he once turned down the chance to go on a Caribbean cruise with his friends at Linwood because it meant missing a whole week of work.

Like many workers with and without autism, Jimmy needs to learn those unspoken rules that determine who gets, keeps, and succeeds in jobs. While these rules may be common sense for many employees, Jimmy needs help and reinforcement in understanding what is and isn't acceptable. For instance, he's learned to control his urge to talk to himself out loud, whether he's pushing shopping carts in the parking lot or resting inside the store.

As someone who's not self-sufficient, Jimmy's ability to thrive on the job is dependent on his support system. For instance, he needs to be reminded to get enough sleep at night; otherwise, he may doze off while standing behind a cart. Once, I picked him up at work a couple of days after Christmas. It was unseasonably warm. Even though temperatures were in the mid-60s, Jimmy was dressed for the mid-20s. He was wearing his knit skull cap, heavy winter coat with five shirts underneath; and long johns under his pants. Making sure this doesn't happen again starts with Pat and me, but it's never easy.

In adulthood, Jimmy encounters new situations, challenges, and people each day. Being able to go off to work every weekday morning is a godsend for Jimmy. The job setting at Walmart provides just the right mixture of structure and independence. His safety in the parking lot remains a concern of ours, no matter what supports are in place. Although he's supervised by a job coach who steps in if there are misunderstandings or problems, he's generally able to work on his own most of the day.

As research shows, Jimmy's ability to work and earn a paycheck each week exposes him to a vast array of opportunities. Walmart and his job coach's expectations are high, but Jimmy has risen to meet those expectations. The diversity of Walmart's employees and customers has been a bonus, accelerating his personal development and broadening his social world.

55 A Jimmy

Dr. Scott Robertson always knew he was different, although he didn't know he was autistic until later in life. At school, he found it difficult to make friends. Other children called him a "retard," and one boy told Scott he was "so weird he shouldn't exist."[191] Today, Dr. Robertson is actively involved in helping adults on the spectrum live more independent, fulfilling lives. It's an uphill struggle, he says. "Most media attention focuses exclusively on young autistic children while commonly ignoring autistic adolescents and adults."[192] "If you ask people on the street about autism, they'll think of children, as though we must disappear as adults."[193]

"All of these young children we are diagnosing and giving early intervention to, they don't stay three, or four, or five (years old)," says Dr. Leann Smith. "Blink-before you know it they're fourteen or fifteen, or twenty-five or thirty, and those individuals on the spectrum and their families need support just as much as three-year-olds and four-year-olds and five-year-olds and their families."[194]

Even though autism is a lifelong condition, interventions for middle-aged and older adults with autism are rarely studied. According to Dr. Rebecca Charlton, we're in the early stages of understanding how autism manifests itself in the later stages of life. Dr. Charlton, who studies aging in developmental disorders, suggests this is because autism is a "relatively new condition…not regularly identified until the 1970s."[195]

Jimmy will somehow manage because of or in spite of what we do. He's a survivor.
    --the daddy

Figure 39 JIMMY AT 40.

J immy is one of a kind, just like each of my daughters. His developmental strengths and shortcomings are unique and unlike any other individual on the autism spectrum. In the autism community, there's a common saying; when you've met one person with autism, you've met one person with autism. The same thing can be said of families who have been personally and profoundly touched by autism. When you encounter one family, you encounter one family.

I can now think of one-hundred reasons why having a son like Jimmy is the best thing that ever happened to me. I still wonder about Jimmy, and what's best for him.
        --the mommy

The weather forecast for today is not a good one as far as Jimmy's concerned. Periods of snow will be arriving this morning, followed by a light wintry mix. Then, there will be a lull, followed by a good chance of sleet and freezing rain. Did I neglect to mention that Jimmy has Special Olympics swim practice at noon today?

It's 8 a.m. Jimmy just called me from his adult living unit. Not surprisingly, he already knew the weather forecast. He wanted to know if swim team practice would be cancelled. His voice was intense, and his questions were pointed; I could ill afford to vacillate. I have learned that answers such as, "I think practice will be cancelled," or "I'm not sure, that depends on your coach" are to be avoided. Being vague simply ramps up his emotional intensity. Consequently, I knew I would have to make a judgement call, even though I might be proven wrong.

In this case, I was fortunate. I had back-up. Allan, his swim team coach, had the foresight to email me the night before. He informed parents and caregivers that he would be keeping watch on the weather and update us on practice early in the morning. I relayed the message from Allan to Jimmy. Did that satisfy Jimmy? Not really, since he was still not certain of his morning schedule nor did he know precisely when Allan would get in touch.

After repeatedly rehashing Allan's email, Jimmy needed reassurance. As he tried to sort out the possibilities, he asked over and over, "Is that right?" Soon, Allan emailed me; practice had been cancelled. I immediately called Jimmy and let him know. Again, Jimmy felt the need to ask a number of questions. "Why was practice cancelled?" "What kind of weather are we having today?" "Why is it dangerous?" "Who is it dangerous for – the athletes, the parents?" "What about next week?" "Will practice be held next week?" "Is this the only practice that will be cancelled?" And so on.

After I got off the phone, I felt exhausted. At that moment, I think I was feeling a bit of "compassion fatigue," or the wear and tear that comes from being there for someone you care about. From start to finish, this entire episode lasted only about 15 minutes, but it had tested my patience. Then I started thinking about Jimmy, and how difficult this had been for him. Trying to put myself in Jimmy's shoes helps me gain much-needed perspective.

What I just described occurred recently; yet it might have taken place more than two or three decades ago. Nevertheless, I see significant progress in Jimmy's ability to deal with uncertainty and cope with changes in his routine. Years ago, for example, Jimmy would have likely "lost it," screaming for a period of time while pounding the daylights out of his napkins. Now, as a middle-aged man, he's much more able to manage his emotions. And he's not at all hesitant to share the pride he feels in this hard-earned ability.

Jimmy demonstrates over and over again that he can indeed achieve realistic goals that at one time seemed unachievable.
--Bill Moss, Executive Director of Linwood Center

Understanding the meanings and implications of a disability such as autism is one thing. Understanding its impact on Jimmy and how he sees himself and the world around him is quite another. To try to explain "a Jimmy" is impossible. As many have said before me, people with autism are the real experts when it comes to making sense of who they are and what it's like to be on the spectrum. As hard as I've tried, recognizing and understanding what Jimmy is thinking and feeling remains a real challenge for me. The best I can do is offer my limited perspective as I grow more attuned to my son and share a few insights from Jimmy and those who know him well.

Not long ago, Pat asked Jimmy a few questions about things I discuss in this book. After he answered, Jimmy had some questions for Pat.

> Jimmy: *"Will this go in Daddy's book?"*
> Pat: *"Yes Jimmy. Is that OK?"*
> Jimmy: *"Sure. Can I have a copy?"*
> Pat: *"Of course."*

Finally, Pat asked him, "What is one thing that you want Daddy to write about in the book?"

> Jimmy: *"How I feel."*

In many ways, it's easier to describe what Jimmy is not, rather than what he is. Clearly, Jimmy is not a tragedy. In a letter to the editor of *The New York Times*, a mother wrote, "My son is not a plague or a tragedy…" and what "really needs to be fixed is how the world looks at autism."[196] Jimmy has never been a tragedy, nor does he live a tragic or lesser life; rather, it's simply a different life. He defies labels; he's not on the low, medium, or high end of the spectrum; nor is he trapped by being on the spectrum. Like me, he's not normal. Actually, using the terms normal and abnormal to describe people, their brains, and their behaviors makes absolutely no sense to me.

Jimmy has a beautiful soul!
--Linda (former counselor at Linwood Center)

Jimmy defies many of the assumptions we hold about autistic people. He's not mentally retarded nor is he a genius. He doesn't talk in a monotone, far from it. He's a people person with a great sense of humor. He likes communicating, and he can be outgoing and empathetic.

Like many of us, Jimmy struggles with the concept of death, especially when it hits close to home. If I inform Jimmy of a close friend's prolonged illness or a family member's serious injury, he'll ask me if that person is going to die. In 2000, one of Jimmy's best friends died. As a volunteer at Linwood, Karen chose to be with our son and regularly took him places. What that meant to both Jimmy and our family is difficult to describe.

Upon her death, Jimmy wrote a letter to her parents:

When I was a teenager Karen took me out places like the mall, riding around, or stayed with my night group. At the mall we looked around at stuff. She took me Xmas shopping for my whole family and for all the birthdays and all the holidays. When she came to Linwood, she would talk to me and my group. When I knew Karen was coming, it was good. Nobody else took me out all by myself. At my Graduation Party, Karen came to visit with me. It was good.
I am sorry she died because she was a good friend. She can't come back because she is in Heaven. I am very sorry. I really wanted to go to Karen's funeral because I wanted to say prayers and say goodbye. Good-bye Karen.
Love,
Jimmy Bucher

Recently, I asked Jimmy, "Are you autistic?" He answered, "Yes." I then asked, "What does that mean?" "Disabled," he said. Then I inquired, "Jimmy, what does disabled mean?" He responded,

"Handicapped." When I asked what handicapped meant, he said, "I don't know, to tell you the truth."

I sometimes wonder what Jimmy would be like if he didn't have autism. To what degree would his values and priorities be different? Would he be as kind and unselfish as he is now? How would he act? Would his personality be radically different? What about his passions?

As much as I try to fully understand Jimmy and how he experiences the world, I know that I never will no matter how hard I try. I have heard some individuals with autism talk about how they feel trapped in their bodies. Does Jimmy feel this way? Does Jimmy feel demeaned by labels and prejudices? Does he resent it when I tell him he should abstain from fiddling with his collection of napkins in certain public places? While I don't know the answers to these questions, I do know this. Even though autism has significantly altered Jimmy's life, it doesn't define him, any more than being a so-called "neurotypical" defines me.

Jimmy is a unique, middle-aged man who can communicate pretty well with those who take the time and make the effort to listen to him. In many ways, Jimmy is no different than the rest of our family. We have our good days and not so good days. We love sports and Broadway musicals. Like me, he is extremely passionate, loves his routine, values his time alone, and occasionally talks out loud to himself. Like my wife, he has a fantastic memory, enjoys music and technology, and loves helping people. He has a distinctive personality and a unique blend of talents. One of his greatest attributes is his ability to bring out the best in other people. Unlike some adults with autism, Jimmy is verbal, can read, use a computer and do basic math. What's more he has a steady job, doesn't drive, and doesn't live independently.

Jimmy has grown into a fine young man who continues to find joy in his life and provide joy to everyone who knows him.
*   --a friend (Trudy Glass)*

Another thing that stands out about Jimmy is his love of life and the miraculous way in which he shares and spreads that love. He has his own way of showing people in his life that he cares deeply about them. Now in his 40's, he's still achieving milestones. And we are still witnessing miracles. Jimmy has never liked hugs. Not long ago, Jimmy hugged his mother for the first time without prompting. Soon thereafter, he walked across the lobby in our church to hug someone with whom he has been building connections. That person happens to be Dana, one of our pastors.

Outside a B&B the summer before last, Jimmy and his mother were walking down a steep hill on some old steps made of railroad ties. Jimmy went first. At one point, he stopped, turned around, and said to his mom, "Watch out! This step is dangerous. You don't want to hurt yourself. It's not a good step." Jimmy could see the step was loose. This was still another miracle, another milestone. Never in her life does Pat remember Jimmy watching out for her like that.

In some ways, Jimmy has not changed all that much. For instance, he remains as hospitable as ever. One of his close friends, the Reverend Judy Emerson, recalls her first encounter with Jimmy when he was a young adult.

I met Jimmy on one of my first few Sundays at Ebenezer United Methodist Church. I had just been

appointed there as the pastor and didn't know anyone in the congregation. Jimmy came through the line to shake my hand after worship and quickly presented me with a greeting card. When I opened it there was a Hallmark greeting for the new pastor and it was signed "Jimmy." From that point forward, Jimmy always remembered me at Christmas, Easter and on my birthday. He would come to church and personally hand me a card and it was always signed "Jimmy."
    --a pastor (Judy Emerson)

While discussing Jimmy, Judy referred me to a passage from the Bible. Hebrews 13:2 says: "Do not neglect to show hospitality to strangers, for by this some have entertained angels without knowing it." As a pastor, she's very aware of the need to show hospitality to others. But she credits Jimmy with teaching her how to *graciously receive* hospitality.

Jimmy's unique in the way he connects with people.
    --the daddy

In an interview with the Autism Support Network, Christina Adams, author of *A Real Boy: A True Story of Autism*, remarked, "A father is socialized to raise a child who's going to grow up to be successful. When they find that there's a possibility their child may not grow up in that mode, it hurts." Fortunately, my socialization has made me very skeptical of broad, exclusive definitions of success that don't begin to do justice to who Jimmy is and how far he's come.

Is Jimmy a success? Curious how he might respond, I asked my 41-year-old son this question. He wasn't sure what it meant to be successful (neither am I) so we talked about it a bit. Grudgingly, he replied, "Yes." When I asked why he felt this way, he mentioned two things; 1) "Working hard and being a good person" and 2) "Being on my own." Personally, I can't think of a better answer.

56   Change for the Better

"My son's autism has made our family life tougher, emotionally and financially...In some sense, this also makes our family closer, because an individual cannot handle the toughness alone." "My marriage is much stronger. We tend to fight less about little things because our focus is on [our son]. We realize the importance of staying together because [our son] benefits from both of our strengths." "My son is, as I have come to realize, my teacher. He is teaching me patience, acceptance, and how to see how much I have, instead of what I am missing." These comments from Dr. Mojdeh Bayat's study point to what can make a family of children with autism stronger or more resilient. Bayat concludes, "The family as a unit, or individuals within the family, often changed for the better, by having learned important lessons which might have life-altering consequences for them."[197]

There is growing interest in family resilience, particularly in families with children who have autism. In the face of extraordinary changes and stressors, families can learn to cope and grow stronger. *Merriam-Webster Dictionary* defines resilience as the ability to bounce back, change and grow from adversity, difficult times, or challenges. Other sources describe it as the capacity to adapt positively to change or develop toughness. Resilience is not only an individual trait; it's a process that involves the entire family *and* their interrelationships. "Developing resilience allows family members to shift attention from oneself to others, develop new coping skills, and adopt a more positive view of life.[198]

Even though my wife and I are both teachers, Jimmy

has been our teacher in many ways. We've learned
so much and changed so much.
      --the daddy

I attended high school in Pleasantville, New York, a suburb of New York City. I fondly remember those years. However, I sometimes wonder if another Pleasantville High School (PHS) student felt the same way about his time at PHS. He was a good student, but I'm not sure how many friends he had. He wore clothes that were out of style, buttoned the top button of his shirts (a fashion faux pas among PHS students at that time), and carried a big black leather briefcase. It seemed as though he was constantly agitated, perhaps that's why he made a habit of picking his skin. Interestingly, he spent time each day asking students, including myself, our birth dates. Then, when he saw me, he would blurt out my birthday with a smile and a sense of pride. Many of us found this behavior kind of strange and a bit humorous. I never ostracized him, but I can't say I ever reached out to him either. He always seemed like he was in another world.

One of the neat or not so neat things about a high school reunion is that it provides an opportunity to go back in time and see how much you and your classmates have changed. When Jimmy was twelve, I attended my twentieth PHS reunion. It didn't take long before Riefe, one of my closest friends, and I started talking about "the good old days" and all the fun we had. Not surprising, we started joking with each other and remembering the crazy things we used to do. Toward the end of our conversation, Riefe said to me, "Buch, you haven't changed a bit." I hesitated and then responded, "Riefe, you have no idea how much I've changed." I didn't go into detail, but my thoughts turned toward Jimmy who was an adolescent at the time.

Later my thoughts turned to my high school classmate who knew my birthday and everybody else's. His uniqueness, including his amazing memory and extreme agitation, remind me of my son. As Jimmy's father, I have a much better sense of what it means to be a social outsider; someone who's perceived as different and is at times invisible to others. In the words of Arturo Madrid, an outsider is someone who "is on the margins," "outside the game," and will "inevitably be seen stereotypically."[199] Over the years, I've become much more aware of social outsiders in our midst, and the importance of advocating for them.

Reflecting back on Jimmy's diagnosis of autism, we were told to temper our expectations. Doctors and professionals let us know in no uncertain terms that raising Jimmy wouldn't be easy by any means. With the exception of Bill Moss, whom Pat and I met during our first visit to Linwood, we were *never* told that raising Jimmy could also be a positive, rewarding experience. Early in Jimmy's life, if someone had the courage to share that message with us, I doubt we would have listened. All of our energy was focused on surviving another day.

When Jimmy was a young boy and we knew almost nothing about autism, I woke up in tears each morning wondering how I was going to get through the day.
--the mommy

Throughout my own childhood and adolescence, one overarching lesson stood with me. If you encounter tough times, don't complain. My dad taught me to address challenges by working harder; somehow that would make things better no matter what. I put this lesson into action when my wife and I came to the realization that Jimmy had a disability. With all of the strength I could summon, I threw myself into my family and my career.

Some of Jimmy's behaviors you're not going to stop. You can guide them, direct them, morph them, but you will not extinguish them.
--the neurologist (Dr. Kenton Holden)

Slowly, I developed the realization that there were things about my son that I couldn't change. For example, I had to accept that as hard as he tried, Jimmy could not tie his shoes, buckle his belt, or button his shirt. His lack of fine motor skills coupled with his minute attention span made these tasks impossible. In order to help Jimmy become more independent, I had to change and adjust my expectations. Following the advice of his occupational therapist, we provided him with slip-on shoes, pants with elastic waists instead of hard-to-manage buckles or hooks, and shirts he could slide over his head. These adjustments allowed Jimmy to do for himself and become more independent.

I never doubted my ability to grow as a parent, nor did I ever doubt the importance of my contribution to Jimmy's growth and development.
--the daddy

Contrary to popular opinion, resilience is not just found in a few, special families. And like many resilient families, we experience doubt and other negative emotions that sap our strength. When I reminisce about powerful lessons we've learned as a family that allow us to come together and grow stronger, many revolve around our children and what they've taught us about life. For instance, we've learned:

1. We can do this. When I say we, I mean our entire family. We close ranks when necessary and understand full well that we have to pool our resources. Furthermore, we're empowered by the belief that if we work together, we can do whatever we need to do regardless of the circumstances.

2. To savor the "miracles." As we have gotten older, our family continues to savor the miracles, no matter how small they may seem to others. A quote from the late Erma Bombeck still resonates with Pat. In discussing what it's like being the mother of a disabled child, Bombeck notes that such a mother will witness miracles and will know it! With Jimmy, we have become aware that nothing is guaranteed. When Jimmy does something for the first time, it's a celebration. When I first saw Jimmy singing with the children's choir at church, I started tearing up. When he first swam "doggie paddle" from point A to point B, it was a miracle. Learning how to roller skate, there was nothing predictable about Jimmy's approach; he must have fallen and gotten up more than fifty times when we took him to the rink for the first time. But to our amazement he somehow managed, with practice, to skate quite well. Again, it was a miracle.

3. To recognize and appreciate all types of diversity. We've developed a newfound comfort zone when it comes to people who

look, think, and act differently. Since childhood, our daughters have been exposed to boys and girls, men and women of diverse social classes, political ideologies, cultural backgrounds, races, religions, lifestyles, and abilities. Eating, laughing, and talking with children who had serious language disabilities, missing limbs, facial disfigurations, and developmental disabilities was no big deal. When Linwood held its annual Christmas party, we all went. Special Olympics was a family affair.

4. To be more patient. Making Jimmy a part of virtually everything we do as a family requires extraordinary patience on everybody's part. When I visit Jimmy, I know I have to prepare myself mentally and ratchet up my patience before I even get there. Pat's patience as a parent carried over to her teaching. Classroom behaviors that would "trip out" other teachers made Pat tune in. Jimmy's patience with himself and his own limitations, especially when he's learning a new skill, is something to behold. With Jimmy, it's important to appear calm even if your insides are exploding. This ability to be in control of one's emotions is a skill we've all worked on and developed because of our unique family dynamics, and we try to model it whenever we can.

As teens, my daughters seemed less preoccupied with their own looks and wants than most girls their age. The lessons they've learned as Jimmy's sisters helped them reevaluate and reorder their priorities and goals in life. Jimmy has further opened their eyes and hearts to a world of pain, misunderstanding, beauty, and potential. And as Katie and Suzy have grown in their faith, they've become more compassionate, caring, and grateful for all they have.

Jimmy's always willing to help people. He doesn't complain when you ask him to do things for you, but he's actually happy to help out. I look up to him as a teacher, a friend, and a brother.
--a sister (Suzy)

Pat is a much different person than she was four decades ago. Before Jimmy was born, she was enamored with achievement and academic excellence. That's what it was all about. Before Jimmy was born, she was insensitive to how others might feel listening to a mother boast about her children. And before Jimmy was born, she was often annoyed by people who took a little too long or weren't efficient enough for her. Pat was also pretty certain that if you worked hard, followed the rules, and did everything right, then nothing bad would happen to you.

I'm happier with myself. I'm much more at ease with the world. I worry less than I used to worry before Jimmy because I found that with faith and family, I can survive whatever comes my way.
--the mommy

No matter how hard or how long the struggle, Jimmy somehow bounces back with a smile on his face. As a little boy, during our annual summer family vacation at New York's Lake George, he wanted absolutely nothing to do with the water or swimming. Even though I was a former lifeguard who taught youngsters how to swim, this was a whole new challenge.

Once we coaxed Jimmy into the lake, he had nothing to hold onto but me. Clinging for dear life, I managed to peel him off me. As I encouraged and helped him move his arms and kick his legs, he screamed "bloody murder." But each day, Jimmy would willingly come into the water only to repeat this scenario. After two weeks, the screaming tapered off somewhat as he became more tolerant of the water. It wasn't too many years before Jimmy was the first one in our family to jump into a frigid Lake George as soon as we arrived.

Now, he absolutely loves swimming. His competence and confidence as a swimmer have improved over time. As I watch Jimmy float in the water and swim backstroke and freestyle as a member of his Special Olympics team, he seems almost relaxed and at peace with the world. I can't help but think back to Lake George.

My wife and I have a rock-solid marriage and a remarkable, giving, and kind family that puts faith and family first.. The incremental changes in our values and priorities over time are now easier for me to see. We continue to have significant physical, psychological, and emotional struggles like anyone else. But our strong faith and family ties have made all the difference. Jimmy, Katie, and Suzy have taught us to never give up, to never lose hope.

Jimmy has enriched your family one-hundred-fold.
    --a grandmother (Jacqueline Bucher)

57   Multiply the Joy

"…my son, he is a joy. He is the life preserver I need when I am drowning in the system…he doesn't initiate conversation unless he means it. *Really* means it. So, when he voluntarily says, 'Mom, I love you!' he means it from the bottom of his little heart. He *feels* it with every fiber of his being every time he says it. They're the most beautiful words I can hear. It took years to hear it…" As the mom of an autistic son, Tracy fights for services and deals with the ignorance of others. As a blogger, she makes time to share the many ways her son brings her joy.[200]

Finding joys in whatever circumstances we encounter isn't enough. Nor is it enough to simply write them down. Rather, research indicates we need to *share* and regularly *discuss* our joys over time. What's more, we grow that much happier and content when we express our gratitude with others, especially those who are supportive and good listeners. After all, we all know what a "downer" it can be when we share a joy and the response is silence, disinterest, or criticism.[201]

As we've gotten older, my wife and I have grown ever more appreciative of all the blessings in our life. Furthermore, we have gotten better at sharing these things with each other as well as relatives, friends, and many in our personal and professional networks, including social media. Not that long ago for instance, my wife found herself talking with her dentist about Jimmy's unique and wonderful relationship with each of his sisters. Around that same time, I had a similar discussion with my mother.

Many of us are hesitant to open up about the joys in our life. Why we feel this way isn't entirely clear. Do we avoid this type of talk in light of all the suffering we see around us? Do we find it easier to bond over complaints than good news? Do the negatives in our life tend to overshadow the positives? As we get used to positive experiences, do they fade into the background?

The neat thing about sharing joy is that it multiplies the more we share it. Certainly, Pat and I think through ahead of time what we're sharing and with whom. Sometimes, we realize it might be better to say nothing. If we think it's appropriate, we try to share our blessings in a thoughtful rather than boastful manner.

My sisters gave me a party with NO parents!
--Jimmy, age 40

A short time ago, Jimmy's sisters took him to Universal Studios to celebrate his 40th birthday. The three of them came to this decision independent of us. The night before the trip they threw him a birthday party. Among other things, he got a "This Guy is 40" tee shirt. The next morning, they got up super early and flew to Orlando for a long weekend. Jimmy had the time of his life.

Figure 40 HAPPY 40TH BIRTHDAY AT UNIVERSAL STUDIOS.

While they were in Florida, the pictures and stories we were sharing with family, neighbors, and friends produced that much more joy. So did the positive responses we got back on Facebook:

> *"Happy Birthday Jimmy!!! What super sisters…they have so much fun with their brother!! Just awesome!!!"*

> *"Woohoo! Enjoy it Jimbo and Happy Happy 40th!"*

> *"SO COOL but wait…Jimmy's 40! How did*

that happen? Katie and Suzy rock!"

Understandably, Katie and Suzy were a bit uncomfortable with all of the attention. When the two of them went to Universal Studios, they just wanted to have some fun with their brother. To quote Katie, "I don't understand why everyone made such a big deal out of it. We certainly don't want people to put us on a pedestal simply because we love our brother."

When they returned, I asked Jimmy what he liked best. He said, "Going clubbing with my sisters." Consider the unique and heartfelt way he expressed his feelings in this note to his sisters.

Dear Katie and Suzy,
Thank you VERY much for all the gifts and taking me to Orlando on my birthday.
I enjoyed staying at the super hotel with my sisters. My room was awesome. And I could sleep every night. The pool was awesome too. I liked swimming alone and I loved the water slide. And I loved the beach spot and the sand on the beach.
I enjoyed all the roller coasters at Universal Studios. I enjoyed all the Harry Potter rides because I could see where everybody was going. I enjoyed going fast. I enjoyed riding the Hulk. It went fast and it made me feel happy, yeah.
I enjoyed all my meals. I loved going out in the dark at night. Thank you for all the fancy drinks at the bars and restaurants.
Thank you for having me by myself. I loved being without mom and dad and just you guys.
Thank you for making me a Birthday iPod. I enjoyed it very much. I loved it all.
It was the very best birthday I ever had.
Love,
Jimmy

Figure 41 READY TO HIT THE PARK IN ORLANDO.

If research is indeed correct and sharing gratitude makes us that much happier, then Jimmy must be one of the happiest people I know.

Gayle got to know Jimmy quite well when she served as our pastor. Somewhere along the way, he chose her as a friend and she became a recipient of his joy. She fondly remembers that when Jimmy started coming to church with his family, "pleasant surprises" began to occur. Gayle recalls:

He started sending me cards for my birthday and other holidays. His cards were always kind and appropriate. I learned that card shopping for his friends and family was something he enjoys doing with his Dad and suggested that Rich was the one to select the cards; to which Rich replied, 'It's all Jimmy.' When I had surgery and Jimmy found out, he insisted that his mother immediately deliver flowers and a card. And as usual, the message inside was, love Jimmy B.

--a pastor (Gayle Annis-Forder)

Julia Bascom describes herself as an autistic woman, writer, and self-advocate. In her book, *The Obsessive Joy of Autism*, Julia describes one of the ways she expresses joy. "Sometimes being autistic means that you get to be *incredibly happy*. And then you get to *flap*. You get to perseverate…flapping your hands *just so* amplifies everything you feel and thrusts it up in the air."[202]

Jimmy embodies joy and shares it in his own unique way. During church service, Gayle would look forward to Jimmy's enthusiasm as he directed the choir from his seat in the third pew. Feeling the vibes from the choir, he'd flap his hands to the sound of the music, all the while smiling gleefully. After the service, he was sure to tell Gayle when he'd be coming to church in the weeks ahead.

But that's not the end of the story. Shortly thereafter, Gayle attended the annual conference for United Methodist clergy and laity. Its theme was "Celebrate the Joy." Throughout the conference, she thought of children of God who are bearers of joy. High on her list was Jimmy. Since then, she's shared her love for Jimmy with people in the community. Gayle continues to celebrate that joy with others and thanks God for bringing Jimmy into her life.

Over the years, Jimmy has taught me so much. I thank God for Jimmy's amazing capacity for joy. Jimmy's joy bubbles up in the love he shows his family, the way he cares for friends, and his delight in a job well done.
--a pastor (Gayle Annis-Forder)

58   Perspective

As a child, Archie was extremely hyperactive and difficult to manage. He didn't seem interested in others, could hear but couldn't speak, and would wander off. He required constant watching. Seeking medical advice, Archie's mother took him to see the family doctor. Harriet, Archie's sister, recalls her mother coming home from the doctor's appointment in tears. The doctor diagnosed 5-year-old Archie as insane and recommended he be sent to a state insane asylum. According to Harriet, "My parents had to go before the county court and he was committed by the court. After that, it was just as if he had died. We never spoke of him."[203]

Archie came from a very intelligent and loving family. He spent the better part of his life "written off" by professionals, moving from institution to institution. Housed with adults, he had no friends and no toys. Since Archie was considered untrainable, nobody tried to teach him even basic skills such as how to dress. Often, he was moved without his family's knowledge. In one state-run institution, Archie bit a staff member for some unknown reason. In order to immediately put a stop to this behavior and ensure it would never happen again, all of his teeth were removed.

After her brother was institutionalized for more than *seven* decades, Harriet happened to read an article on autism by Dr. Ruth Sullivan that made her question Archie's diagnosis. Harriet asked Dr. Sullivan, co-founder of what is now the Autism Society of America, to interview Archie. Harriet was right; Archie was not insane or retarded; rather, he was autistic. With Dr. Sullivan's assistance, Harriet secured Archie's release from a mental hospital. He was admitted to a group home where he lived with five other autistic adults. There he learned to take care of himself, tend to his own flower garden, and open up to people. Also, Archie enjoyed attending church, going to the park, and taking in country music concerts. He died at the age of 83.[204]

R eflecting on the past can provide much-needed perspective. The U.S. and other parts of the world have a long history of misdiagnoses and inhumane treatment of people with autism. When Archie Casto was first institutionalized, there was no such thing as a diagnosis of autism. Deemed a "clinical idiot," he was warehoused with other children who were considered hopeless social misfits, burdens on society and their families. As Archie grew older, his skills regressed. Institutional staff kept him alive, but that was about it. Overcrowding and limited funding meant education, therapy, and any hope for some measure of independence was a pipe dream.

During the better part of the twentieth century, autism was mistakenly identified as childhood schizophrenia, mental retardation, or perhaps dementia. One hundred years ago, doctors would have in all likelihood described my son as an "ignoramus" or "idiot," "feebleminded," or perhaps a "lunatic." Long before a diagnosis of autism was even possible, doctors might have latched on to the term "attachment disorder" to describe Jimmy's inability to form "normal relationships" with primary caregivers such as Pat and me. As his parents, we would have to accept blame for Jimmy's "social deficits." Like others with intellectual disabilities, there's a good chance he would spend part or all of his life in a psychiatric hospital, perpetually drugged for some condition he never had. To make sure he didn't have any children, Jimmy might have been forced to undergo sterilization After all, the sterilization of residents in state-run institutions was perfectly legal in many states in the early 1900s. Advocates of sterilization saw it as necessary to protect society from defective or "weak genes."

Early in Jimmy's life, medical misdiagnoses and recommendations were still all too common. Autism was supposedly a real rarity, or at least that's what we were led to believe. Those who were diagnosed were still largely hidden from public view. Had we listened to one doctor in particular, there's a good chance Jimmy would have been institutionalized at a young age. A specialist of great renown encouraged us to put Jimmy away and "get on with our lives." Fortunately for Jimmy, his family, friends, and community, we didn't listen.

When I was a student at Colgate University in the 1960s, I remember taking an education class. Part of the course requirement was doing field work at various sites. I chose to travel to Utica, New York each week and work with patients at Utica State Hospital, formerly called the New York State Lunatic Asylum at Utica. The hospital, one of the first state-run institutions for the mentally ill in the U.S., was opened in the mid-1800s.

For some reason, I remember being the only student in my class who wanted to work with patients in the adult rather than the children's ward. I use the word "work" loosely. The ward, whose walls were stark white; seemed cold, impersonal, and sterile. Patients watched TV, took their allotted meds, played board games, and passed a great deal of time just ambling around and staring into space. Although I tried, striking up a conversation with them was challenging to say the least. Smoking was allowed, even encouraged. After all, it helped patients occupy themselves and gave them something to do. Most of them would smoke their allotted cigarettes right down to the filter, often burning their fingers. To keep this from happening, much of my time on the ward was spent removing lit cigarettes from their fingers. A short while after I completed my field work at Utica State Hospital, they shut it down and transferred patients to other facilities.

In the mid-1800s, Dr. Amariah Brigham, Utica State Hospital's first director, didn't care for the standard practice of using chains to restrain patients. Instead, he invented something called "The Utica Crib." The dimensions of the Utica Crib were similar to a regular bed, about six feet long, three feet wide, and one and one-half feet deep; but with a hospital mattress at the crib's base that left only about 12 inches of space for the patient. The Crib, with slats on the side, a mattress on the bottom, and a hinged top that could be locked, allowed a small staff to control patients and keep them from wandering off during the day and night. Sometimes it was used for hours at a time and sometimes for days. One woman at an Illinois institution was confined to the Crib for fourteen years. While some physicians touted it as safe, therapeutic, and practical, critics described the Crib as barbarous, even though it was considered an upgrade from straitjackets and leather straps used to tie patients to their beds. In 1887, Utica State Hospital removed all Utica Cribs.[205]

Not long ago, I came across a blog titled, "Restraining Wanderers – A Little History." Written by autistic advocate Savannah Logsdon-Breakstone, it elaborates on the abuses of the Utica Crib *and* its relationship to wandering and autism. One of the main functions of the Crib was to keep patients from wandering off. The "most common image of a wanderer is an older adult with dementia," Savannah says, but like many with autism, Savannah has a history of wandering.[206] Thinking back to patients hidden, housed, and abused in hospitals, asylums, and training schools for the mentally ill, how many were in fact autistic and wanderers who had no business being there? How many were locked in a Utica Crib, scarred for life?

Figure 42 THE UTICA CRIB. (by permission of the HRSH Historical Museum)

Children diagnosed with autism today have so many more opportunities than Archie Casto or even Jimmy had when they were young. Autistic children are much less likely to be neglected and dumped somewhere as a matter of convenience or because appropriate services and supports aren't available. But it's a mistake to think that adults like Archie Casto, who was diagnosed with autism much later in life, are a thing of the past. Today, the reality is that very little is known about autism and aging in the U.S. and abroad. Researchers are still discovering adults and senior citizens who are autistic but have never been diagnosed, and in some cases, those who have been misdiagnosed and aren't autistic at all.[207]

59 When We're Gone, Then What?

Siblings find it is next to impossible to talk with their parents about it. Avoiding this topic creates more stress and makes it harder to discuss. Frustrated by her mother, one sibling (Siobnan) made it her business to find out what she needs to know. "...at this stage, yes, my mother will get upset, but really I don't care anymore if she wants to cry through the whole conversation, because it needs to be addressed." When siblings want to talk about this topic, parents often react with "anxiety and distress." What topic do siblings and their parents dread discussing? Not terribly surprising, it's what happens when parents can no longer provide support for their autistic child.[208]

Research shows every family's situation is unique. A sister, for example, shares her thoughts about caring for her 10-year-old autistic brother (Mitch). She tells her mom, "I don't really want to do this all my life when I'm older; when I'm married, have kids." Sensing her daughter's anxiety about the future, her mom tries to offer reassurance, saying, "That's why we try to help and all that good stuff...You're supposed to have your life and he's supposed to have his. We're not saying blow him off, but keep in touch, have help, be there once a week."[209]

However, siblings do not necessarily share the same personalities, priorities, and perspectives. When Marion, the older sister of a child on the spectrum learned she was accepted by Harvard University, she wasn't sure she wanted to attend. Marion seriously considered turning down the offer, since as she put it, "I couldn't abandon Elena when I was literally my sister's keeper."[210]

Regardless of their future roles, siblings are in dire need of more information. "I'd love to go to a workshop with other people who have siblings with Down syndrome or autism or any sort of disability because we're at the next stage now of his life…So I think it would be great to have even an information day about, you know, what should we be doing now." This same study found siblings took issue with overprotective parents. For them, they wanted to care for their brothers and sisters with special needs; and they did not see this responsibility as a burden.[211]

One of the biggest mistakes I made as a young mother was worrying about Jimmy's future.
        --the mommy

As my wife and I ease into retirement, we've gradually cut back on Jimmy's family visits. Once Jimmy moved into a Linwood adult living unit when he turned 21, one of us or one of his sisters made sure to visit him virtually every weekend. Given Jimmy's penchant for routines, changing something that's been in place for years has never been easy. We have gradually decreased our visits, making sure Linwood staff gets him involved in meaningful activities the weekends we don't see our son. In so doing, we are trying to prep him for the fact that we won't be able to visit him every weekend forever.

The death of a loved one is difficult for all of us, but for someone with autism it poses extraordinary challenges. So too can other major life events, such as divorce, retirement, and moving, all of which can seriously mess up one's routine and emotional equilibrium. When a mother shared with me that she had recently divorced, she noted just how difficult it was for her autistic son to comprehend what took place and cope with feelings of confusion and anxiety, to the point where he contemplated suicide. Barry Prizant, a clinician who helps families "reframe their experience with autism," explains that the neurology of autistic people is different but not abnormal. But this difference makes it exceptionally difficult for them to stay emotionally and physiologically regulated in the midst of a life-changing event such as this.[212]

While our marriage is as strong as ever, I sometimes think about what will happen when we're gone. However, my wife recently confided in me that she no longer "goes there." The reason is simple. She wasted a lot of time in the past; the things Pat worried about early in his life took care of themselves. Now that he's in Linwood's adult program, the future is clear to her: "God will take care of Jimmy according to his plan."

However, Pat and I fully understand we can't totally ignore the future. Rather, we must plan as best as we can and "pray with our feet." Because of Linwood, we know who will care for Jimmy. Because of his sisters, we know who will manage his finances, who will be there for him no matter what, and who will make sure his needs are met and "love him to death."

Due to his lack of independence along with his inability and reluctance to self-advocate, some questions still linger in my mind. Will caregivers have the patience to listen to his endless stream of questions and pick out the important stuff? When he fails to disclose he's seriously sick, who will pick up on that and how long will it take? Who will take long walks with him when he feels the need to burn some energy? Who will monitor the small stuff that can become big stuff, like whether he's getting the help he needs to brush and floss his teeth? How will Jimmy adjust as his routines change and his physical abilities diminish? Who will be there to intervene when he encounters issues at work? How will he spend his days when he retires, and so on and so on?

Fortunately, Jimmy is able to make certain key decisions for himself. At one point, as Jimmy neared age 21, we considered declaring him "incompetent" so we could become his legal guardians. Bill Moss, Linwood's Director, advised us not to take this action. He reminded us that declaring Jimmy "incompetent" would not allow Jimmy to make decisions for himself that he's capable of making. As limited as his abilities might be, Jimmy is able to verbalize his basic needs and wants. For example, Jimmy is able to decide and express where he wants to live, where he wants to work, who he wants to care for him, and who he doesn't want to care for him. We don't want to take these critical choices away from him.

Because autism is a lifelong disability, Jimmy will require extensive support for the rest of his life. My wife and I understand and appreciate the absolutely critical role his sisters play in Jimmy's development and care. However, we've been very conscious of trying not to put too much responsibility on the shoulders of his sisters and their families. After all, they have their own lives and their own families.

Whatever we do, we've always tried to ensure that all family members are taken into consideration. Recently, we started revisiting the idea of wills, Jimmy's future at Linwood, and his financial situation once we die. Based on our experiences, it's a very good idea to seek legal advice if possible, and not just from any attorney. Ideally, the attorney should be well-versed in planning for special needs children and adults, an area of the law that can be complex and challenging. In Jimmy's case, it's a matter of making sure he gets whatever inheritance we leave him without losing his benefits.

Soon after we started this process, Katie

started asking questions about Jimmy's wants and needs once he gets older, his rights, and how much say she and Suzy will have when we're gone? Emotionally wrought questions such as these take on a greater sense of urgency now that Pat and I are getting on in years. Needless to say, this is never an easy conversation.

Understandably, numerous questions from Katie and Suzy dealt with finances and elderly care. "When Jimmy can't work anymore, how will his financial situation change? What about a special needs trust, can that be spent on him? What about when he's old and needs to be cared for differently?" The fact that Pat and I are learning too, both in terms of the big picture and the details of what happens when we're gone, makes this discussion that much more difficult. But fortunately, communicating openly and honestly with our daughters about Jimmy is nothing new.

As we plan for the future, it's reassuring to know that our daughters love spending time with their brother and vice versa. High on their list of fun things to do are getaways, eating out, church, sleepovers, shopping, ice-skating, amusement parks, or just 'chillin.' Even our grandchildren have developed a very close bond with Uncle Jimmy. The stereotype that people with autism would rather be alone and avoid human contact whenever possible certainly doesn't apply to Jimmy. When we depart from this world, we have peace of mind knowing that his sisters will continue to watch over his needs, whatever that might entail.

I have never thought about moving away. He's a Bucher, and this is my life.
    --a sister (Suzy)

60 Thankfulness and Gratitude

As your autistic child grows up, the seemingly endless demands, stress and challenges *can* make it that much harder to be grateful. However, studies show that parents do indeed find positive meaning in their child's disability. For instance, they tend to appreciate little things more. Often, they experience a spiritual awakening or strengthening. Moreover, scientific analysis reveals the perceptions of parents who have children on the spectrum impact a family's ability to come together and develop a "greater appreciation of life in general."[213]

Research finds reasons for gratitude vary. For example, one mother comments, "Autism has made me more aware for my reason and purpose of existing." Trying to make sense of it all, a father said, "…I feel if there is a God, he meant to create my son and gave me the honor to be his father."[214] In another study, parents talked about appreciating the "little things" and not taking things for granted. One mother wrote, "He has made us 'see the light' and reprioritize."[215]

The word gratitude comes from the Latin word gratia, meaning grace, gratefulness, or graciousness. *Webster's New World Dictionary* defines gratitude as "a feeling of thankful appreciation for favors or benefits received." Some researchers who take issue with this definition argue that gratitude and thankfulness aren't quite the same. For instance, Professor Paul Mills says gratitude isn't that specific;

rather, it's broader, deeper, and goes to our very soul.[216] To illustrate, I may be thankful for a warm house or a beautiful day. But a feeling of gratitude tends to be more permanent; it exists regardless of what I have or don't have at any given moment.

The latter definition of gratitude is something I feel each and every day. However, my gratitude can certainly waver or temporarily evaporate under the strain of a crisis or one stressful event after another. For me, praying and expressing my genuine appreciation to others, including Jimmy, helps me foster a state of being what Dr. Robert Emmons might describe as an "attitude of gratitude." Being grateful, according to Dr. Emmons, is a choice which allows me to focus on others rather than myself.[217] When I feel exhausted and demoralized, gratitude has the power to energize me and help me cope.

During the first twenty years of Jimmy's life, feeling gratitude was difficult but necessary for my wife. As she confided in me, "His autism was a living nightmare. I survived by seeking out those things for which I was thankful." Deep in her heart she felt eternally grateful that we had a Jimmy, knowing full well we almost lost him five different times.

To this day, my wife and I don't take for granted that Jimmy is such a loving, joyful person. Indeed, Jimmy is one of the most thankful people we know. Furthermore, he has a wonderful ability to express his thankfulness for almost anything. "Thank you, daddy, for taking me out to lunch." "Thank you for buying me grapefruit." "Thank you for vacuuming my room." "Thank you for finding my favorite TV station." "Thank you, mommy, for giving me an extreme makeover" (note: this entails a face and neck shave, haircut, and spray gel). After walking through a state park in western Maryland on a hot and humid summer day, I looked at Jimmy. He was sweating profusely, and his tee shirt was soaked with perspiration. I said kiddingly, "Jimmy, you sweat like a pig." His straight-faced response was simply, "Thank you."

Jimmy is grateful for everything; for where he is and what he's doing at any moment.
--the mommy

Another way in which Jimmy expresses his attitude of gratitude is through his thank you notes. Very early in life, Jimmy got into the habit of writing thank-you's. Both Pat and I grew up in families that constantly reminded us to express our thanks. When he was five, Pat special-ordered a rubber stamp. While Jimmy could not write at this age, he could use this stamp. A little boy appeared on the stamp along with Jimmy's name. He used this stamp to sign his notes after dictating them to us.

Figure 43 JIMMY'S STAMP

As an adult, Jimmy still finds such joy in writing

these notes of thanks to anybody who does anything for him. For example, he wrote to the person who checked him in at Mandalay Bay Hotel in Las Vegas, simply because she was so nice to him. He thanked Deanna, the University of Maryland employee who helped us get tickets to a football game. And he sends thank-you's to each of his Special Olympics coaches after the season ends. The list goes on and on and grows each year.

Jimmy has an uncanny way of expressing his thanks. Two of his thank you notes follow; one to his uncle Jerry and one to his sister Suzy.

Dear Uncle Jerry,
Thank you VERY much for taking me on your boat and taking me behind your boat to go tubing. I enjoyed going over the high waves very fast and holding onto the bar zooming. Thank you for speeding.
Love,
Jimmy B.

Dear Suzy,
Thank you very, very much for taking me to Disney World. I had a blast riding all the buses to the drop-offs, and especially the ferry boat ride to Magic Kingdom. The boat ride was awesome. The Rock n Roller Coaster was outstanding and also Space Mountain. And I was not afraid while we were riding it splitting up.
The Tower of Terror was fabulous and I was not afraid of the movie at all. I had fun riding the slide with you.
The Muppet 3d movie was excellent and I enjoyed my glasses. Yes it did – it made me laugh. I enjoy

having you as my sister. I enjoyed the trip with you. I love you very much.
Love,
Jimmy B.

In so many ways, this book is an expression of gratitude. To paraphrase my daughter Katie, we have learned to appreciate the uniqueness of our family and the gifts that Jimmy has given us. When gifts are difficult to acknowledge and appreciate, my wife and I find it helpful to go back in time. For instance, when Jimmy is bombarding us non-stop with questions, we recollect when we weren't sure if he would ever talk. There were times when I caught myself looking longingly at my neighbor's son helping out with raking leaves or shoveling snow off the driveway, two things Jimmy cannot physically do because of his lack of motor control. Then I think of all those times when Jimmy offers to help and cheerfully do whatever he can at a moment's notice.

If Pat and I experience a lengthy delay at an airport, it's pretty easy to keep things in perspective. We vividly remember a five-hour delay we had at Fort Worth airport years ago, with Jimmy (age 7) and 3-year-old Katie in tow. After that experience, during which Jimmy required nonstop "entertainment" and attention to avoid a meltdown, and Katie somehow managed, any layover now is no big deal. Over the years, emergency care has taken on a whole new meaning for Pat and me. One day soon after he was born, Jimmy stopped breathing while he was breastfeeding. After giving him mouth-to-mouth resuscitation, Pat called 911. When she entered the emergency room with Jimmy, nurses grabbed him and ran. A life and death situation like this colors your perception of an "emergency," and why it might be necessary to wait for extended periods of time in an emergency room.

We're so grateful he's alive. How many times did we (Rich and I) sit waiting in a hospital thinking Jimmy might die?
    --the mommy

As Jimmy's parents, both Pat and I see the world differently, and that's a blessing. As an example, Jimmy has increased our capacity for joy, even in the smallest things. We have learned to be grateful for what we have and who we are. Jimmy could care less about physical attributes, material things, and popularity. He isn't hung up on what others think about how he looks or the way he acts.

Our son has made it possible for us to adjust and connect with others in a deeper and more meaningful way. Because of Jimmy's generosity, we have learned about the joy of giving, with absolutely no expectation of getting something in return. He has provided us with the motivation to understand people better and move past those superficial labels that have a way of dividing us. In essence, Jimmy has provided us with a far greater understanding of what it's like to be treated as different; and what it's like to be embraced and accepted unconditionally.

Because of Jimmy, I developed an appreciation for special children and adults. So many are kind, patient, noncompetitive, and sincere; so many have the best human traits.
    --the mommy

Because of my Jimmy, I run a lot deeper. A 'meaningful life' now means something quite different to me.
    --the daddy

61 The Journey Together

My name is James Bucher. My birthday is October 26, 1976. I live at Linwood. I live with Pom and Jon and Linda and Aaron. I like to watch game shows, Muppet Shows, Full House, and Sesame Street on YouTube. I like to listen to Sirius Oldies on 5. I like to watch videos, Muppet Show with Jim Henson, Disney, and Full House on DVD and all. On the TV I like to watch the Game Show Channel. I like to swim and kayak with Special Olympics because I'm a good swimmer and a good kayaker. I also like the picnics and award ceremonies.

I work at Wal-Mart. I push carts, so people can have them. I like all the people there and I stay away from people if needed. I like working outside. I've been working there for a long time [since 2000]. I like it when they leave me alone to push my carts. I love the holiday decorations at Wal-Mart. I like buying greeting cards for my sisters, parents, and family and friends too there. I work in all kinds of weather. Sometimes I need to wear long johns. It's very hot in the summer. I wear my regular Walmart hat, work gloves, and sunblock and drink lots of water. The weather does not bother me at all.

I like to go on vacations. I like to go on whatever is available. Some of my fav vacations are Deep Creek (Maryland), Ithaca, Disney World, Universal Studios. I like very scary rides. I love to go to Broadway shows. What I like best is chill: sometimes alone and sometimes with other people.
--Jimmy, age 41

I love being a father. I love watching my children grow; knowing I had something to do with it. I love each of them and make a point of telling them that every chance I get. I marvel at the kindness, caring, and warmth they show each other, friends, and complete strangers. In today's world, I hear some parents complain about the drudgery of being a parent and the toll it takes on you. Certainly, I'm not immune to those kinds of feelings, but they're short-lived and superficial. Deep down, there are few things in this world that give me as much pleasure and contentment as being a parent.

No word or phrase sufficiently captures our family's journey and growth since Jimmy was born. One dictionary definition of journey is "progress from one stage to another." As we all know, progress or growth has its ups and downs. While positives may be hard to find in the literature on autism, they are readily apparent in the life of each member of our family. Our journey involves things that can be difficult to capture over time, such as the development of character, humility, knowledge, awareness, and appreciation, as well as the ability to bring out the best in oneself and others.

Hardship, pain, and suffering have been part of the growing process as well. So has acceptance. In one new study, fathers of children on the spectrum describe their experiences as a "path," a journey with "milestones along the way." During the journey, these fathers found it difficult to make sense of their experiences. But once they reached "the point of acceptance," they could look back, express their frustrations and feelings of grief along the way, and adopt a more positive perspective.[218]

I enjoy being "totally there" for my son and the rest of my family. While it can be a slow, exhausting grind, it's also who I am and why I love getting up each morning. For my wife and me, what has worked for us is maintaining an unbelievable work ethic, making our marriage and family a priority, consuming knowledge and using it whenever possible, broadening our support system, and strengthening our relationship with God.

I remember reading a handwritten storybook my wife put together for Jimmy when he was young. Recently, I found it buried under videos and keepsakes in his room. *Jimmy and His Tonsils* had the look of a book that was read many, many times. Created by my wife, it helped to lessen Jimmy's anxiety once we told him that he needed his tonsils out. It begins, "Once there was a boy named Jimmy. He was a good boy who liked to read books, watch TV, and play with his octopus…" As I turned each page, I read more and more about Jimmy and the fact that he kept getting strep throat.

Written in plain simple language, *Jimmy and His Tonsils* took our son through a difficult, scary process. It brought back memories of going to the hospital, checking Jimmy into his own room, and watching him ride down the hall in "a special bed with special wheels." Once in the operating room, Dr. Alderman put on a "black mask with a balloon. He told Jimmy to try to blow up the balloon. Jimmy put the mask over his mouth and nose and breathed in and out. Soon he was asleep, and Dr. Alderman took out his tonsils."

Next came the recovery. "When Jimmy woke up, his throat hurt a lot. He was thirsty, but it hurt his throat to drink anything. The nurse said he had to drink, or he wouldn't get better. Jimmy felt mad but drank the coke, so he would get well and go back to sleep. The next day he felt much better, had lots of ice cream, and went home."

Researching, writing, illustrating, and then

reading and rereading *Jimmy and His Tonsils* to our son is one small but significant example of my wife's limitless love, patience, and unselfishness. Yes, it took her a great deal of time to put it together, but that didn't matter. After all, her main motivation was to respect Jimmy's right and need to know, and calmly address the questions and fears that kept spilling out of him.

To be honest, creating this book (Jimmy and His Tonsils) was not totally unselfish on my part. I needed it to survive.
     --the mommy

In the course of writing *A Mommy, A Daddy, Two Sisters, and a Jimmy*, I've felt a tremendous sense of debt and responsibility. As Katie recently shared, the subject matter is "so raw, so personal, and so important." Parents, scientists, activists, and other pioneers, some autistic and some not, have made it possible for Jimmy and our family to enjoy the life we have. Without Linwood, we might still be looking for much-needed structure and support in Jimmy's life. In particular, we are indebted to Tai Mitchell, a counselor at Linwood who for more than twenty years provided our son with the discipline and care he needed, and the guidance of a "big brother." We love you Tai.

Throughout, I have tried to do justice to my amazing family and tell their stories as truthfully as I can. This book was made possible by their patience and understanding, and in particular, the ability and willingness of my wife and daughters to go back in time and relive memories, both pleasant and excruciating.

Because autism is a lifelong disability, active parenting is still very much a part of our lives; whether it's answering his multiple daily phone calls, making certain he's communicating with Linwood staff about his basic, daily needs, visiting, or going on a trip.

To celebrate Jimmy's 42ⁿᵈ birthday, we took him on a cruise (his first) to Bermuda; another new leap of faith. The first three days were magical. The ship had shows, roller skating, bumper cars, and five pools. He did it all. The ship was full of spectacular, high-tech visuals and sounds. He loved it all. Once we arrived in Bermuda and he got off the ship to go to the beach, he looked around and said loudly, "This is the life time!!" We totally agreed.

Then on the fourth day, we went to the dolphin park – at Jimmy's request. He was a totally different person. He was uncooperative and said "NO" loudly while waving his arms to each and every little thing he was asked to do. And at each step, Rich and I were fighting to control our exploding emotions and frustrations as we gently and kindly encouraged him, until he acquiesced. By the end, he had gone in the water with the dolphins, fed them, and petted them. He was very proud of himself. Rich and I were absolutely and completely drained. From that time on we felt like we were walking on eggshells until we were home.

Figure 44 SWIMMING WITH THE DOLPHINS.

In some ways I felt like this trip was a microcosm of our journey with our son; extraordinary joy, satisfaction, and a powerful sense of accomplishment as Jimbo goes way beyond his comfort zone with fantastic success. Then, when we least expect it, there is a sudden turn of events and our lives become extraordinarily difficult, exhausting, and emotionally painful for a while. It's just our life. And it's not only a good life, it's a spectacularly wonderful life. And it's all part of our ongoing journey.
    --the mommy

As I've gotten older, I've learned more and more about my son, other members of my family, and myself. I have a better feel for why *he* does what *he* does, and some of the things *I* can and should do differently. If I don't understand something Jimmy does, I'm now much more inclined to keep asking myself, "Why?" What purpose does it serve? Does research provide me with any clues?

Writing this book, I think, has strengthened my relationship with my children and my wife. It has made me more aware of the pivotal role each member of our growing family plays in our journey together, including our sons-in-law (Tom and Clayton) and grandchildren (Tommy, Aubrey, and Tay-Tay). Without "a Jimmy," I doubt our family would be nearly as strong and as caring as we are. But without Pat, Katie and Suzy and the rest of the gang, the same holds true. Like other families, we are intensely interconnected, both emotionally and spiritually. That interdependence is a tremendous source of strength and love. Indeed, we are blessed.

Figure 45 A RECENT FAMILY GET-TOGETHER IN UPSTATE NEW YORK.

Yes, Jimmy was the center of our lives for the longest time and out of necessity, we were consumed by his autism. But things are markedly different now; there are more different agendas to consider and now Jimmy has to stand in line more often to get his needs met. And that's okay. For instance, planning our family vacation at a nearby lake is no longer all about Jimmy's needs. We ask for everybody's input, including all our children, their spouses, and even grandchildren before we decide how to spend this special time together. While we still need a schedule of sorts, it's more flexible than in the past and *everybody* knows they might have to adjust at a moment's notice, even Jimmy.

As Pat and I look back at our journey, do we have regrets? Sure, but they're far and few between. Not long ago, someone asked my wife, "Do you ever think you could have done more?" She answered with a definitive, "No!" As Jimmy's father, I feel the exact same way; and that's a good feeling to have whenever we reflect on how far we've come and how much we've grown, individually and as a family.

Lastly, I feel a deep sense of gratitude to all those outside of our family who have contributed to our story in one way or another. Too often, there's a tendency to look at a family like ours and think that we alone are responsible for what has transpired over the years. That shortsighted point of view ignores the fact that we've had help, lots of it. Our family could not and cannot do it alone; rather, it has taken an ever-growing "village" to support and nurture us along the way. It's my sincere hope that in some small way *A Mommy, A Daddy, Two Sisters, and A Jimmy* has captured the love and kindness of friends, families, professionals, and others too numerous to mention, as well as the critical roles they have all played in our journey together.

About the Author

For more than 40 years, Dr. Richard Bucher has been a professor, speaker, consultant and author in the field of diversity. Rich's interest in this field began academically as an undergraduate student at Colgate University, and continued at New York University (M.A.) and Howard University (Ph.D. in sociology). His scholarly work in diversity turned personal when his firstborn child was born with autism in 1976.

Besides being a deeply involved father, Rich is the author of **Diversity Consciousness: Opening Our Minds to People, Cultures, and Opportunities**, now in its fourth edition, and **Cultural Intelligence: Nine Megaskills.** When he retired from teaching at Baltimore City Community College, Rich's thoughts, energy, research and writing turned to his family's personal journey. By weaving the latest scientific studies on autism into story upon story in his new book, it becomes clear that Rich's family experiences aren't at all unique.

Rich lives with his wife Pat in Frederick, MD. He's the father of three children, Jimmy, Katie and Suzy, who all live nearby. When he isn't writing and spending time with his growing family, he's exercising and working with youth in his community.

Profits from the sale of the book will go to Linwood Center, Ellicott City, Maryland (linwoodcenter.org)

Why Linwood

For more than 60 years, Linwood Center has sought to "create the possibility of extraordinary lives for children and adults living with autism." It's one of only a handful of programs throughout the U.S. that provides comprehensive education and residential programs from elementary school through old age. Linwood's staff works one-on-one to cultivate autistic students' personal growth, self-advocacy, and autonomy. Its school currently serves more than fifty students from extremely diverse backgrounds. Linwood, recognized world-wide as a pioneering leader in the field of autism, has expanded its reach to support individuals and families affected by autism. One of Linwood's core beliefs is that all individuals should be treated with dignity and respect, and all individuals have a right to live in an environment full of encouragement and opportunity.

What Linwood Means to Me

My son, whom I've always loved so dearly, by age ten was so out-of-control, such a danger to himself and others, and constantly going through these horrible panic/anxiety attacks that made me feel completely helpless. Even though I'd been able to teach him math and reading, when schools couldn't, these behaviors were "out of my league" and getting worse. Public school couldn't handle him anymore. To say Jimmy's presence dominated my whole family's existence is a massive understatement.

When we first visited Linwood, I poured out my soul; informing staff of every socially unacceptable thing my son did. I was so tired of him being rejected by schools (23 in all) that I was putting it all out there. When their response was that they WANTED Jimmy and COULD HELP him – the relief was so amazing I hardly dared feel it. Over the next 30 years, as we raised him together, he has grown into a very pleasant, polite, helpful man with a steady job. He lives in a Linwood group home where he's not only well-cared for, but very, very happy.

During his early childhood years, I saw my future as a woman who would stay home to care for her son for the rest of my life. Instead, I went on to a teaching career, helping low-achieving high school students from difficult backgrounds become successful in math. While Jimmy lived at Linwood during the weekdays, I got to enjoy my wonderful daughters and husband, spending time with just them. Then on the weekends Jimmy and I were able to have our special time together.

And now, as I move through my sixties, I don't have to carry around worry and fear for my two daughters' futures, because Linwood is still there and always will be for our Jimmy.

--Pat Bucher (the mommy)

When I think of Linwood, I think of family. By any definition, a family is made up of people you can count on, trust in; people you grow to love and who love you back. For Jimmy and our entire family, Linwood's all that and more.

    --Rich Bucher (the daddy)

Linwood's adult program has given my mom and dad time and flexibility in Jimmy's adult life. They are able to not only spend quality time with each other, but to visit and spend quality time with our families.
For me personally, Linwood has allowed them to have the ability to be an important part of my children's lives.

    --Katie Hessen (a sister)

When I think of Linwood, I think of opportunity. I think of my parents having the opportunity to be working parents and send my sister and me to college. I think of Jimmy having the opportunity to build a life of his own and have a job. I think of the opportunity for my parents to finally have a sense of relief and know that their son is receiving proper care.

    --Suzette Painter (a sister)

People [at Linwood] are very nice, kind, polite, and very special. They take very good care of me at all times. I feel very happy and proud when they do this. When I first came to Linwood I would cry, get upset, and I would lose my bag of cards and napkins because I had not done a good job at all. Yes I have learned a very good lesson with that. I would NEVER try that again. Linwood has helped a lot. By helping me grow with the world and giving me specific directions.

    --Jimmy Bucher (a Jimmy)

A Note about Language and Research

Language

As an author, professor, and sociologist, I'm well aware that the way we refer to someone matters. The language we use to describe autism can play a key role in shaping how we view this disability. Words such as dysfunctional, derangement, disease, abnormal, affliction, impairment, and deficiency still find their way into the headlines and literature on autism. If we look up the definitions of these terms in the dictionary, they're overwhelmingly negative, deceptively simple, and most importantly inaccurate.

Does that mean he's irregular? (a half-joking response when told her son was not like regular children)
>   *--a friend (Fran Dunn, a member of my wife's support group for parents of special needs children)*

"Person-first language" puts the person before the disability. For example, I may refer to *people with autism* to emphasize that someone with a disability like autism is first and foremost a person. However, I can also appreciate why many people with autism reject person-first language and strongly prefer "identity-first language." Jim Sinclair states in no uncertain terms, "I am not a 'person with autism,' I am an autistic person." He continues, "Autism is hard-wired into the ways my brain works."[219] "Autism is not an appendage," says Sinclair. It is a "way of being."[220]

Across the world, many prefer identity-first language. There are also those who use person-first and identity-first language interchangeably, as I do in this book. Others identify themselves as "on the autism spectrum," or prefer any number of terms, including "Aspie" and "awe-tism." Some dismiss the importance of language or don't care. What really matters, they say, is what people think and how they act. In fact, there is no *one* universally accepted guideline. Whatever our preference, we need to respect and be open to other points of view.

Research

As parents of a child with autism, it seemed like we always had more questions than answers. And often, we felt like we were "driving in a fog," going with our gut instincts and learning from trial and error. While we still feel that way to some extent, research has gradually filled some of the knowledge gaps.

Not that long ago, many subscribed to the belief that poor parenting caused autism. The blame was placed at the feet of "refrigerator mothers" who were characterized as cold and unfeeling. Years later, a parent of a child with autism by the name of Dr. Bernie Rimland conducted research that proved this belief was hogwash. We've come a long way since then, but we've got a long way to go.

Solid scientific research on autism moves us beyond personal experiences and expands our knowledge and understanding. Rather than assume something is true because it's "common sense" (whatever that is) or makes sense to us, research in the U.S. and abroad takes an idea or a treatment and repeatedly tests it under controlled conditions; giving us more confidence that an idea is valid, a strategy is worth pursuing, or a treatment actually works.

Since Jimmy was born, research on autism has increased exponentially, although much of it is still uneven and incomplete. For instance, research on the development of autistic individuals is apt to focus on his or her risk factors, symptoms and so-called impairments. Relatively few studies examine the impact of environmental influences, including families, peers, schools, jobs, places of worship, and neighborhoods. Further, there is much more research on autism and its effects early in life as opposed to later in the life span. We don't know nearly enough about what happens as autistic individuals move through middle age and become senior citizens.

Research still tends to focus on deficits, disadvantages, and challenges of autism. For instance, studies examine so-called problem behaviors, their impact, and how to correct or lessen the effect of such behaviors. In other words, fix the individual. Despite the tremendous diversity that exists within the autistic population, there are surprisingly few studies on the strengths of individuals with autism and the critical role of siblings, extended families, and peers.

There are many different forms, dimensions, and symptoms of autism. Scientific literature tells us that people with autism don't fit into neat, clear cut categories. That's certainly true of our son Jimmy who makes a habit of defying expectations. Lorna Wing, a psychiatrist, researcher, *and* a mother of an autistic child, introduced the term autism "spectrum" to emphasize the remarkable variability of autism. No two individuals with autism are the same, just as there is no one right or effective way to treat autism. According to Dr. Stephen Scherer, a world class geneticist who studies differences in autism, recent findings show that "each child with autism is like a snowflake – unique from the other."[221]

What we know about autism changes every day. Being a scientist, I'm well aware of how biases can unknowingly creep into research, and how data can be manipulated. Like all scientific research, the diverse and thought-provoking studies in this book need to be critically evaluated; however, they represent some of the most current and important research on autism available today.

ENDNOTES

[1] Suzy Bucher, "I Look Up to You, Jimmy," *The Exceptional Parent*, 30, Issue 5, May 2000.

[2] Some scientists now use the terms "the autisms" as well as "the autism spectrum disorders" to emphasize the uniqueness of each individual.

[3] Tessa Prebble, "Blog: As Long As It's Healthy," Oct. 30, 2014, accessed Aug. 15, 2017. Available: **http://theoneinamillionbaby.com/about-us/**.

[4] Joyce Ann Wright, "Transcendence: Phenomenological Perspective of the Mother's Experience of Having a Child with a Disability" (Doctoral dissertation, Widener University, 2002).

[5] Jim Sinclair, "Don't Mourn For Us," *Our Voice*, 1, No. 3, 1993.

[6] Alysia Abbott, "Love in the Time of Autism," *Psychology Today*, July 2, 2013.

[7] Alexander Burrell, Jonathan Ives, and Gemma Unwin, "The Experiences of Fathers Who Have Offspring with Autism Spectrum Disorder," *Journal of Autism Developmental Disorders*, 47(4), Jan. 28, 2017, 1135-1147.

[8] Alysia Abbott, "Love in the Time of Autism," July 2, 2013. Available: **https://www.psychologytoday.com/articles/201307/love-in-the-time-autism.**

[9] Bruno Bettelheim. *The Empty Fortress: Infantile Autism and the Birth of the Self* (NY: Free Press, 1972).

[10] Theresa Schmidt, "Autism Mom: Ruth Christ Sullivan Part 1," kplctv.com, 2014.

[11] Forward by Bertram A. Ruttenberg, M.D. as found in Jeanne Simons and Sabine Oishi, *The Hidden Child: The Linwood Method for Reaching the Autistic Child* (Bethesda, MD: Woodbine House, 1987).

[12] Marina Sarris, "Families Face Autism, Stigma, Isolation," posted February 4, 2016. Available: **https://iancommunity.org/ssc/families-face-autism-stigma-isolation.**

[13] Frank Roylance and Meredith Cohn, "Alternative Autism Treatments Can Be Appealing to Desperate Parents," *The Baltimore Sun*, May 11, 2011. Available: **http://www.baltimoresun.com/health/bs-md-autism-parents-therapy-20110511-story.html.**

[14] Andrew Solomon. *Far From the Tree: Parents, Children, and the Search for Identity*, (NY: Scribner, 2012).

[15] Frank Roylance and Meredith Cohn, "Alternative Autism Treatments Can Be Appealing to Desperate Parents," *The Baltimore Sun*, May 11, 2011.

[16] Centers for Disease Control and Prevention, "CDC Estimates 1 in 68 Children Has Been Identified With Autism Spectrum Disorder." Available: **http://www.cdc.gov/media/releases/2014/p0327-autism-spectrum-disorder.html**, Mar. 27, 2014.

[17] U. S. Census Bureau, National Center for Health Statistics, "2014 National Health Interview Survey."

[18] "Autism Diagnosis: Slipping through the Cracks in Some Communities," *Parents and Kids Magazine*, accessed March 9, 2017. Available: **http://www.gulfcoast-parents-kids.com/index.php/current-issue/latest-issue/761-autism-diagnosis-slipping-through-the-cracks-in-some-communities.**

[19] Pew Research Center survey of parents with children under 18, Sept. 15-Oct 13, 2015, Q95, 96.

[20] Bronnie Ware. *The Top Five Regrets of the Dying* (NY: Hay House, 2012).

[21] Melissa Milkie, Kei Nomaguchi, and Kathleen Denny, "Does the Amount of Time Mothers Spend With Children or Adolescents Matter?" *Journal of Marriage and Family*, 77, Issue 2, April 2015, 355-372.

[22] Brigid Schulte, "Pushing For Dad Time," *The Washington Post*, July 20, 2014, G1+.

[23] Terry Keller, Julie Ramisch, and Marsha Carolan, "Relationships of Children with Autism Spectrum Disorders and their Fathers," *The Qualitative Report*, 19, Article 66, 2014, 1-15.

[24] Carrie Braithwaite, "New Study Highlights the Importance of Fathers in the Care of Children with Autism," posted Nov. 1, 2016. Available: http://www.leedsbeckett.ac.uk/news/1116-new-study-highlights-the-importance-of-fathers-in-the-care-of-children-with-autism/.

[25] David Smukler, "Unauthorized Minds: How 'Theory of Mind' Theory Misrepresents Autism," *Mental Retardation*, American Association of Intellectual and Developmental Disabilities, 43 (1), 20-21, Feb. 2005.

[26] Donna Williams. *Nobody Nowhere: The Remarkable Autobiography of an Autistic Girl* (London, UK: Jessica Kingsley Publishers, 1998).

[27] R. Ginny and B. Norwich, "Dilemmas, Diagnosis, and De-stigmatization: Parental Perspectives on the Diagnosis of Autism Spectrum Disorders," *Clinical Child Psychology and Psychiatry*," 17(2), 229-245, in Stasha Stobbs, "My Greatest Joy and My Greatest Heartache: A Narrative Analysis Exploring Mothers' Experiences of Having a Child on the Autism Spectrum," Manchester Metropolitan University, March, 2014. Available: https://e-space.mmu.ac.uk/576484/1/Stasha%20STOBBS.pdf.

[28] Costanza Giuffrida and Emilia Barakova, "Time Processing Ability and Anxiety in Children With Autism: Evaluation of the Effects of Music Using Music Timer PLAYtime," International Association of Societies of Design Research (IASDR), 2013, Aug. 26-30, Tokyo, Japan.

[29] Donna Williams. *Nobody Nowhere: The Extraordinary Autobiography of an Autistic* (New York: Times Books, 1992).

[30] Jim Sinclair, "Don't Mourn For Us," *Our Voice*, Number 3, 1993.

[31] Darold Treffert, "Rain Man, the Movie/Rain Man, Real Life," Wisconsin Medical Society, accessed 9/15/2017. Available: **https://www.wisconsinmedicalsociety.org/professional/savant-syndrome/resources/articles/rain-man-the-movie-rain-man-real-life/**.

[32] Ginny Russell, *University of Exeter guest blog: Screen Talks*, "Savants and Stereotypes: Barry Levinson's Rain Man." Available http://blogs.exeter.ac.uk/screentalks/blog/2013/04/, posted April 9, 2013.

[33] Anders Nordahl-Hansen, Ronald Oien, and Sue Fletcher-Watson, "Pros and Cons of Character Portrayals of Autism on TV and Film," *Journal of Autism and Developmental Disorders*, February 2018, 48, Issue 2, pp. 635-636.

[34] Ruth Sullivan, personal communication, October 18, 2016.

[35] Michael Staton, "Researchers Examine Effects of Compression Clothing on Children with Autism," posted Feb. 22, 2017. Available: http://newsstand.clemson.edu/mediarelations/researchers-examine-effects-of-compression-clothing-on-children-with-autism/.

[36] Autism Speaks, "Study Suggests Repetitive Behaviors Emerge Early in Autism," May 15, 2014. Available: **https://www.autismspeaks.org/science/science-news/study-suggests-repetitive-behaviors-emerge-early-autism**.

[37] Temple Grandin and Margaret Scariano. E*mergence: Labeled Autistic*, reissue edition (NY: Warner Books, 1996).

[38] Kim Parker, Pew Research Center, "6 Facts about American Fathers," posted June 15, 2017. Available: http://www.pewresearch.org/fact-tank/2017/06/15/fathers-day-facts/.

[39] Micelle Flippin and Elizabeth Crais, "The Need for More Effective Father Involvement in Early Autism Intervention: A Systematic Review and Recommendations, *Journal of Early Intervention*, 33(1), 24-50, 2011.

[40] University of Illinois at Urbana-Champaign, "Dad's Parenting of Children with Autism Improves Moms' Mental Health: Fathers' Engagement in Literacy, Caregiving Activities Reduces Mothers' Depression, Stress," *Science Daily*, July 14, 2015. Available: **www.sciencedaily.com/releases/2015/07/150714131600.htm.**

[41] Sigan Hartley, Marsha Mailick Seltzer, Lara Head, and Leonard Abbeduto, "Psychological Well-being in Fathers of Adolescents and Young Adults with Down Syndrome, Fragile X Syndrome, and Autism," *Family Relations*, 61 (2), April 1, 2012, 327-342.

[42] Alexander Burrell, Jonathan Ives, and Gemma Unwin, "The Experiences of Fathers Who Have Offspring with Autism Spectrum Disorder," *Journal of Autism Developmental Disorders*, 47 (4), Jan. 28, 2017, 1135-1147.

[43] Kim Parker, Pew Research Center, "6 Facts about American Fathers," posted June 15, 2017. Available: http://www.pewresearch.org/fact-tank/2017/06/15/fathers-day-facts/.

[44] David Elkind. *The Power of Play: How Spontaneous, Imaginative Activities Lead to Happier, Healthier Children* (Da Capo Press, 2007); Edward Miller and Joan Almon, *Crisis in the Kindergarten: Why Children Need to Play in School, 2009.*

[45] Noah Sasson, Daniel Faso, Jack Nugent, Sarah Lovell, Daniel Kennedy, and Ruth Grossman, "Neurotypical Peers Are Less Willing to Interact with Those with Autism Based on Thin Slice Judgments," *Scientific Reports* 7, February 1, 2017. Available: **https://www.nature.com/articles/srep40700.**

[46] Connie Kasari, *The Journal of Child Psychology and Psychiatry,* 57, Issue 2, 171-179, Feb., 2016.

[47] Lena Rivkin, Autism Support Network, "Autism and Sibling Guilt," accessed Oct. 10, 2018, available: http://www.autismsupportnetwork.com/news/autism-and-sibling-guilt-story-2374892.

[48] Maureen Angell, Hedda Meadan, and Julia Stoner, "Experiences of Siblings of Individuals with Autism Spectrum Disorders," *Autism Research and Treatment*, Vol. 2012, 2011. Available: https://www.hindawi.com/journals/aurt/2012/949586/.

[49] Katie Bucher, "My Brother Jimmy," *Exceptional Parent*, March, 1990.

[50] "Street Gang," *Wikipedia* (Nov. 28, 2016). Available: **https://en.wikipedia.org/wiki/Street_Gang.**

[51] Marie-Louise Mares and Zhongdang Pan, *Journal of Applied Developmental Psychology*, "Effects of *Sesame Street*: A Meta-analysis of Children's Learning in 15 Countries," 2013

[52] Erin DeBoer, "Sesame Workshop Announces Initiative Focused on Autism," October 22, 2015.

[53] Mary Papenfuss, "Meet the New Kid on Sesame Street: Julia, A Muppet with Autism," *Huff Post*, posted 3/20/17. Available: **http://www.huffingtonpost.com/entry/autism-muppet-sesame-street_us_58cf5f15e4b0be71dcf5b455**.

[54] Marissa Martinelli, "An Autism Advocate Explains How She Helped *Sesame Street* Create Its New Autistic Muppet," posted April 12, 2017. Available: **http://www.slate.com/blogs/browbeat/2017/04/12/autistic_self_advocacy_network_s_julia_bascom_on_sesame_street_s_new_muppet.html.**

[55] Malcolm Gladwell. *The Tipping Point: How Little Things Can Make a Big Difference* (New York: Little Brown and Co., 2000).

[56] *Medscape Psychiatry*, "Autism First-Hand: An Expert Interview with Temple Grandin, PhD," 10 (1), 2005.

[57] Jennifer Cook O'Toole, *Asperkids: An Insider's Guide to Loving, Understanding, and Teaching Children with Asperger's Syndrome* (London, UK: Jessica Kingsley Publishers, 2012).

58 C. Nicolaidis, D. M. Raymaker, E. Ashkenazy, K. E. McDonald, S. Dern, A. E. Baggs, S. K. Kapp, M. Weiner, and W. C. Boisclair, "Respect the Way I Need to Communicate with You: Healthcare Experiences of Adults on the Autism Spectrum," *Autism: The International Journal of Research and Practice*, 19, 7, 2015, 824-831.

59 O. Zerbo, M. L. Massolo, Y. Qian, and L. A. Croen, "A Study of Physician Knowledge and Experience with Autism in Adults in a Large Integrated Healthcare System," Journal of Autism and Developmental Disorders, 45 (12), 2015, 4002-4014.

60 "New NHS Treatment Helps Children with Autism Overcome Fears," *EurekAlert! The Global Source for Science News*, February 10, 2017. Available: **https://www.eurekalert.org/pub_releases/2017-02/nu-nn021017.php.**

61 Leo Kanner, "Autistic Disturbances of Affective Contact," *Nervous Child*, 2, 1943, 217-250.

62 "New NHS Treatment Helps Children with Autism Overcome Fears," *EurekAlert! The Global Source for Science News*, February 10, 2017. Available: **https://www.eurekalert.org/pub_releases/2017-02/nu-nn021017.php.**

63 Susan Mayes, Susan Calhoun, Richa Aggarwal, Courtney Baker, Santosh Mathapati, Sarah Molitoris, and Rebecca Mayes, "Unusual Fears in Children With Autism," *Research in Autism Spectrum Disorders*, 7 (1), 151-158, Jan., 2013.

64 Sinéad Lydon, Olive Healy, Orla O'Callaghan, Teresa Mulhern, and Jennifer Holloway, "A Systematic Review of the Treatment of Fears and Phobias Among Children with Autism Spectrum Disorders," *Review Journal of Autism and Developmental Disorders*, 2, Issue 2, June 2015. Available: **https://link.springer.com/article/10.1007/s40489-014-0043-4.**

65 Mary Rowe, "Micro-affirmations and Micro-inequities," Jan., 2008. Available:

https://www.researchgate.net/publication/265450386_Micro-affirmations_Micro-inequities.

[66] O. Shtayermman, "An Exploratory Study of the Stigma Associated with a Diagnosis of Asperger's Syndrome: The Mental Health Impact on the Adolescents and Young Adults Diagnosed with a Disability with a Social Nature," *Journal of Human Behavior in the Social Environment*, 19, 2009, 298-313.

[67] Center for Autism Research - The Children's Hospital of Philadelphia, "The Importance of Self-Esteem." Available: https://www.carautismroadmap.org/the-importance-of-self-esteem/?print=pdf.

[68] Iman Rastegari and Leah Shafer, "Accentuate the Positive," posted Dec. 22, 2016. Available: https://www.gse.harvard.edu/news/uk/16/12/accentuate-positive.

[69] National Institute of Mental Health, "Most Children with ASD Diagnosed after Age 5 Use Multiple Services and Medications," May 24, 2012. Available: https://www.nimh.nih.gov/news/science-news/2012/most-children-with-asd-diagnosed-after-age-5-use-multiple-services-and-medications.shtml.

[70] M. L. McPheeters, Z. Warren, Bruzek Sathe, S. Krishnaswami, R. N. Jerome, and J. Veenstra-Vanderweele, "A Systematic Review of Medical Treatments for Children With Autism Spectrum Disorders," *Pediatrics*, May, 2011, 1312-1321.

[71] Anne Roux, Paul Shattuck, Jessica Rast, Julianna Rava, and Krisy Anderson. *National Autism Indicators Report: Transition into Young Adulthood* (Philadelphia, PA: Life Course Outcomes Research Program, A.J. Drexel Autism Institute, Drexel University, 2015).

[72] Drexel University, "A Quarter of Adults with Autism on Disability Services Don't Have Work or Activities, New Report Shows," *Science Daily*, May 24, 2017. Available: https://www.sciencedaily.com/releases/2017/05/170524110016.htm#.

[73] Abbey Clow, "Growing Together: Stories of Resilience in Families of Children with Autism," April 2016. Available: https://e-space.mmu.ac.uk/617775/1/Clow%20(Abbey)%202016%20(Manchester%20Metropolitan)%20Qualitative.pdf.

[74] "Circle of Moms," posted 8/29/09. Available: http://www.circleofmoms.com/autismaspergerspdd-awareness/autism-why-all-the-repetitive-questions-i-am-going-crazy-365741.

[75] C. Hughes, R. Bernstein, L. Kaplan, C. Reilly, N Brigham, J Cosgriff, and M. Boykin, "Increasing Conversational Interactions between Verbal High School Students with Autism and Their Peers." *Focus on Autism and Other Developmental Disabilities*," 28, 2013, 241-254.

[76] Christina Nicolaidis, What Can Physicians Learn from the Neurodiversity Movement?" *Virtual Mentor: AMA Journal of Ethics*, June 2012, 14 (6), 503-510.

[77] Barry Prizant. *Uniquely Human: A Different Way of Seeing Autism* (New York: Simon and Schuster, 2015).

[78] Marya Dumke, "Autism and the Impact of the Siblings' Identities," 2015, *Master of Social Work Clinical Research Papers*, Paper 438. Available: http://sophia.stkate.edu/msw_papers/438, p. 42.

[79] Barry Prizant. *Uniquely Human: A Different Way of Seeing Autism* (New York: Simon and Schuster, 2015).

[80] Janine Montgomery, Toby Martin, Shahin Shooshtari, Brenda Stoesz, and Dustin Heinrichs, "Interventions for Challenging Behaviors of Students with Autism Spectrum Disorders and Developmental Disabilities: A Synthesis Paper," *Exceptionality Education International*, 23, Issue 1, 2013, 2-21.

[81] Phone conversation with a retired senior citizen who described himself as a "former Linwood student who later became successful," Aug., 2017.

[82] Jeanne Simons and Sabine Oishi, *The Hidden Child: The Linwood Method for Reaching the Autistic Child* (Bethesda, MD: Woodbine House, 1987).

[83] Ibid.

[84] Joe Holley, "Jeanne Simons, Pioneer for Autistic Children, Dies," *The Washington Post*, March 12, 2005, B06.

[85] "From People with Autism, Lessons for Scientists on Love, Compassion," *Spectrum*, Dec. 22, 2017. Available: https://www.spectrumnews.org/features/special-report/people-autism-lessons-scientists-love-compassion/.

[86] Simon Baron-Cohen. *Mindblindness: An Essay on Autism and Theory of the Mind* (Cambridge, MA: MIT Press, 1995).

[87] Mike Falcon, "Stars 'CAN-do' about defeating autism," *USA Today*, April 10, 2002. Available: **http://usatoday30.usatoday.com/news/health/spotlight/2002/04/10-autism.htm**.

[88] Roy Q. Sanders, "The Experts Speak: Hard Times Come Again No More, posted April 20, 2011. Available: **https://autismspeaksblog.wordpress.com/2011/04/20/experts-reflect-on-parenthood-finale.**

[89] Simon Baron-Cohen. *The Science of Evil: On Empathy and the Origins of Cruelty* (NY: Basic Books, 2011).

[90] Barbara Myers, Virginia MacIntosh, and Robin Goin-Kochel, "My Greatest Joy and My Greatest Heart Ache: Parents' own words on how having a child in the autism spectrum has affected their lives and their families' lives," *Research in Autism Spectrum Disorders*, July-September, 2009. Available: **https://www.sciencedirect.com/science/article/pii/S1750946709000051**.

[91] Sara Ryan, "'Meltdowns,' Surveillance and Managing Emotions: Going Out with Children with Autism," *Health and Place*, September, 2010. Available: https://www.ncbi.nlm.nih.gov/pmc/articles/PMC2927009/.

[92] The National Autistic Society, "Shrinking Worlds," *Too Much Information*, accessed 4/15/17. Available: **file:///C:/Users/Rich/Downloads/TMI_Campaign_Report_FINAL_290316 %20(2).pdf.**

[93] Temple Grandin and Debra Moore. *The Loving Push: How Parents and Professionals Can Help Spectrum Kids Become Successful Adults* (Arlington, TX: Future Horizons, 2015), ix.

[94] Marina Sarris, "The Stigma of Autism: When All Eyes Are Upon You," Interactive Autism Network (IAN), January 15, 2015. Available: **https://iancommunity.org.**

[95] United Nations, "Secretary-General's Message for World Autism Awareness Day," April 2, 2014. Available: **www.un.org/en/events/autismday/2014/sgmessage.shtml.**

[96] Carl Bainbridge, "Parents of Children with Autism: How to Deal with Pain Management," *YMC: Motherhood Unfiltered*, accessed 1/18/2018. Available: **http://www.yummymummyclub.ca/health/wellness/20160417/parents -of-children-with-autism-how-to-deal-with-pain-management-bc?qt-contests_minitab=0&qt-newest_and_trending_tabs=0.**

[97] Sarah Deweerdt, "Unseen Agony: Dismantling Autism's House of Pain," *Spectrum*, posted May 21, 2015. Available: https://spectrumnews.org/features/deep-dive/unseen-agony-dismantling-autisms-house-of-pain/**.**

[98] C. S. Allely, "Pain Sensitivity and Observer Perception of Pain in Individuals with Autism Spectrum Disorder," *Scientific World Journal*, posted June 13, 2013. Available: **https://core.ac.uk/download/pdf/16459727.pdf.**

[99] Connie Anderson, J. Kiely Law, Amy Daniels, Catherine Rice, David Mandell, Louis Hagopian, and Paul Law, "Occurrence and Family Impact of Elopement in Children With Autism Spectrum Disorders," *Pediatrics*, October 12, 2012.

[100] Autism Speaks, "Study Confirms Autism Wandering Common and Scary," Oct. 8, 2012. Available: **https://www.autismspeaks.org/science/science-news/study-confirms-autism-wandering-common-scary.**

[101] Marina Sarris, "Understanding Research: An Autism Researcher Answers Your Questions," posted Feb. 20, 2017. Available: iancommunity.org.

[102] Wendy Fournier, "New Study Highlights Mortality and Risk in Autism Wandering/Elopement," April 3, 2017. Available: http://nationalautismassociation.org/new-study-highlights-lethal-risks-of-missing-persons-with-autism/**.**

[103] Olga Solomon and Mary Lawlor, "'And I Look Down and He Is Gone:' Narrating Autism, Elopement and Wandering in Los Angeles," *Social Science Medicine*, October, 2013. Available: **https://www.ncbi.nlm.nih.gov/pubmed/23890970.**

[104] R. P. Hastings and H. M. Taunt, "Positive Perceptions in Families of Children with Developmental Disabilities," *American Journal of Mental Retardation*, 107(2), Mar., 2002, 116-27; M. Bayat, "Evidence of Resilience in Families of Children with Autism," *Journal of Intellectual Disability Research*, 51, 2007, 702-714; Ashley Hartmann, "Autism and its Impact on Families," 2012, *Master of Social Work Clinical Research Papers*, Paper 35, Available: **https://sophia.stkate.edu/msw_papers/35/.**

[105] Annie Lubliner Lehmann. *The Accidental Teacher: Life Lessons From My Silent Son* (Ann Arbor, MI: University of Michigan Press, 2009).

[106] Barbara Myers, Virginia MacIntosh, and Robin Goin-Kochel, "My Greatest Joy and My Greatest Heart Ache: Parents' Own Words on How Having a Child in the Autism Spectrum Has Affected their Lives and their Families' Lives," *Research in Autism Spectrum Disorders* 3, 2009, 670-684.

[107] Anne Haddad, "Teen Gains an Unlikely Insider's Perspective on Prejudice," *The Sun – Carroll County and Maryland*, March 22, 1993, B1.

[108] Melanie Yergeau, "Socializing Through Silence," in Julia Bascom (ed.), *Loud Hands: Autistic People, Speaking* (Washington, DC: The Autistic Press, 2012).

[109] Ariane Buescher, Zuleyha Cidav, Martin Knapp, and David Mandell, "Costs of Autism Spectrum Disorders in the United Kingdom and the United States," *JAMA Pediatrics*, 168 (8), August 2014, 721-728.

[110] Chris Taylor, "Raising an Autistic Child: Coping with the Costs," *Money*, June 24, 2014. Available: *http://time.com/money/2918134/cost-raising-autistic-child.*

[111] Ibid., 111

[112] Katherine Pickard and Brooke Ingersoll, "Quality vs. quantity: The role of socioeconomic status on parent-reported service knowledge, service use, unmet service needs, and barriers to service use," *Autism*, 20 (1), 2016, 106-115.

[113] Hend Hamed, "Tourism and Autism: An Initiative Study for How Travel Companies Can Plan Tourism Trips for Autistic People," *American Journal of Tourism Management*, 2013, 2(1), 1-14.

[114] Jeanne Simons and Sabine Oishi, *The Hidden Child: The Linwood Method For Reaching The Autistic Child* (Bethesda, MD: Woodbine House, 1987), 241.

[115] Ibid., 232.

[116] Vicky Hallett, "Certain Characteristics Prove Advantageous for People with Autism Who Enjoy Running," *The Washington Post*, May 9, 2017, E3.

[117] Marina Sarris, Interactive Autism Network, "The Challenge of Physical Fitness for People with Autism," Nov. 17, 2014. Available: **https://iancommunity.org/ssc/autism-physical-fitness.**

[118] Alison Wade, "For Many with Autism, Running Is a Sport That Fits," *Runner's World*, 2017. Available: https://www.runnersworld.com/special-report/for-many-with-autism-running-is-a-sport-that-fits.

[119] Ibid.

[120] Ibid.

[121] Geraldine Dawson and Michael Rosanoff, "Sports, Exercise, and the Benefits of Physical Activity for Individuals with Autism," *Autism Speaks*, posted February 19, 2009. Available: https://www.autismspeaks.org/science/science-news/sports-exercise-and-benefits-physical-activity-individuals-autism.

[122] Roseann Schaaf, Susan Toth-Cohen, Stephanie Johnson, Gina Outten, and Teal Benevides, "The Everyday Routines of Families of Children with Autism," *Autism*, 15(3), 373-389, May 2011.

[123] Ibid.

[124] Ibid.

[125] Amy Lennard Goehner, "Travel Tips" TIME Magazine 2009.

[126] Molly Shields Bagby, Virginia Dickie, and Grace Baranek, "How Sensory Experiences of Children with and Without Autism Affect Family Occupations," *American Journal of Occupational Therapy,* 66 (1), Jan-Feb, 2012, 78-86.

[127] Ibid, 82.

[128] Temple Grandin, Case history, "My Experiences as an Autistic Child." Available: http://orthomolecular.org/library/jom/1984/pdf/1984-v13n03-p144.pdf, 1984.

[129] Cynthia Kim, "Musings of an Aspie: One Woman's Thoughts about Life on the Spectrum, posted May 24, 2013. Available: https://musingsofanaspie.com/2013/05/24/sensory-seeking/.

[130] Kennedy Krieger Institute, "80 Percent Autism Divorce Rate Debunked in First-Of-Its Kind Scientific Study," posted May 19, 2010. Available: https://www.kennedykrieger.org/overview/news/80-percent-autism-divorce-rate-debunked-first-its-kind-scientific-study.

[131] Sigan Hartley, Erin Barker, Marsha Seltzer, and Jan Greenberg, "Marital Satisfaction and Parenting Experiences of Mothers and Fathers of Adolescents and Adults with Autism," *American Journal on Intellectual and Developmental Disabilities*, 116 (1), 81-95, Jan., 2011.

[132] "Parents of Kids with Autism May Sacrifice 'Couples Time,'" *HealthDay*, March 31, 2017. Available: https://consumer.healthday.com/cognitive-health-information-26/autism-news-51/parents-of-kids-with-autism-may-sacrifice-couples-time-721106.html.

[133] Brian Freedman, Luther Kalb, Benjamin Zablotsky, and Elizabeth Stuart, "Relationship Status Among Parents of Children with Autism Spectrum Disorders: A Population-Based Study," *Journal of Autism and Developmental Disorders*, 42 (4), 539-548.

[134] S.L. Hartley, E.T. Barker, M.M. Seltzer, F. Floyd, J. Greenberg, G. Orsmond, and D. Bolt, *Journal of Family Psychology*, 24 (4), Aug., 2010, 449-457.

[135] Laurel Joss, "Scott Robertson Advocates for Autistic Adults," *Autism Daily Newscast*, June 1, 2017. Available: http://www.autismdailynewscast.com/scott-robertson-advocates-for-autistic-adults/3170/laurel-joss/.

[136] Marsha Mailick Seltzer and Marty W. Krauss - Principal Investigators, *Report #2: A Profile of Adolescents and Adults with Autism Spectrum Disorder*, May 23, 2016, Madison, WI: Lifespan Family Research Program. Available: http://www.waisman.wisc.edu/family/study_autism.html.

[137] Marina Sarris, "Coming of Age: Autism and the Transition to Adulthood," Autism Network at Kennedy Krieger Institute, posted April 8, 2014. Available: https://iancommunity.org/ssc/autism-transition-to-adulthoodInteractive.

[138] Barbara Myers, Virginia MacIntosh, Robin Goin-Kochel, "My Greatest Joy and My Greatest Heart Ache: Parents' own words on how having a child in the autism spectrum has affected their lives and their families' lives," *Research in Autism Spectrum Disorders* 3, 2009, 670-684.

[139] Ibid., 676

[140] Elena Delle Donne, *The Players' Tribune*, "Lizzie," posted Aug. 12, 2015. Available: https://www.theplayerstribune.com/elena-delle-donne-sister/.

[141] Melissa Isaacson, "Elena Delle Donne Continues to Spred the Word of Acceptance," June 8, 2016. Available: http://www.espn.com/espnw/culture/article/16049634/elena-delle-donne-continues-spread-word-acceptance.

[142] Marsha Mailick Seltzer and Marty W. Krauss, *Adolescents and Adults with Autism: A Study of Family Caregiving*, "Report #3: Reflections from Adult Siblings who have a Brother or Sister with an Autism Spectrum Disorder." Available: http://www.waisman.wisc.edu/family/reports/autism/aaareport3.pdf.

[143] Marsha Mailick Seltzer and Marty W. Krauss, *Adolescents and Adults with Autism: A Study of Family Caregiving*, "Report #1: A Book of Quotes: Shared Experiences from Families of Adolescents and Adults with Autism." Available: http://www.waisman.wisc.edu/family/reports/autism/aaareport1.pdf.

[144] Barbara Myers, Virginia MacIntosh, and Robin Goin-Kochel, "'My Greatest Joy and My Greatest Heart Ache': Parents' own words on how having a child in the autism spectrum has affected their lives and their families' lives," *Research in Autism Spectrum Disorders* 3, 2009, 670-684.

[145] Marya Dumke, "Autism and the Impact of the Siblings' Identities," 2015, *Master of Social Work Clinical Research Papers,* 438. Available: **https://sophia.stkate.edu/msw_papers/438/.**

[146] Amy Lennard Goehner, "Challenges Siblings of Children with Autism Face," *World of Autism,* accessed 4/11/2018. Available: **http://www.worldofautism.com/ASD/Challenges_siblings-of-children_with_autism_face.html.**

[147] Scott Michaux, "Star of Spieth Family is Ellie," *Masters,* Mar. 20, 2016.

[148] Jennifer Sarrett, "Trapped Children: Popular Images of Children with Autism in the 1960s and 2000s," *Journal of Medical Humanities,* 32, 141-153, January 12, 2011.

[149] Ibid.

[150] Alshaba Billawalla and Gregor Wolbring, "Analyzing the Discourse Surrounding Autism in the New York Times Using an Ableism Lens," *Disability Studies Quarterly,* 34 (1), 2014.

[151] Lu Tang and Bijie Bie, "The Stigma of Autism in China: An Analysis of Newspaper Portrayals of Autism between 2003 and 2012, *Health Communication,* 31 (4), 2016, 445-452.

[152] Chantelle Wood and Megan Freeth, "Students' Stereotypes of Autism," *Journal of Educational Issues,* 2016, 2 (2). Available: **https://files.eric.ed.gov/fulltext/EJ1127546.pdf.**

[153] Claire Allen, Autism South Africa, "When Your Child Has Autism: Tips for Parents," accessed Dec. 15, 2016. Available: **http://aut2know.co.za/wp/wp-content/uploads/10-Tips-for-Parents.pdf**, p. 2 of 4.

[154] Kate Masters, "Grandin Celebrates Learners with Special Needs," *The Frederick News-Post,* January 19, 2018, 1+.

[155] C. Crawford, J. Burns, B.A. Fernie, Psychosocial Impact of Involvement in the Special Olympics," *Research in Developmental Disabilities*, Oct.-Nov. 2015, 45-46.

[156] Joanne Kersh and Gary Siperstein, "The Positive Contributions of Special Olympics to the Family" (Boston, MA: Special Olympics Global Collaborating Center, University of Massachusetts, 2012).

[157] Special Olympics, *Serving Athletes, Families, and the* Community, 2009. Available: **http://www.specialolympics.org/uploadedFiles/LandingPage/WhatWeD o/Research_Studies_Desciption_Pages/Impact%20Policy%20Brief_feb3. pdf.**

[158] Joanne Kersh and Gary Siperstein, "The Positive Contributions of Special Olympics to the Family," Boston, MA: Special Olympics Global Collaborating Center, University of Massachusetts, 2012.

[159] *2014 Reach Report*, "Special Olympics Research Overview." Available: **http://media.specialolympics.org/resources/research/Special-Olympics-Research-Overview.pdf.**

[160] Elena Delle Donne, *The Players' Tribune*, "Lizzie," posted Aug. 12, 2015. Available: **https://www.theplayerstribune.com/elena-delle-donne-sister/.**

[161] M. J. Ault, B. C. Collins, and E. W. Carter, "Factors Associated with Participation in Faith Communities for Individuals with Developmental Disabilities and Their Families," *Journal of Religion, Disability, and Health* 17, 2013, 184-211; M. J. Ault, B. C. Collins, and E. W. Carter, "Congregational Participation and Supports for Children and Adults with Disabilities: Parent Perceptions," *Intellectual and Developmental Disabilities*, 51 (1), Feb., 2013, 48-61.

[162] Elizabeth E. O'Hanlon, "Religion and Disability: The Experiences of Families of Children with Special Needs," *Journal of Religion, Disability, and Health*, 17, 42-61, 2013.

[163] Marina Sarris, "Autism and Faith: Inclusion and Acceptance at Places of Worship," posted March 4, 2014. Available: **https://iancommunity.org/ssc/autism-and-faith.**

[164] Marsha Mailick Seltzer and Marty W. Krauss, "Report #3: Reflections from Adult Siblings who have a Brother or Sister with an Autism Spectrum Disorder." Available: **http://www.waisman.wisc.edu/family/reports/autism/aaareport3.pdf.**

[165] Ranit Mishori, "Autism Can Have Large Effects, Good and Bad, on a Disabled Child's Siblings," *The Washington Post*, September 3, 2012. Available: **https://www.washingtonpost.com/national/health-science/autism-can-have-large-effects-good-and-bad-on-a-disabled-childs-siblings/2012/08/31/e35a82e2-b956-11e1-abd4-aecc81b4466d_story.html?utm_term=.b2237866c764.**

[166] Barbara Fredrickson. *Positivity* (New York, NY: Crown, 2009).

[167] John Donvan and Caren Zucker, "Autism's First Child," *The Atlantic*, October, 2010. Available: **https://www.theatlantic.com/magazine/archive/2010/10/autisms-first-child/308227/.**

[168] Ibid.

[169] E. J. Mundell, "Common Sports, Hobbies Often Popular Among People with Autism," *HealthDay*, May 13, 2015.

[170] Connie Anderson, *IAN Research Report #14: Grandparents of Children with ASD, Part 1*, April 2010. Available: **https://iancommunity.org/cs/ian_research_reports/ian_research_report_apr_2010.**

[171] Serena Gordon, "Grandparents Play Vital Role for Autistic Children," April 30, 2010. Available: **http://news.healingwell.com/index.php?p=news1&id=638183.**

[172] Ibid.

[173] Marlo G. Hode, "The Tyranny of Neuronormality: Questioning Neurotypical Privilege in Communication," University of Missouri, Columbia, May 7, 2012.

[174] Amy Sequenzia, "Non-Speaking Autistic Speaking," posted 8/13/2013. Available: **http://nonspeakingautisticspeaking.blogspot.com/**.

[175] Amy Sequeniza, "Non-Speaking, 'Low Functioning.'" in Julia Bascom (ed.), *Loud Hands* (Washington, DC: The Autistic Press, 2012).

[176] autistictic, "Ableism/Disablism –What it is and how it feels," posted July 31, 2015. Available: **https://www.youtube.com/watch?v=iV-VxnF8-xQ**.

[177] Nicole Caruso, "A Qualitative Investigation into Posttraumatic Growth in Mothers of Children with Autism Spectrum Disorder," accessed 7/4/17. Available: **http://www.autismsa.org.au/Media/Default/Research%20Documents/3%20%20COPY%20OF%20FINAL%20REPORT.pdf**.

[178] Jane Johnson, "Editorial: Parental Stress and Autism Spectrum Disorders," *Autism Research Review International*, Fall, 2013.

[179] Research Autism, "Caregiver Stress Project," May 26, 2015. Available: researchautism.net/caregiver-stress-project.

[180] Sheri, "Autism Bullying Story," Hope Center for Autism, posted September 9, 20013. Available: **http://www.hopecenter4autism.org/autism-bullying-story/**.

[181] Anahad O'Connor, "Autistic Pupils Face Far More Bullying," *The New York Times*, 9/04/2012, D7.

[182] Dana Roc, "Author, Teacher, and Autism Education Pioneer, Soma Mukhopadhyay." Available: danaroc.com/inspiring_041910soma.html.

[183] *"The Mind Tree*: A Review," accessed 7/05/2017. Available: **http://teenautism.com/2008/09/18/the-mind-tree-a-review/**.

184 Noah Sasson, Daniel Faso, Jack Nugent, Sarah Lovell, Daniel Kennedy, and Ruth Grossman, "Neurotypical Peers are Less Willing to Interact with Those with Autism Based on Thin Sliced Judgments," *Scientific Reports*, Feb. 1, 2017. Available: **https://www.nature.com/articles/srep40700.**

185 Kyoko Tanaka, Tokio Uchiyama, and Fumio Endo, "Informing Children about Their Sibling's Diagnosis of Autism Spectrum Disorder: An Initial Investigation into Current Practices," *Research in Autism Spectrum Disorders*, 5, 1421 -1429, Oct-Dec 2011.

186 Ibid.

187 Organization for Autism Research, *Brothers, Sisters, and Autism: A Parent's Guide to Supporting Siblings*, Summer, 2014. Available: **https://researchautism.org/wp-content/uploads/2016/04/OAR_SiblingResource_Parents_2015.pdf.**

188 Shira Rubin, "The Israeli Army Unit That Recruits Teens with Autism," *The Atlantic*, Jan. 6, 2016. Available: **https://www.theatlantic.com/health/archive/2016/01/israeli-army-autism/422850/.**

189 Ibid.

190 Rachel Ewing, "Young Adults on the Autism Spectrum Face Tough Prospects for Jobs and Independent Living," *Health – Society and Culture*, September 4, 2013.

191 Laurel Joss, "Scott Robertson Advocates for Autistic Adults," *Autism Daily Newscast*, posted March 15, 2017. Available: **http://www.autismdailynewscast.com/scott-robertson-advocates-for-autistic-adults/3170/laurel-joss/.**

192 Jennifer Van Pelt, "Autism Into Adulthood – Making the Transition," *Social Work Today*, 8 (5), 12.

193 Laurel Joss, "Scott Robertson Advocates for Autistic Adults," *Autism Daily Newscast*, posted March 15, 2017. Available:

http://www.autismdailynewscast.com/scott-robertson-advocates-for-autistic-adults/3170/laurel-joss/.

[194] Jenny Price, "Coming of Age," *OnWisconsin Magazine*. Available: www.onwisconsin.uwalumni.com/features/coming-of-age.

[195] Rebecca Ann Charlton, "What Happens When People With Autism Grow Old?" *The Conversation*, October 18, 2016. Available: http://theconversation.com/what-happens-when-people-with-autism-grow-old-65572.

[196] Jeanne Kelly, Letter to *The New York Times* Editor, 2004, in Alshaba Billawalla and Gregor Wolbring, "Analyzing the Discourse Surrounding Autism in the New York Times Using an Ableism Lens," *Disability Studies Quarterly*, 34 (1), 2014.

[197] M. Bayat, "Evidence of Resilience in Families of Children with Autism," *Journal of Intellectual Disability Research*, 51, 2007, 702-714.

[198] Seieun Oh and and Sun Ju Chang, "Concept Analysis: Family Resilience," *Open Journal of Nursing*, 4, 980-990, 2014.

[199] Arturo Madrid, "Diversity and Its Discontents," from *Intercultural Communication: A Reader,* 7th ed., eds. Larry Samovar and Richard Porter, (Belmont, CA: Wadsworth, Inc., 1994), 127-131.

[200] Tracy B. Smith, "The 8 Best Ways My Son with Autism Brings Me Joy," *The Mighty*, August 31, 2015. Available: https://themighty.com/2017/06/what-i-want-people-who-say-you-dont-look-autistic-to-know/.

[201] Nathaniel Lambert, A. Marlea Gwinn, Roy Baumeister, Amy Strachman, Isaac Washburn, Shelly Gable, and Frank Fincham, "A Boost of Positive Affect: The Perks of Sharing Positive Experiences," *Journal of Social and Personal Relationships*, 30, (1), February, 2013, 24-43.

[202] Julia Bascom, "Just Stimming...The Obsessive Joy of Autism," posted April 5, 2011. Available:

https://juststimming.wordpress.com/2011/04/05/the-obsessive-joy-of-autism/.

[203] Martha Bryson Hodel, "Autistic Man Finds Life After 70 Years," *Los Angeles Times*, November 17, 1991. Available: http://articles.latimes.com/1991-11-17/news/mn-211_1_state-hospital.

[204] Ibid.

[205] Webster, Dennis. *Old Main: New York State Lunatic Asylum at Utica, N.Y.* (Utica, NY: North Country Books, 2015)

[206] Savannah Logsdon-Breakstone, "Restraining Wanderers – A Little History," posted Mar. 28, 2012, *disabilityrightnow*. Available: https://disabilityrightnow.wordpress.com/2012/03/28/restraining-wanderers-a-little-history.

[207] UNC Health Talk, "The Atlantic Tells the Story of Adult Autism Through Research at UNC," Dec. 10, 2015. Available: http://cidd.unc.edu/Registry/Research/Docs/30.pdf.

[208] Máire Lane, Anna Kingston, and Claire Edwards, "Adult Siblings of Individuals with Intellectual Disability/Autism Spectrum Disorder: Relationships, Roles, and Support Needs," December, 2016. Available: http://nda.ie/nda-files/Adult-Siblings-of-Individuals-with-Intellectual-Disability-Autistic-Spectrum-Disorder;-Relationships-Roles-Support-Needs.pdf.

[209] Melissa McVicker, "The Sisters' Experience of Having a Sibling with an Autism Spectrum Disorder," (Antioch University Repository and Archive, Dissertations and Theses), 2013.

[210] Barbara Cain, "Autism's Invisible Victims: The Siblings," *Time*, November 30, 2012.

[211] Máire Lane, Anna Kingston, and Claire Edwards, "Adult Siblings of Individuals with Intellectual Disability/Autism Spectrum Disorder: Relationships, Roles, and Support Needs," December 2016. Available: http://nda.ie/nda-files/Adult-Siblings-of-Individuals-with-Intellectual-

Disability-Autistic-Spectrum-Disorder;-Relationships-Roles-Support-Needs.pdf.

[212] Barry Prizant. *Uniquely Human: A Different Way of Seeing Autism* (New York: Simon and Schuster, 2015).

[213] M. Bayat, "Evidence of Resilience in Families of Children with Autism," *Journal of Intellectual Disability Research*, 51, Part 9, September 2007, 702-714.

[214] Ibid.

[215] Barbara Myers, Virginia MacIntosh, and Robin Goin-Kochel, "My Greatest Joy and My Greatest Heart Ache: Parents' own words on how having a child in the autism spectrum has affected their lives and their families' lives," *Research in Autism Spectrum Disorders* 3, 2009, 677.

[216] American Psychological Association, "A Grateful Heart is a Healthier Heart," posted April 9, 2015. Available: http://www.dailygood.org/story/532/how-gratitude-can-help-you-through-hard-times-robert-emmons/.

[217] Robert Emmons, "How Gratitude Can Help You through Hard Times," *DailyGood*, posted September 12, 2013. Available: http://www.dailygood.org/story/532/how-gratitude-can-help-you-through-hard-times-robert-emmons/.

[218] Alexander Burrell. Jonathan Ives, and Gemma Unwin, "The Experiences of Fathers Who Have Offspring with Autism Spectrum Disorder," *Journal of Autism Developmental Disorders*, 47(4), Jan. 28, 2017, 1135-1147.

[219] Jim Sinclair, "Autism Mythbusters: Why I dislike 'person-first' language,'" accessed July 31, 2017. Available: http://autismmythbusters.com/general-public/autistic-vs-people-with-autism/jim-sinclair-why-i-dislike-person-first-language/.

[220] Jim Sinclair, "Don't Mourn For Us," *Our Voice*, 1, (3), 1993.

[221] Autism Speaks, "Largest-Ever Autism Genome Study Finds Most Siblings Have Different Autism-Risk Genes," *Science Daily*, January 26, 2015. Available: https://www.sciencedaily.com/releases/2015/01/150126124604.htm.

BIBLIOGRAPHY
(for clickable version see www.ajimmy.com)

2014 Reach Report, "Special Olympics Research Overview." Available: **http://media.specialolympics.org/resources/research/Special-Olympics-Research-Overview.pdf.**

Abbott, Alysia, "Love in the Time of Autism," *Psychology Today*, July 2, 2013. Available: **http://www.psychologytoday.com/articles/201306/love-in-the-time-autism.**

"Ableism/Disablism –What it is and how it feels," posted July 31, 2015. Available: **https://autistictic.com/2015/07/31/ableism-disablism/.**

Allely, C. S., "Pain Sensitivity and Observer Perception of Pain in Individuals with Autism Spectrum Disorder," *Scientific World Journal*, posted June 13, 2013. Available: **https://core.ac.uk/download/pdf/16459727.pdf.**

Allen, Claire, Autism South Africa, "When Your Child Has Autism: Tips for Parents," accessed Dec. 15, 2016. Available: **http://aut2know.co.za/wp/wp-content/uploads/10-Tips-for-Parents.pdf**, p. 2 of 4.

American Psychological Association, "A Grateful Heart is a Healthier Heart," posted April 9, 2015. Available: **http://www.dailygood.org/story/532/how-gratitude-can-help-you-through-hard-times-robert-emmons/.**

Anderson, Connie, *IAN Research Report #14: Grandparents of Children with ASD, Part 1*, April 2010. Available: **https://iancommunity.org/cs/ian_research_reports/ian_re search_report_apr_2010**.

Anderson, Connie, J. Kiely Law, Amy Daniels, Catherine Rice, David Mandell, Louis Hagopian, and Paul Law, **"Occurrence and Family Impact of Elopement in Children with Autism Spectrum Disorders,"** *Pediatrics*, October 12, 2012.

Angell, Maureen, Hedda Meadan, and Julia Stoner, "Experiences of Siblings of Individuals with Autism Spectrum Disorders," *Autism Research and Treatment*, 2012. Available: **https://www.hindawi.com/journals/aurt/2012/949586/**.

Ault, M. J., B. C. Collins, and E. W. Carter, **"Factors Associated with Participation in Faith Communities for Individuals with Developmental Disabilities and Their Families,"** *Journal of Religion, Disability, and Health* 17, 2013, 184-211; M. J. Ault, B. C. Collins, and E. W. Carter, "Congregational Participation and Supports for Children and Adults with Disabilities: Parent Perceptions," *Intellectual and Developmental Disabilities*, 51 (1), Feb., 2013, 48-61.

"Autism Diagnosis: Slipping through the Cracks in Some Communities," *Parents and Kids Magazine*, accessed March 9, 2017. Available: **http://www.gulfcoast-parents-kids.com/index.php/current-issue/latest-issue/761-autism-diagnosis-slipping-through-the-cracks-in-some-communities**.

Autism Speaks, "Largest-Ever Autism Genome Study Finds Most Siblings Have Different Autism-Risk Genes," *Science Daily*, January 26, 2015. Available: **https://www.sciencedaily.com/releases/2015/01/15012612 4604.htm**.

Autism Speaks, "Study Confirms Autism Wandering Common and Scary," Oct. 8, 2012. Available: **https://www.autismspeaks.org/science/science-news/study-confirms-autism-wandering-common-scary.**

Autism Speaks, "Study Suggests Repetitive Behaviors Emerge Early in Autism," May 15, 2014. Available: **https://www.autismspeaks.org/science/science-news/study-suggests-repetitive-behaviors-emerge-early-autism.**

Bagby, Molly Shields, Virginia Dickie, and Grace Baranek, "**How Sensory Experiences of Children with and Without Autism Affect Family Occupations**," *American Journal of Occupational Therapy*, 66 (1), Jan-Feb, 2012, 78-86.

Bainbridge, Carl, "Parents of Children with Autism: How to Deal with Pain Management," *YMC: Motherhood Unfiltered*, accessed 1/18/2018. Available: **http://www.yummymummyclub.ca/health/wellness/20160417/parents-of-children-with-autism-how-to-deal-with-pain-management-bc?qt-contests_minitab=0&qt-newest_and_trending_tabs=0.**

Baron-Cohen, Simon. *Mindblindness: An Essay on Autism and Theory of the Mind* (Cambridge, MA: MIT Press, 1995).

Baron-Cohen, Simon. *The Science of Evil: On Empathy and the Origins of Cruelty* (NY: Basic Books, 2011).

Bascom, Julia, "Just Stimming…The Obsessive Joy of Autism," posted April 5, 2011. Available: **https://juststimming.wordpress.com/2011/04/05/the-obsessive-joy-of-autism/.**

Bayat, M., "**Evidence of Resilience in Families of Children with Autism**," *Journal of Intellectual Disability Research*, 51, 2007, 702-714.

Bettelheim, Bruno. *The Empty Fortress: Infantile Autism and the Birth of the Self* (NY: Free Press, 1972).

Billawalla, Alshaba and Gregor Wolbring, **"Analyzing the Discourse Surrounding Autism in the New York Times Using an Ableism Lens,"** *Disability Studies Quarterly*, 34 (1), 2014.

Braithwaite, Carrie, "New Study Highlights the Importance of Fathers in the Care of Children with Autism," posted Nov. 1, 2016. Available: **http://www.leedsbeckett.ac.uk/news/1116-new-study-highlights-the-importance-of-fathers-in-the-care-of-children-with-autism/.**

Bucher, Katie, "My Brother Jimmy," *Exceptional Parent*, March, 1990. No link available.

Bucher, Suzy, **"I Look Up to You, Jimmy,"** *The Exceptional Parent*, **30, Issue 5, May 2000.**

Buescher, Ariane, Zuleyha Cidav, Martin Knapp, and David Mandell, **"Costs of Autism Spectrum Disorders in the United Kingdom and the United States,"** *JAMA Pediatrics*, 168 (8), August 2014, 721-728.

Burrell, Alexander, Jonathan Ives, and Gemma Unwin, **"The Experiences of Fathers Who Have Offspring with Autism Spectrum Disorder,"** *Journal of Autism Developmental Disorders*, 47(4), Jan. 28, 2017, 1135-1147.

Cain, Barbara, **"Autism's Invisible Victims: The Siblings,"** *Time*, November 30, 2012.

Caruso, Nicole, "A Qualitative Investigation into Posttraumatic Growth in Mothers of Children with Autism Spectrum Disorder," accessed 7/4/17. Available: **http://www.autismsa.org.au/Media/Default/Research%20Documents/3%20%20COPY%20OF%20FINAL%20REPORT.pdf.**

CBS 60 Minutes Overtime: "Temple Grandin: Understanding Autism," July 15, 2012. Available: **http://www.cbsnews.com/news/temple-grandin-understanding-autism/.**

Center for Autism Research - The Children's Hospital of Philadelphia, "The Importance of Self-Esteem." Available: **https://www.carautismroadmap.org/the-importance-of-self-esteem/?print=pdf.**

Centers for Disease Control and Prevention, "CDC Estimates 1 in 68 Children Has Been Identified with Autism Spectrum Disorder." Available: **http://www.cdc.gov/media/releases/2014/p0327-autism-spectrum-disorder.html**, Mar. 27, 2014.

Charlton, Rebecca Ann, "What Happens When People With Autism Grow Old?" *The Conversation*, October 18, 2016. Available: **http://theconversation.com/what-happens-when-people-with-autism-grow-old-65572.**

"Circle of Moms," posted 8/29/09. Available: **http://www.circleofmoms.com/autismaspergerspdd-awareness/autism-why-all-the-repetitive-questions-i-am-going-crazy-365741.**

Clow, Abbey, "Growing Together: Stories of Resilience in Families of Children with Autism," April 2016. Available: **https://e-space.mmu.ac.uk/617775/1/Clow%20(Abbey)%202016%20(Manchester%20Metropolitan)%20Qualitative.pdf**.

Crawford, C., J. Burns, and B.A. Fernie, **Psychosocial Impact of Involvement in the Special Olympics,**" *Research in Developmental Disabilities*, Oct.-Nov. 2015, 45-46.

Dawson, Geraldine and Michael Rosanoff, "Sports, Exercise, and the Benefits of Physical Activity for Individuals with Autism," *Autism Speaks*, posted February 19, 2009. Available: **https://www.autismspeaks.org/science/science-news/sports-exercise-and-benefits-physical-activity-individuals-autism.**

DeBoer, Erin, **"Sesame Workshop Announces Initiative Focused on Autism,"** October 22, 2015.

Delle Donne, Elena, *The Players' Tribune*, "Lizzie," posted Aug. 12, 2015. Available: **https://www.theplayerstribune.com/elena-delle-donne-sister/**.

Deweerdt, Sarah, "Unseen Agony: Dismantling Autism's House of Pain," *Spectrum*, posted May 21, 2015. Available: **https://spectrumnews.org/features/deep-dive/unseen-agony-dismantling-autisms-house-of-pain/**.

Donvan, John and Caren Zucker, "Autism's First Child," *The Atlantic*, October, 2010. Available: **https://www.theatlantic.com/magazine/archive/2010/10/autisms-first-child/308227/**.

Drexel University, "A Quarter of Adults with Autism on Disability Services Don't Have Work or Activities, New Report Shows," *Science Daily*, May 24, 2017. Available: **https://www.sciencedaily.com/releases/2017/05/170524110016.htm**.

Dumke, Marya, "Autism and the Impact of the Siblings' Identities," 2015, *Master of Social Work Clinical Research Papers*, 438. Available: **https://sophia.stkate.edu/msw_papers/438/**.

Elkind, David. *The Power of Play: How Spontaneous, Imaginative Activities Lead to Happier, Healthier Children* (Da Capo Press, 2007); Edward Miller and Joan Almon, *Crisis in the Kindergarten: Why Children Need to Play in School, 2009*.

Emmons, Robert, "How Gratitude Can Help You through Hard Times," *DailyGood*, posted September 12, 2013. Available: **http://www.dailygood.org/story/532/how-gratitude-can-help-you-through-hard-times-robert-emmons/**.

Ewing, Rachel, "**Young Adults on the Autism Spectrum Face Tough Prospects for Jobs and Independent Living**," *Health – Society and Culture*, September 4, 2013.

Falcon, Mike, "Stars 'CAN-do' about defeating autism," *USA Today*, April 10, 2002. Available: **http://usatoday30.usatoday.com/news/health/spotlight/2 002/04/10-autism.htm**.

Flippin, Micelle and Elizabeth Crais, "**The Need for More Effective Father Involvement in Early Autism Intervention: A Systematic Review and Recommendations**, *Journal of Early Intervention*, 33(1), 24-50, 2011.

Fournier, Wendy, "New Study Highlights Mortality and Risk in Autism Wandering/Elopement," April 3, 2017. Available: **http://nationalautismassociation.org/new-study-highlights-lethal-risks-of-missing-persons-with-autism/**.

Fredrickson, Barbara. *Positivity* (New York, NY: Crown, 2009).

Freedman, Brian, Luther Kalb, Benjamin Zablotsky, and Elizabeth Stuart, "**Relationship Status Among Parents of Children with Autism Spectrum Disorders: A Population-Based Study**," *Journal of Autism and Developmental Disorders*, 42 (4), 539-548.

"From People with Autism, Lessons for Scientists on Love, Compassion," *Spectrum*, Dec. 22, 2017. Available: **https://www.spectrumnews.org/features/special-report/people-autism-lessons-scientists-love-compassion/**.

Ginny, R. and B. Norwich, "Dilemmas, Diagnosis, and De-stigmatization: Parental Perspectives on the Diagnosis of Autism Spectrum Disorders," *Clinical Child Psychology and Psychiatry*," 17(2), 229-245, in Stasha Stobbs, "My Greatest Joy and My Greatest Heartache: A Narrative Analysis Exploring Mothers' Experiences of Having a Child on the Autism Spectrum," Manchester Metropolitan University, March, 2014. Available: **https://e-space.mmu.ac.uk/576484/1/Stasha%20STOBBS.pdf**.

Giuffrida, Costanza and Emilia Barakova, "**Time Processing Ability and Anxiety in Children with Autism: Evaluation of the Effects of Music Using Music Timer PLAYtime**," Tokyo, Japan: International Association of Societies of Design Research (IASDR), 2013.

Gladwell, Malcolm. *The Tipping Point: How Little Things Can Make a Big Difference* (New York: Little Brown and Co., 2000).

Goehner, Amy Lennard, "Challenges Siblings of Children with Autism Face," *World of Autism*, accessed 4/11/2018. Available: **http://www.worldofautism.com/ASD/Challenges_siblings-of-children_with_autism_face.html.**

Goehner, Amy Lennard, "**Travel Tips**" TIME Magazine 2009.

Gordon, Serena, "Grandparents Play Vital Role for Autistic Children," April 30, 2010. Available: **http://news.healingwell.com/index.php?p=news1&id=638183.**

Grandin, Temple and Debra Moore. *The Loving Push: How Parents and Professionals Can Help Spectrum Kids Become Successful Adults* (Arlington, TX: Future Horizons, 2015), ix.

Grandin, Temple and Margaret Scariano. *Emergence: Labeled Autistic*, reissue edition (NY: Warner Books, 1996).

Grandin, Temple, "My Experiences as an Autistic Child and Review of Selected Literature." Available: **http://orthomolecular.org/library/jom/1984/pdf/1984-v13n03-p144.pdf**, 1984.

Haddad, Anne, "**Teen Gains an Unlikely Insider's Perspective on Prejudice,**" *The Sun – Carroll County and Maryland*, March 22, 1993, B1.

Hallett, Vicky, "These Runners Have Autism, and That's a Quite Good Combination," *The Washington Post*, May 9, 2017, E3. Available: **https://www.washingtonpost.com/national/health-science/these-runners-have-autism-and-thats-a-quite-good-combination/2017/05/05/64c60064-2e81-11e7-8674-437ddb6e813e_story.html?utm_term=.c12c8933f2b9.**

Hamed, Hend, "**Tourism and Autism: An Initiative Study for How Travel Companies Can Plan Tourism Trips for Autistic People**," *American Journal of Tourism Management*, 2013, 2(1), 1-14.

Hartley, S.L., E.T. Barker, M.M. Seltzer, F. Floyd, J. Greenberg, G. Orsmond, and D. Bolt, "The Relative Risk and Timing of Divorce in Families of Children with an Autism Spectrum Disorder," *Journal of Family Psychology*, 24 (4), Aug., 2010, 449-457.

Hartley, Sigan, Erin Barker, Marsha Seltzer, and Jan Greenberg, "**Marital Satisfaction and Parenting Experiences of Mothers and Fathers of Adolescents and Adults with Autism**," *American Journal on Intellectual and Developmental Disabilities*, 116 (1), 81-95, Jan., 2011.

Hartley, Sigan, Marsha Mailick Seltzer, Lara Head, and Leonard Abbeduto, "**Psychological Well-being in Fathers of Adolescents and Young Adults with Down Syndrome, Fragile X Syndrome, and Autism**," *Family Relations*, 61 (2), April 1, 2012, 327-342.

Hastings, R. P. and H. M. Taunt, "Positive Perceptions in Families of Children with Developmental Disabilities," *American Journal of Mental Retardation*, 107(2), Mar., 2002, 116-27; M. Bayat, "Evidence of Resilience in Families of Children with Autism," *Journal of Intellectual Disability Research*, 51, 2007, 702-714; Ashley Hartmann, "Autism and its Impact on Families," 2012, *Master of Social Work Clinical Research Papers*, Paper 35, Available: **https://sophia.stkate.edu/msw_papers/35/.**

Hode, Marlo G., "The Tyranny of Neuronormality: Questioning Neurotypical Privilege in Communication," University of Missouri, Columbia, May 7, 2012.

Hodel, Martha Bryson, "Autistic Man Finds Life After 70 Years," *Los Angeles Times*, November 17, 1991. Available: http://articles.latimes.com/1991-11-17/news/mn-211_1_state-hospital.

Holley, Joe, "Jeanne Simons, Pioneer for Autistic Children, Dies," *The Washington Post*, March 12, 2005, B06.

Hughes, C., R. Bernstein, L. Kaplan, C. Reilly, N Brigham, J Cosgriff, and M. Boykin, "Increasing Conversational Interactions between Verbal High School Students with Autism and Their Peers." *Focus on Autism and Other Developmental Disabilities*," 28, 2013, 241-254.

Isaacson, Melissa, "Elena Delle Donne Continues to Spred the Word of Acceptance," June 8, 2016. Available: http://www.espn.com/espnw/culture/article/16049634/elena-delle-donne-continues-spread-word-acceptance.

Johnson, Jane, "Editorial: Parental Stress and Autism Spectrum Disorders," *Autism Research Review International*, Fall, 2013.

Joss, Laurel, "Scott Robertson Advocates for Autistic Adults," *Autism Daily Newscast*, June 1, 2017. Available: http://www.autismdailynewscast.com/scott-robertson-advocates-for-autistic-adults/3170/laurel-joss/.

Kanner, Leo, "Autistic Disturbances of Affective Contact," *Nervous Child*, 2, 1943, 217-250.

Kasari, Connie, Erin Rotheram-Fuller, Jill Locke, and Amanda Gulsrud, "Making the Connection: Randomized Controlled Trial of Social Skills at School for Children with Autism Spectrum Disorders," *The Journal of Child Psychology and Psychiatry and Allied Disciplines*, 57, Issue 2, 171-179, Feb., 2016.

Keller, Terry, Julie Ramisch, and Marsha Carolan, **"Relationships of Children with Autism Spectrum Disorders and their Fathers,"** *The Qualitative Report*, 19, Article 66, 2014, 1-15.

Kelly, Jeanne, Letter to *The New York Times* Editor, 2004, in Alshaba Billawalla and Gregor Wolbring, **"Analyzing the Discourse Surrounding Autism in the *New York Times* Using an Ableism Lens,"** *Disability Studies Quarterly*, 34 (1), 2014.

Kennedy Krieger Institute, "80 Percent Autism Divorce Rate Debunked in First-Of-Its Kind Scientific Study," posted May 19, 2010. Available: **https://www.kennedykrieger.org/overview/news/80-percent-autism-divorce-rate-debunked-first-its-kind-scientific-study.**

Kersh, Joanne and Gary Siperstein, **"The Positive Contributions of Special Olympics to the Family,"** Boston, MA: Special Olympics Global Collaborating Center, University of Massachusetts, 2012.

Kim, Cynthia, "Musings of an Aspie: One Woman's Thoughts about Life on the Spectrum, posted May 24, 2013. Available: **https://musingsofanaspie.com/2013/05/24/sensory-seeking/.**

Lambert, Nathaniel, A. Marlea Gwinn, Roy Baumeister, Amy Strachman, Isaac Washburn, Shelly Gable, and Frank Fincham, **"A Boost of Positive Affect: The Perks of Sharing Positive Experiences,"** *Journal of Social and Personal Relationships*, 30, (1), February, 2013, 24-43.

Lane, Máire, Anna Kingston, and Claire Edwards, "Adult Siblings of Individuals with Intellectual Disability/Autism Spectrum Disorder: Relationships, Roles, and Support Needs," December 2016. Available: **http://nda.ie/nda-files/Adult-Siblings-of-Individuals-with-Intellectual-Disability-Autistic-Spectrum-Disorder;-Relationships-Roles-Support-Needs.pdf.**

Lehmann, Annie Lubliner. *The Accidental Teacher: Life Lessons from My Silent Son* (Ann Arbor, MI: University of Michigan Press, 2009).

Logsdon-Breakstone, Savannah, "Restraining Wanderers – A Little History," *disabilityrightnow*, posted Mar. 28, 2012, Available: **https://disabilityrightnow.wordpress.com/2012/03/28/res training-wanderers-a-little-history.**

Lydon, Sinéad, Olive Healy, Orla O'Callaghan, Teresa Mulhern, and Jennifer Holloway, "A Systematic Review of the Treatment of Fears and Phobias Among Children with Autism Spectrum Disorders," *Review Journal of Autism and Developmental Disorders*, 2, Issue 2, June 2015. Available: **https://link.springer.com/article/10.1007/s40489-014-0043-4.**

Madrid, Arturo, "Diversity and Its Discontents," from *Intercultural Communication: A Reader,* **7th ed.**, eds. Larry Samovar and Richard Porter (Belmont, CA: Wadsworth, Inc., 1994), 127-131.

Martinelli, Marissa, "An Autism Advocate Explains How She Helped *Sesame Street* Create Its New Autistic Muppet," posted April 12, 2017. Available: **http://www.slate.com/blogs/browbeat/2017/04/12/autisti c_self_advocacy_network_s_julia_bascom_on_sesame_s treet_s_new_muppet.html.**

Masters, Kate, "**Grandin Celebrates Learners with Special Needs,**" *The Frederick News-Post*, January 19, 2018, 1+.

Mayes, Susan, Susan Calhoun, Richa Aggarwal, Courtney Baker, Santosh Mathapati, Sarah Molitoris, and Rebecca Mayes, "**Unusual Fears in Children with Autism,**" *Research in Autism Spectrum Disorders*, 7 (1), 151-158, Jan., 2013.

McPheeters, M. L., Z. Warren, Bruzek Sathe, S. Krishnaswami, R. N. Jerome, and J. Veenstra-Vanderweele, "**A Systematic Review of Medical Treatments for Children with Autism Spectrum Disorders,**" *Pediatrics*, May, 2011, 1312-1321.

McVicker, Melissa, "**The Sisters' Experience of Having a Sibling with an Autism Spectrum Disorder**" (Antioch University Repository and Archive, Dissertations and Theses), 2013.

Medscape Psychiatry, "**Autism First-Hand: An Expert Interview with Temple Grandin, PhD,**" 10 (1), 2005.

Michaux, Scott, "**Star of Spieth Family is Ellie,**" *Masters*, Mar. 20, 2016.

Milkie, Melissa, Kei Nomaguchi, and Kathleen Denny, "**Does the Amount of Time Mothers Spend With Children or Adolescents Matter?**" *Journal of Marriage and Family*, 77, Issue 2, April 2015, 355-372.

Mishori, Ranit, "Autism Can Have Large Effects, Good and Bad, on a Disabled Child's Siblings," *The Washington Post*, September 3, 2012. Available: **https://www.washingtonpost.com/national/health-science/autism-can-have-large-effects-good-and-bad-on-a-disabled-childs-siblings/2012/08/31/e35a82e2-b956-11e1-abd4-aecc81b4466d_story.html?utm_term=.b2237866c764.**

Montgomery, Janine, Toby Martin, Shahin Shooshtari, Brenda Stoesz, and Dustin Heinrichs, "**Interventions for Challenging Behaviors of Students with Autism Spectrum Disorders and Developmental Disabilities: A Synthesis Paper,**" *Exceptionality Education International*, 23, Issue 1, 2013, 2-21.

Mundell, E. J., "**Common Sports, Hobbies Often Popular Among People with Autism,**" *HealthDay*, May 13, 2015.

Myers, Barbara, Virginia MacIntosh, and Robin Goin-Kochel, "My Greatest Joy and My Greatest Heart Ache: Parents' own words on how having a child in the autism spectrum has affected their lives and their families' lives," *Research in Autism Spectrum Disorders*, July-September, 2009. Available: **https://www.sciencedirect.com/science/article/pii/S17509 46709000051.**

National Institute of Mental Health, "Most Children with ASD Diagnosed after Age 5 Use Multiple Services and Medications," May 24, 2012. Available: https://www.nimh.nih.gov/news/science-news/2012/most-children-with-asd-diagnosed-after-age-5-use-multiple-services-and-medications.shtml.

"New NHS Treatment Helps Children with Autism Overcome Fears," *EurekAlert! The Global Source for Science News*, February 10, 2017. Available: https://www.eurekalert.org/pub_releases/2017-02/nu-nn021017.php.

Nicolaidis, C., D. M. Raymaker, E. Ashkenazy, K. E. McDonald, S. Dern, A. E. Baggs, S. K. Kapp, M. Weiner, and W. C. Boisclair, "**Respect the Way I Need to Communicate with You: Healthcare Experiences of Adults on the Autism Spectrum**," *Autism: The International Journal of Research and Practice*, 19, 7, 2015, 824-831.

Nicolaidis, Christina, "**What Can Physicians Learn from the Neurodiversity Movement?**" *Virtual Mentor: AMA Journal of Ethics*, June 2012, 14 (6), 503-510.

Nordahl-Hansen, Anders, Ronald Oien, and Sue Fletcher-Watson, "**Pros and Cons of Character Portrayals of Autism on TV and Film**," *Journal of Autism and Developmental Disorders*, February 2018, 48, Issue 2, pp. 635-636.

O'Connor, Anahad, "**Autistic Pupils Face Far More Bullying**," *The New York Times*, 9/04/2012, D7.

O'Hanlon, Elizabeth E., "**Religion and Disability: The Experiences of Families of Children with Special Needs**," *Journal of Religion, Disability, and Health*, 17, 42-61, 2013.

O'Toole, Jennifer Cook, *Asperkids: An Insider's Guide to Loving, Understanding, and Teaching Children with Asperger's Syndrome* (London, UK: Jessica Kingsley Publishers, 2012).

Oh, Seieun and and Sun Ju Chang, "Concept Analysis: Family Resilience," *Open Journal of Nursing*, 4, 980-990, 2014.

Organization for Autism Research, *Brothers, Sisters, and Autism: A Parent's Guide to Supporting Siblings*, Summer, 2014. Available: https://researchautism.org/wp-content/uploads/2016/04/OAR_SiblingResource_Parents_2015.pdf.

Papenfuss, Mary, "Meet the New Kid on Sesame Street: Julia, A Muppet with Autism," *Huff Post*, posted 3/20/17. Available: http://www.huffingtonpost.com/entry/autism-muppet-sesame-street_us_58cf5f15e4b0be71dcf5b455.

"Parents of Kids with Autism May Sacrifice 'Couples Time,'" *HealthDay*, March 31, 2017. Available: https://consumer.healthday.com/cognitive-health-information-26/autism-news-51/parents-of-kids-with-autism-may-sacrifice-couples-time-721106.html.

Parker, Kim, Pew Research Center, "6 Facts about American Fathers," posted June 15, 2017. Available: http://www.pewresearch.org/fact-tank/2017/06/15/fathers-day-facts/.

Pew Research Center, "Survey of parents with children under 18," Sept. 15 -Oct 13, 2015, Q95, 96.

Pickard, Katherine and Brooke Ingersoll, "Quality vs. quantity: The role of socioeconomic status on parent-reported service knowledge, service use, unmet service needs, and barriers to service use," *Autism*, 20 (1), 2016, 106-115.

Prebble, Tessa, "Blog: As Long As It's Healthy," Oct. 30, 2014, accessed Aug. 15, 2017. Available: http://theoneinamillionbaby.com/about-us/.

Price, Jenny, "Coming of Age," *OnWisconsin Magazine*. Available: www.onwisconsin.uwalumni.com/features/coming-of-age.

Prizant, Barry. *Uniquely Human: A Different Way of Seeing Autism* (New York: Simon and Schuster, 2015).

Rastegari, Iman and Leah Shafer, "Accentuate the Positive," posted Dec. 22, 2016. Available: **https://www.gse.harvard.edu/news/uk/16/12/accentuate-positive**.

Research Autism, "Caregiver Stress Project," May 26, 2015. Available: **researchautism.net/caregiver-stress-project**.

Roc, Dana, "Author, Teacher, and Autism Education Pioneer, Soma Mukhopadhyay." Available: **http://danaroc.com/inspiring_041910soma.html**.

Roux, Anne, Paul Shattuck, Jessica Rast, Julianna Rava, and Krisy Anderson. *National Autism Indicators Report: Transition into Young Adulthood* (Philadelphia, PA: Life Course Outcomes Research Program, A.J. Drexel Autism Institute, Drexel University, 2015).

Rowe, Mary, "Micro-affirmations and Micro-inequities," Jan., 2008. Available: **https://www.researchgate.net/publication/265450386_Micro-affirmations_Micro-inequities**.

Roylance, Frank and Meredith Cohn, "Alternative Autism Treatments Can Be Appealing to Desperate Parents," *The Baltimore Sun*, May 11, 2011. Available: *http://www.baltimoresun.com/health/bs-md-autism-parents-therapy-20110511-story.html*.

Rubin, Shira, "The Israeli Army Unit That Recruits Teens with Autism," *The Atlantic*, Jan. 6, 2016. Available: **https://www.theatlantic.com/health/archive/2016/01/israeli-army-autism/422850/**.

Russell, Ginny, *University of Exeter guest blog: Screen Talks*, "Savants and Stereotypes: Barry Levinson's Rain Man." Available **http://blogs.exeter.ac.uk/screentalks/blog/2013/04/**, posted April 9, 2013.

Ryan, Sara, "'Meltdowns,' Surveillance and Managing Emotions: Going Out with Children with Autism," *Health and Place*, September, 2010. Available: **https://www.ncbi.nlm.nih.gov/pmc/articles/PMC2927009/**.

Sanders, Roy Q., "The Experts Speak: Hard Times Come Again No More, posted April 20, 2011. Available: **https://autismspeaksblog.wordpress.com/2011/04/20/experts-reflect-on-parenthood-finale**.

Sarrett, Jennifer, **"Trapped Children: Popular Images of Children with Autism in the 1960s and 2000s**," *Journal of Medical Humanities*, 32, 141-153, January 12, 2011.

Sarris, Marina, "Autism and Faith: Inclusion and Acceptance at Places of Worship," posted March 4, 2014. Available: **https://iancommunity.org/ssc/autism-and-faith**.

Sarris, Marina, "Coming of Age: Autism and the Transition to Adulthood," Autism Network at Kennedy Krieger Institute, posted April 8, 2014. Available: **https://iancommunity.org/ssc/autism-transition-to-adulthoodInteractive**.

Sarris, Marina, "Families Face Autism, Stigma, Isolation," posted February 4, 2016. Available: *https://iancommunity.org/ssc/families-face-autism-stigma-isolation*.

Sarris, Marina, "The Stigma of Autism: When All Eyes Are Upon You," Interactive Autism Network (IAN), January 15, 2015. Available: **https://iancommunity.org**.

Sarris, Marina, "Understanding Research: An Autism Researcher Answers Your Questions," posted Feb. 20, 2017. Available: **iancommunity.org**.

Sarris, Marina, Interactive Autism Network, "The Challenge of Physical Fitness for People with Autism," Nov. 17, 2014. Available: **https://iancommunity.org/ssc/autism-physical-fitness**.

Sasson, Noah, Daniel Faso, Jack Nugent, Sarah Lovell, Daniel Kennedy, and Ruth Grossman, "Neurotypical Peers Are Less Willing to Interact with Those with Autism Based on Thin Slice Judgments," *Scientific Reports* 7, February 1, 2017. Available: **https://www.nature.com/articles/srep40700.**

Schaaf, Roseann, Susan Toth-Cohen, Stephanie Johnson, Gina Outten, and Teal Benevides, "**The Everyday Routines of Families of Children with Autism**," *Autism*, 15(3), 373-389, May 2011.

Schmidt, Theresa, "**Autism Mom: Ruth Christ Sullivan Part 1,**" kplctv.com, 2014.

Schulte, Brigid, "More Than a Paycheck: New Dads Want Paid Leave to Be Caregivers," *The Washington Post*, July 20, 2014, G1+. **https://www.washingtonpost.com/local/more-than-a-paycheck-new-dads-want-paid-leave-to-be-caregivers/2014/07/18/f607dcfe-f1b8-11e3-bf76-447a5df6411f_story.html?utm_term=.8a658fe1fc62.**

Seltzer Marsha Mailick and Marty W. Krauss, *Adolescents and Adults with Autism: A Study of Family Caregiving: Report #1: A Book of Quotes: Shared Experiences from Families of Adolescents and Adults with Autism*, 2002. Available: **http://www.waisman.wisc.edu/family/reports/autism/aa areport1.pdf.**

Seltzer, Marsha Mailick and Marty W. Krauss, *Adolescents and Adults with Autism: A Study of Family Caregiving: Report #3: Reflections from Adult Siblings who have a Brother or Sister with an Autism Spectrum Disorder*, 2002. Available: **http://www.waisman.wisc.edu/family/reports/autism/aa areport3.pdf.**

Seltzer, Marsha Mailick and Marty W. Krauss, *Report #2: A Profile of Adolescents and Adults with Autism Spectrum Disorder,* May 23, 2016, Madison, WI: Lifespan Family Research Program, 2002. Available: **http://www.waisman.wisc.edu/family/study_autism.html.**

Seltzer, Marsha Mailick and Marty W. Krauss, *Report #3: Reflections from Adult Siblings who have a Brother or Sister with an Autism Spectrum Disorder.* Available: **http://www.waisman.wisc.edu/family/reports/autism/aaareport3.pdf.**

Sequeniza, Amy, **"Non-Speaking, 'Low Functioning.'"** in Julia Bascom (ed.), *Loud Hands* (Washington, DC: The Autistic Press, 2012).

Sequenzia, Amy, "Non-Speaking Autistic Speaking," posted 8/13/2013. Available: **http://nonspeakingautisticspeaking.blogspot.com/.**

Sheri, "Autism Bullying Story," Hope Center for Autism, posted September 9, 20013. Available: **http://www.hopecenter4autism.org/autism-bullying-story/.**

Shtayermman, O., **"An Exploratory Study of the Stigma Associated with a Diagnosis of Asperger's Syndrome: The Mental Health Impact on the Adolescents and Young Adults Diagnosed with a Disability with a Social Nature,"** *Journal of Human Behavior in the Social Environment,* 19, 2009, 298-313.

Simons, Jeanne and Sabine Oishi, *The Hidden Child: The Linwood Method for Reaching the Autistic Child* (Bethesda, MD: Woodbine House, 1987).

Sinclair, Jim, "Autism Mythbusters: Why I dislike 'person-first' language,'" accessed July 31, 2017. Available: **http://autismmythbusters.com/general-public/autistic-vs-people-with-autism/jim-sinclair-why-i-dislike-person-first-language/.**

Sinclair, Jim, **"Don't Mourn For Us,"** *Our Voice,* **1, (3), 1993.**

Smith, Tracy B., "The 8 Best Ways My Son with Autism Brings Me Joy," *The Mighty*, August 31, 2015. Available: **https://themighty.com/2017/06/what-i-want-people-who-say-you-dont-look-autistic-to-know/.**

Smukler, David, "**Unauthorized Minds: How 'Theory of Mind' Theory Misrepresents Autism**," *Mental Retardation*, American Association of Intellectual and Developmental Disabilities, 43 (1), 20-21, Feb. 2005.

Solomon, Andrew. *Far from the Tree: Parents, Children, and the Search for Identity*, (NY: Scribner, 2012).

Solomon, Olga and Mary Lawlor, "'And I Look Down and He Is Gone:' Narrating Autism, Elopement and Wandering in Los Angeles," *Social Science Medicine*, October, 2013. Available: **https://www.ncbi.nlm.nih.gov/pubmed/23890970.**

Special Olympics, *Serving Athletes, Families, and the* Community, 2009. Available: **http://www.specialolympics.org/uploadedFiles/Landing Page/WhatWeDo/Research_Studies_Desciption_Pages/I mpact%20Policy%20Brief_feb3.pdf.**

Staton, Michael, "Researchers Examine Effects of Compression Clothing on Children with Autism," posted Feb. 22, 2017. Available: **http://newsstand.clemson.edu/mediarelations/researche rs-examine-effects-of-compression-clothing-on-children-with-autism/.**

"Street Gang," *Wikipedia* (Nov. 28, 2016). Available: **https://en.wikipedia.org/wiki/Street_Gang.**

Tanaka, Kyoko, Tokio Uchiyama, and Fumio Endo, "**Informing Children about Their Sibling's Diagnosis of Autism Spectrum Disorder: An Initial Investigation into Current Practices**," *Research in Autism Spectrum Disorders*, 5, 1421 -1429, Oct-Dec 2011.

Tang, Lu and Bijie Bie, "**The Stigma of Autism in China: An Analysis of Newspaper Portrayals of Autism between 2003 and 2012**, *Health Communication*, 31 (4), 2016, 445-452.

Taylor, Chris, "Raising an Autistic Child: Coping with the Costs," *Money*, June 24, 2014. Available: *http://time.com/money/2918134/cost-raising-autistic-child.*

"The Mind Tree: A Review," accessed 7/05/2017. Available: **http://teenautism.com/2008/09/18/the-mind-tree-a-review/.**

The National Autistic Society, "Shrinking Worlds," *Too Much Information*, accessed 4/15/17. Available: **https://www.scribd.com/document/357237318/TMI-Campaign-Report-FINAL-290316.**

Treffert, Darold, "Rain Man, the Movie/Rain Man, Real Life," Wisconsin Medical Society, accessed 9/15/2017. Available: **https://www.wisconsinmedicalsociety.org/professional/savant-syndrome/resources/articles/rain-man-the-movie-rain-man-real-life/.**

U. S. Census Bureau, National Center for Health Statistics, "**2014 National Health Interview Survey**."

UNC Health Talk, "The Atlantic Tells the Story of Adult Autism Through Research at UNC," Dec. 10, 2015. Available: **http://cidd.unc.edu/Registry/Research/Docs/30.pdf.**

United Nations, "Secretary-General's Message for World Autism Awareness Day," April 2, 2014. Available: **www.un.org/en/events/autismday/2014/sgmessage.shtml.**

University of Illinois at Urbana-Champaign, "Dad's Parenting of Children with Autism Improves Moms' Mental Health: Fathers' Engagement in Literacy, Caregiving Activities Reduces Mothers' Depression, Stress," *Science Daily*, July 14, 2015. Available: **www.sciencedaily.com/releases/2015/07/150714131600.htm.**

Van Pelt, Jennifer, **"Autism Into Adulthood – Making the Transition,"** *Social Work Today*, 8 (5), 12.

Wade, Alison "For Many with Autism, Running Is a Sport That Fits," *Runner's World*, 2017. Available: **https://www.runnersworld.com/special-report/for-many-with-autism-running-is-a-sport-that-fits.**

Ware, Bronnie. *The Top Five Regrets of the Dying* (NY: Hay House, 2012).

Webster, Dennis. *Old Main: New York State Lunatic Asylum at Utica, N.Y.* (Utica, NY: North Country Books, 2015).

Williams, Donna. *Nobody Nowhere: The Extraordinary Autobiography of an Autistic* (New York: Times Books, 1992).

Williams, Donna. *Nobody Nowhere: The Remarkable Autobiography of an Autistic Girl, Revised Edition* (London, UK: Jessica Kingsley Publishers, 1998).

Wood, Chantelle and Megan Freeth, "Students' Stereotypes of Autism," *Journal of Educational Issues*, 2016, 2 (2). Available: **https://files.eric.ed.gov/fulltext/EJ1127546.pdf.**

Wright, Joyce Ann, **"Transcendence: Phenomenological Perspective of the Mother's Experience of Having a Child with a Disability"** (Doctoral dissertation, Widener University, 2002).

Yergeau, Melanie, "Socializing Through Silence," in Julia Bascom (ed.), *Loud Hands: Autistic People, Speaking* (Washington, DC: The Autistic Press, 2012).

Zerbo, O., M. L. Massolo, Y. Qian, and L. A. Croen, "A Study of Physician Knowledge and Experience with Autism in Adults in a Large Integrated Healthcare System," *Journal of Autism and Developmental Disorders*, 45 (12), 2015, 4002-4014.

Made in the USA
Middletown, DE
15 September 2021